D0488106

Oxford Socio-Legal Studies

Just Lawyers

R

JUST LAWYERS

Regulation and Access to Justice

CHRISTINE PARKER

RD

RESS

xford OX2 6DP

t of the University of Oxford.
It furthers the University's objective of excellence in research, scholarship,
and education by publishing worldwide in

Oxford New York

Athens Auckland Bangkok Bogotá Buenos Aires Calcutta
Cape Town Chennai Dar es Salaam Delhi Florence Hong Kong Istanbul
Karachi Kuala Lumpur Madrid Melbourne Mexico City Mumbai
Nairobi Paris São Paulo Singapore Taipei Tokyo Toronto Warsaw

and associated companies in Berlin Ibadan

Oxford is a registered trade mark of Oxford University Press
in the UK and in certain other countries

Published in the United States
by Oxford University Press Inc., New York

First published 1999

British Library Cataloguing in Publication Data

Data available

Library of Congress Cataloging in Publication Data

Parker, Christine, Ph.D.
Just lawyers : regulation and access to justice / Christine Parker.
p. cm.—(Oxford socio-legal studies)
Includes bibliographical references and index.
1. Lawyers. 2. Practice of law. 3. Legal ethics
4. Justice, Administration of. I. Title. II. Series
K117.P37 1999 174′.3—dc21 99–37268

ISBN 0–19–826841–6

1 3 5 7 9 10 8 6 4 2

Typeset in Baskerville
by Hope Services (Abingdon) Ltd.
Printed in Great Britain
on acid-free paper by
Bookcraft Ltd., Midsomer Norton, Somerset

To Joyce and David Parker and to the Caxton Legal Centre

Preface

Lawyers and justice often have little to do with one another. This book rethinks the regulation and organization of lawyers, guided by ideals of access to justice, and analysis of existing legal institutions. Certainly legal institutions are limited in accomplishing what ordinary people would see as justice, and it is dangerous to give legal professionals too much weight in justice arrangements. This does not mean that the quest for ways to reform legal professions so that they contribute to justice should be abandoned. We cannot effectively reform and regulate lawyers without a broader vision of doing justice. This book therefore moves from grand political theory to explanatory analyses of legal professional institutions, from the broad arrangements that seek to guarantee social justice for citizens to the narrower institutions affecting the regulation of legal professions. I propose a practical model for improving access to justice which incorporates lawyers' justice, but goes beyond it—the institutionalization of justice without lawyers balanced against the reformed regulation of lawyers' justice.

This book has benefited from the useful comments and kind help of many friends and colleagues during my time as Ph.D. student at the Law Program, Research School of Social Sciences, Australian National University and later as Postdoctoral Research Fellow in the Law Faculty, University of New South Wales. Susanne Corcoran, Jim Davis, Adrian Evans, Marcia Neave, Guy Powles, and Philippa Weeks were invaluable accomplices in my attempts to find lawyers for the Chapter 6 interviews. Toni Makkai helped me settle into the peculiarities of the Research School of Social Sciences in 1994. Both Julian Disney and Stephen Parker were always ready to make useful comments on draft chapters; and the work was also greatly improved by conversations with, or suggestions from, Valerie Braithwaite, Andrew Brien, Ann Daniel, Peter Drahos, Andrew Goldsmith, Marcia Neave, Philip Pettit, Deborah Russell, Peter Sack, Colin Scott, Robert Shelly, and Leon Wolff. The administrative support of Chris Treadwell, Ann Robinson, and, as Head of Department, Paul Finn was vital, as was the companionship and intellectual stimulation of the other students, especially Jennifer Balint, Nathan Harris, and Anne Jenkins. In 1997, the Law Faculty at the University of New South Wales provided me with an intellectual home in which to complete this work for publication. David Dixon provided advice and encouragement throughout the revision and publication process. Martin Krygier went well beyond the duties of a new colleague in reading and commenting on the whole manuscript, and the comments of the two anonymous referees for Oxford University Press also greatly improved the manuscript.

Eliza Kaczynska-Nay shared many long discussions of both personal and intellectual aspects of the manuscript. Without her friendship, it would not have been as enjoyable to write this book. I owe the greatest debt of gratitude to my mentor and Ph.D. supervisor John Braithwaite for his inspiration, support, and commitment to the project. My parents Joyce and David Parker attentively nurtured the skills and sensibilities that led me to this project. My love and affection belongs to Greg Restall for continuing to be my support and anchor even in the most difficult times. It also belongs to the circle of friends who welcomed us to Canberra where this work began, especially Lorraine Hatfield and Jennifer Collier, for keeping me sane despite their doubts about the sanity of embarking on a project aimed at improving lawyers. The book is dedicated to my parents and to Brisbane's Caxton Legal Centre where, as a law student, I first struggled with whether it was possible to be a just lawyer.

Sydney *C.E.P.*
March 1999

Contents

1 Doorkeepers to Many Rooms

LAWYERS' JUSTICE

Reforming the legal profession

The ominous statement which begins Kafka's famous parable of the futility of modern law—'Before the law stands a doorkeeper' (Kafka 1992: 285)—sums up much of our knowledge of access to legal justice.[1] His villainous doorkeeper with 'big sharp nose and long, thin, black Tartar beard' (Kafka 1992: 285) fits well the gloomy picture of the legal profession painted by much contemporary socio-legal scholarship and by many advocates for the reform of the profession's (self-) regulation. According to this picture, the rich and sophisticated gain easy access to 'justice' through a legal profession only too willing to bend the law to suit the purposes of those who can pay (e.g. McBarnet 1994, Mann 1985). Yet lawyers are frequently unavailable, unaffordable, or unhelpful to 'downsiders' (Cain 1994)—the poor and the different. Because lawyers do their most careful and creative work for the rich, the discourse of law becomes increasingly irrelevant, and oppressive, to those who have little access to it (Cain 1994, McBarnet 1994, Powell 1993). It reflects the concerns of those who use it most, vivid in the technicalities of tax avoidance or takeovers; and excludes those who use it least, biased against women and ethnic minorities in language and content.

Far from fighting for justice against these tendencies, the profession as a whole seems engaged in a cynical attempt to manipulate the exclusionary capacities of lawyers' justice in the attempt to further their own market advantage and social status (Abel 1988*a*, 1989*a*). If they are not actively antipathetic to community concerns about justice, they are

[1] This grim parable forms the climax of Kafka's novel *The Trial*, which was first published in German in 1925. A man 'from the country' comes seeking the radiant justice of law, in the naive belief that it should be 'accessible at all times and to everyone'. The doorkeeper tells him that he cannot be allowed entry 'at the moment', and that if the man ignores his veto, he will only meet opposition from a series of more terrible gatekeepers who guard the inner sanctums of the law. Despite his many bribes and wearisome attempts to be admitted, the doorkeeper always refuses to allow the man in, until eventually the man has sacrificed everything in attempts to bribe the gatekeeper. As he dies, the doorkeeper announces that the gate will now be shut because it was meant only for him.

apathetic, showing little concern for the unjust effects of their work. Sociological and economic critiques of the profession have been strong on motivating competition reform and accountability mechanisms in order to prevent restrictive and self-serving professional practices (Abel 1988*a*, 1989*a*, Weisbrot 1990), and legal professions have been substantially reformed over the last thirty years. Yet the critics have, to date, been weak on suggesting what positive role lawyers might play in helping citizens achieve justice.

In response to the limitations of the market control critique, some scholars have looked for normative ideals for lawyers in the traditional elements of legal professionalism. In a paper on the 'redemption of professionalism', Gordon and Simon (1992: 231) write that 'after both the weaknesses of the [legal professional] ideal and the bar's faithlessness to it are acknowledged there remains a residuum of the professional vision with significant normative appeal and, though this is far more speculative, social potency'. In other work, Gordon has excavated a historical republican ideal of lawyering which could motivate better advocacy for the poor and more social responsibility in the way the rich are served in contemporary contexts (1985, 1988, 1990; see also Luban 1988). In *Beyond Monopoly*, Halliday (1987) finds that legal professions have a capacity not only to pursue market projects, but also to assist the state in governing more effectively by taking responsibility for rationalizing and improving the law; and in *Lawyers and the Rise of Western Political Liberalism*, Halliday and Karpik (1997) show how lawyers have historically helped to preserve and strengthen the rule of law and the separation of powers and therefore kept political liberalism alive. Dingwall and Fenn (1987) and Paterson (1996) also see potential for the social contract between profession and state to be revitalized to ensure that the profession improves its self-regulation.

These approaches attempt to rehabilitate traditional functionalist theories of the professions (Durkheim 1992, Parsons 1954*a*, 1954*b*) by using elements of them as normative ideals rather than empirically accurate analytic descriptions (see Freidson 1992). While they provide some positive ideals for lawyers, on the whole they remain too bounded by the narrow domain of traditional legal culture. Failures of lawyers' justice do not necessarily reflect the failures of individual lawyers, but the bankruptcy of a whole system that predicates its understanding of justice on what happens in just one room, the courtroom. Their conceptions therefore remain unsatisfying in the wider context of citizens' aspirations for justice and the inevitable failure of lawyers to provide it.

Law and society research describes a procedural and remote system of legal justice which often has little meaning to ordinary citizens, is ineffectual in speaking to the culture and consciousness of everyday life, and is only utilized effectively by the rich and powerful. Legalism steals disputes from the control of individuals and communities and provides solutions that are at best irrelevant and at worst oppressive (Auerbach 1983, Christie 1977, Goldberg et al. 1985, Macdonald 1990, Merry 1990, 1993, Merry & Milner 1993). Legal norms that might promote justice prove incapable of penetrating and changing everyday injustices unless supported by existing cultural norms, or supplemented with concerted and persuasive social and political action (Galanter 1981, Krygier 1997, Rosenberg 1991). Yet the coercion of law is an effective tool of oppression in the hands of powerful players who are able to subvert it to their own purposes and even dictate its content through domination of political and legal processes (Fitzpatrick 1992, Galanter 1974, Norrie 1993).

In the following chapters I will argue that while recent reforms to legal professions have achieved much, it is only when reformers and policy-makers move their focus towards the doing of justice 'in many rooms' (Galanter 1981) that we are likely to be able to improve the doing of justice by lawyers in the one room for which they are directly responsible. To the extent lawyers' justice remains uncoupled from other justice mechanisms, it remains unsatisfactory. Since 'people experience justice (and injustice) not only (or usually) in forums sponsored by the state, but also at the primary institutional locations of their activity—home, neighbourhood, workplace, business setting and so on' (Galanter 1981: 162), it is there that justice must be improved. Yet currently informal justice in everyday locations tends to entrench community dominations or mimic the rigidity and control of law (Abel 1982*b*, Cain 1985, Nader 1980). I will argue that access to justice should occur in the interaction between courtroom justice and informal everyday justice in companies, shops, sports clubs, and family homes. Like Selznick (1980: 219), I argue that 'the distinction between formal and informal is only a starting point for social analysis . . . It is the interplay of the two that counts.' It should be in that interaction that lawyers' justice educates people's justice to improve the justice quality of everyday relationships and transactions. It should also be in that interaction that community concerns (including community access to justice concerns) reshape lawyers' regulation, organization, and practices.

This book proposes a model of justice as the deliberative mechanisms by which citizens decide how to organize their lives together and contest actions and decisions that are not made according to shared ideals. It joins deliberative democratic theory with the law and society tradition of research on the limits and possibilities of law in achieving justice. It proposes a model of justice that is more than law, and a normative theory in which law and lawyers facilitate the doing of justice as an everyday practice. It also shows how this broad understanding of access to justice might revitalize the narrower domain of legal professionalism with realistic ideals for the practice of justice. It evaluates the different strategies that are available for regulating the legal profession to achieve these goals, and suggests a model for rendering lawyers themselves subject to the justice of deliberative democracy.

Between facts and norms

The failure of the dominant political theories of 'bourgeois liberal republic' has been failure of the technological capacity for institutional design—the 'failure to specify an array of institutions and practices capable of furnishing its subjects with security of life and capable of protecting that array against internal and external threat' (Dunn 1994: 222). This book attempts to remedy the failure of democratic institutional design in the domain of lawyers and access to justice through an analysis founded on constant dialogue between normative and explanatory theory. Much political theory falls into the trap of ignoring the realities of social life, while much social science fails for want of sufficient interest in normative ideals to supply visionary answers to policy problems. As Habermas (1996: 66) writes,

> The philosophical discourse of justice misses the institutional dimension, toward which the sociological discourse on law is directed from the outset. Without the view of law as an empirical action system, philosophical concepts remain empty. However, insofar as the sociology of law insists on an objectivating view from the outside, remaining insensitive to the symbolic dimension whose meaning is only internally accessible, sociological perception falls into the opposite danger of remaining blind.

Rather than a more orthodox social scientific presentation (where a powerful explanatory theory of an empirical phenomenon is presented and rounded off with a few normative implications) or a political theory (where a strong normative thesis is established and then garnished with one or two comments on how it might apply in practice), this book maintains a contextualized dialogue between the normative and the explanatory throughout. It is a 'pragmatic' project in the Deweyan sense in which abstract reason cannot be divorced from practical experience, and facts and values must shape each other in the ongoing experiment of life (see Selznick 1992: 23). It does not attempt to rewrite the democratic theories of writers like Pettit and Habermas, but to enter into dialogue with their work in the attempt to develop a theory about lawyers, justice, and professional regulation.

In her empirical sociological work, Vaughan (1992, 1996) utilizes a 'theory elaboration method' for adjusting explanatory concepts developed by reference to research in one organizational form (perhaps at a macrolevel) against theories developed by reference to another (perhaps a microlevel case study). The concepts are then re-evaluated in a macrolevel iteration of the analysis, a process that could be repeated through many case studies to produce an explanatory theory powerful enough to apply generally.[2] The model of 'iterated adjustment' between the normative and explanatory adapted from Vaughan in this book is a discipline against, on the one hand, choosing categories in the normative theory of justice that can never map onto a powerful explanatory theory, and, on the other, pursuing explanation devoid of the ability to address crucial normative questions. In Habermas's (1996) words, the method adopted moves 'between facts and norms'. It seeks to avoid the pitfalls of both the 'objectivist disenchantment' (Habermas 1996: 43) of the sociology of law, and the 'sociologically naive' (Bohman 1994: 912) philosophy of justice (see Habermas 1996: 42–81), and to produce (at a rather more modest level of abstraction than Habermas) a policy-oriented theory of lawyers and their regulation for access to justice that is uncompromisingly pragmatic in its normativity. Thus, the book moves from a summary of research on community complaints about lawyers, to the normative theory of access to justice in deliberative democracy, to empirical research on the regulation and nature of the legal profession, and back to questions of deliberative democracy.

Rather than treating the design of regulatory institutions for the legal profession as a case study in regulatory policy, the following chapters see it equally as an application of normative political theory. In place of a focus on technical rules and specific structures, I develop a broad-based theory of the policies, processes, and institutions that ought to

[2] Also see Scheff's (1990: 31, 180–1) method of 'abduction' which shuttles back and forth between observation and imagination, induction and deduction, and relates the specific to the general, the part to the whole, and theory to research.

inform the regulation of legal professions in a variety of places, times, and contexts. Instead of seeing regulatory issues as narrowly confined to the legal, disciplinary, or market structures governing the profession, I look at the many ways, formal and informal, by which we can ensure that lawyers behave according to access to justice norms. And rather than concluding with a static model of lawyer regulation, I propose a dynamic theory for regulating the legal profession according to the requirements of deliberative democracy—a deliberative democracy to which lawyers themselves contribute the justice of law.

CHAPTER OUTLINE

The book begins with the facts that both lawyers' regulation and access to justice are urgent issues of law reform throughout the common law world, and the intuition that they ought to be related as a matter of institutional design. Chapter 2 finds that community and client concerns about lawyers are related to concerns about access to justice, a concern that raises both normative and empirical questions of whether access to justice is an important goal, whether it is relevant to lawyers, and how it might be achieved. The remainder of the book addresses the challenge that client and community complaints raise—of ensuring that the practice of lawyering and the goal of citizens' access to justice are married in theory and policy.

States and reformers have attempted to guarantee access to justice through four waves of reform over the last thirty years: legal aid, public interest law, alternative dispute resolution, and competition policy. The concept of access to justice is defined and adjusted by reference to democratic theory and research on the operation of justice in Chapter 3. It uses deliberative democratic theory together with law and society research on the limits of law and the significance of communal orderings to outline what we can reasonably expect law and lawyers to contribute to the practice of justice in democracy. It concludes that while law is a fundamental mechanism of a just democracy, justice is often done better through informal dispute resolution, social movement politics, formal political action, and dialogic, persuasive, and moralizing means of social control.

Communitarian face-to-face justice and social and political action have been seen as disparate alternatives or subordinate supplements to legal justice rather than complementary pieces of a whole picture of just democracy. Chapter 4 proposes an integrated access to justice policy in which access to informal and political means of doing justice are explicitly seen to be as important as access to law. The relative merits of formal and informal justice, of legal and political justice, have been much debated, but this model integrates them so that (1) the potential for doing justice without law but under the shadow of law is maximized, and (2) individualized justice flows into collective action for justice, and collective justice movements shape and participate in individual claims for justice (see Fig. 4.3).

Chapter 5 turns to the discussion of how lawyers might be regulated to contribute their part to the practice of justice. It shows that lawyers' traditions of ethical self-regulation already provide ideals the profession has used to promote itself as having an access to justice role: the liberal advocacy ideal, the social responsibility ideal, the justice ideal, and the ideal of professional community or collegiality. These ideals are reformulated to address the problems of lawyers' conduct identified in previous chapters and to provide a set of goals according to which the contemporary profession could be governed. The crucial question, however, is what techniques are required to implement them.

Chapter 6 uses sociological theory and empirical evidence about the legal professions of common law countries to show that the profession is an ambiguous target of regulation; segmented, fractured, and diffuse. It has a special power of knowledge and trained competence in the crucial institutions of the law that warrants trust. It has a power from cartelization that warrants distrust. Only a responsive regulatory strategy (see Ayres & Braithwaite 1992) that flows from the kind of deliberation that enables it to be contextually flexible is likely to comprehend this ambiguity. These findings converge with data from a study of reform to the Australian legal profession which show that although lawyers' immediate responses to proposed reform might be defensive and conservative, if reformist regulators use a deliberative process, are prepared to adopt a mix of regulatory strategies, and work with rather than against lawyers' devotion to traditional professional norms, lawyers can be much more responsive to community concerns.

Chapter 7 outlines a normative theory for the design of regulatory institutions of the legal profession based on deliberation between profession, state, and community. It shows that within a deliberative process regulatory techniques of professional community, self-regulation, market reform, and institutions of accountability can complement and balance one another to achieve improvements in access to justice. First, decisions about which regulatory strategies to use and when should be based on judgments about how they will help lawyers fulfil the ethical ideals aimed at justice outlined in Chapter 5. Secondly, each of the regulatory mechanisms used should be subject to continual, contextual deliberation and evaluation in which community and consumer voices are as important as state and professional ones. Thirdly, policy-makers should focus on improving justice as an integrated strategy and then asking where lawyers or legal advisers will fit into that (if at all), rather than assuming access to justice means access to lawyers and allowing existing conceptions of legal service delivery to limit reforms.

Chapter 8 focuses on the problem of legalism's stranglehold on practical access to justice institutions and proposes a possible fifth wave of access to justice reform which implements the insights of the previous chapters. The fifth wave would focus on improving access to justice in the institutions where people transact their daily lives—schools, workplaces, shops, government departments, and families. Such a strategy escapes the reliance of access to justice policy-making on formal legalistic processes and lawyers' services, by requiring these institutions to develop and refine their own access to justice policies which link internal justice processes with external and independent oversight. The fifth wave is posited as not only a desirable development, but also a feasible one given the impetus of mandated self-regulation and the rubric of the new regulatory state (Hood & Scott 1996, Majone 1994).

This book therefore addresses two separate problems, one mainly exogenous to the legal profession, one mainly endogenous: (1) the profession's place in the world from the external perspective of access to justice and (2) the issue of how to regulate lawyers given the nature of the profession and the regulatory techniques available. Chapter 9 concludes the bilateral dialogue by putting the regulation of the legal profession and the theory of deliberative democracy together, summarizing how each can inform the other. The political theory of deliberative democracy helps us understand what role lawyers' justice might play in achieving just social and political relations and how processes of democratic regulation can effectively remedy lawyers' domination. But political theory itself is often too focused on lawyers' justice, on formal participation in the public political sphere, and on the need to remedy abuse of public (not private) power to provide a complete conception of what roles lawyers should play (and not play) in contributing to justice.

The detailed study of the legal profession and access to justice institutions challenges the idealistic democratic and legal theory of writers like Pettit (1997) and Habermas (1996) to grapple with the facts that law and lawyers are integral to achieving justice, yet are very limited in what they can achieve. Therefore, (1) justice must be done in many rooms and through many means; (2) citizens may be able to share in the government of their communities and the practice of justice by realistic participation in local and private institutions, not just in public deliberation that feeds into central law-making processes; (3) the limiting of private power should be as important as the limiting of public power in any theory of how a just democracy should be organized.

By contrast, in another area of scholarly endeavour, reformers and researchers advocate the privileging of the 'lifeworld', of diffuse local and individualized means of face-to-face justice without lawyers, as a solution to the limitations of centralized law in doing justice. This approach to justice is also flawed. As writers like Abel point out, it contains too little law and too little politics to solve fundamental injustices (Abel 1982*b*, Cain 1985, Nader 1980). It does not address adequately the permeation of structures of domination throughout whole communities (making idyllic communal justice impossible). Nor does it have a normative vision of political and legal institutions for alleviating that domination.

This book advocates a bi-directional approach to doing justice in which it is recognized that the centralized justice of law and state politics will only ever be directly applied to a handful of injustices, while the diffuse and decentralized justice (or injustice) of face-to-face relations in families, schools, workplaces, neighbourhoods, and community organizations will apply to many daily situations. A credible architecture of access to justice must be about how what happens in one room affects what happens in others. The model developed here gives each form of justice a role in conditioning and supplementing the other; the few cases which are the subject of formal politics and lawyers' justice create the norms and the potential for coercive enforcement that alleviate domination among informal and diffuse local means of justice. The space for local and informal justice to grow can enable a more practical, democratic architecture of justice where voices from the basement are more audible and the doorkeepers of the law less dominating.

2 Judgments on Lawyers

INTRODUCTION

In popular culture, writes Robert Post, 'the most striking aspect of the image of the lawyer . . . is the intense hostility with which it is invested' (Post 1987: 379). On the one hand movies portray lawyers as heroes of justice. As the authors of one study of the characterization of law and lawyers in film concluded,

> A crucial feature of many of the films examined is the function of the lawyer; the legal process is the means to deliver justice and the lawyer is the bearer of the metaphorical sword. The indispensable central figure is the lawyer who ensures that equity and fairness are distributed to the deserving plaintiff or innocent defendant. (Greenfield & Osborn 1995: 115)

On the other hand, as Post and others point out, lawyer 'bashing' and lawyer jokes permeate our cultures (see Galanter 1994). On the whole people who use a lawyer are in fact satisfied with his or her performance (Galanter 1994: 663, Lafontaine 1985: 177). Yet surveys of public attitudes in the USA, Canada, England, and Australia consistently reveal that lawyers arouse amongst the most negative opinions or impressions of any occupation or profession (Daniel 1983: 118–22, Galanter 1994, Weisbrot 1990: 18, Yale 1982).

Over the last thirty years public concerns about the legal profession have motivated substantial critique and reform of the profession. This chapter and the next outline the major contours of judgment and reform that have faced common law legal professions. In this chapter the focus is on critiques of the profession's failures. The data used are existing empirical literature on lawyers' ethical breaches and offences, on client complaints, and on public attitudes towards lawyers. The purpose is not to argue that the whole legal profession is worse than any other profession or occupation, or that overall legal practice is of a low standard. This chapter simply focuses attention on what can potentially go wrong with legal professionals' delivery of legal services. The design of regulatory institutions (including disciplinary, ethical, and socializing processes) for legal professions must be based in an empirical understanding of what wrongs lawyers can possibly do and how regulation has sometimes failed adequately to deal with them in the past.

The evidence summarized in this chapter shows that clients and community complain when lawyers fail to provide good-quality, consumer-oriented legal services. Traditional regulatory processes, however, ignored those issues and concentrated instead on breaches of professional community and trust account fraud. Abandonment of the regulation of the quality of legal services to the market had profoundly unequal effects. Lawyers generally provide better, more cost-effective services for the rich than the poor, an outcome that has led to great community dissatisfaction with inequality of access to legal services. This dissatisfaction is in turn compounded by evidence that the profession as a whole does not merely provide superior service to the rich, but that they are in the business of distorting justice for the rich.

Public complaints and concerns with lawyers sometimes appear deeply inconsistent. As Robert Post (1987: 380) argues, and the evidence in this chapter will confirm, lawyers 'are simultaneously praised and blamed for the very same actions'. We praise them for effectively following our wishes and using the law to articulate our perspectives, but condemn them for using the legal system to satisfy the desires of other clients. The apparent inconsistency makes it seem that clients and communities are unclear about what they want of lawyers and incapable of making cogent judgments about either the quality of lawyers' work or their role in society. In fact, public attitudes are inchoate but insistent in requiring of lawyers a definite and pivotal role in facilitating and preserving the justice that law is supposed to help us achieve in our societies. As Post argues,

> [We live] in a wildly pluralistic culture, in which individuals constantly struggle to achieve recognition for the legitimacy of their private perspectives. We have organised our legal system so that lawyers speak for the particular and specific sides of this struggle . . . we both want and in some respects have a universal, common culture, and we simultaneously want that culture to be malleable and responsive to the particular and often incompatible interests of individual groups and citizens. We expect lawyers to fulfil both desires, and so they are a constant irritating reminder that we are neither a peaceable kingdom, nor a land of undiluted individual autonomy, but somewhere disorientingly in between. Lawyers, in the very exercise of their profession, are the necessary bearers of that bleak winter's tale, and we hate them for it. (Post 1987: 385, 386)

Lawyers stand at an awkward intersection between law and justice. By purveying legality, lawyers regularly both implement and destroy people's notions of justice and community values (see Post 1987: 382–3). Over the last thirty years judgments on the way lawyers have performed that task have set the agenda for significant reforms.

LACK OF CONSUMER ORIENTATION

Traditionally the structure, organization, and regulation of legal practice in common law countries was governed by the professional associations of barristers and solicitors without community or state interference. This tradition derives from the practice of English barristers who, from at least the end of the fifteenth century, were self-regulated by the strict hierarchies of Inns of Court where students, barristers, and benchers lived together (Disney et al. 1986: 6, Pound 1953: 82 ff.). The Law Societies were set up by solicitors and attorneys in the nineteenth century in an attempt to emulate the success of the Inns of Court at inculcating common standards of professional conduct and ethics through self-regulation (Holdsworth 1937: 443).

The self-regulatory project inherited by today's lawyers was conceived by solicitors in the middle of the nineteenth century at a time when the state was much less interventionist in its regulatory policy, and the community less demanding in its expectation of dynamic democratic involvement in private governments than they are today.[1] By the 1970s professional self-regulation appeared to be an unjustifiably statist bargain that was undemocratic in its incapacity to countenance community concerns about access to justice, consumer service, and controlling costs. Legal professions became vulnerable to government intervention and community criticism. The first (and perhaps most compelling) challenge to the self-regulatory bargain came in the early 1970s with the widespread recognition that lawyers' justice was not available, affordable, or accessible to the poor and the disadvantaged. The private profession was criticized from without by reformist governments and from within by a rapidly growing movement of activist lawyers influenced by the welfarist new left politics of the day. This coincided with the genesis of the access to justice movement described in Chapter 3.

As attention turned more directly to the practices of the legal profession, one of the issues that received most attention from researchers

[1] See Brazier et al. 1993: 198, Tuohy 1976 for the concept of legal professional associations as 'private governments'.

and reformers was the traditional lack of consumer orientation of many lawyers as individual service providers, which was compounded by the lack of concern shown by self-regulatory and disciplinary bodies for consumer complaints about lawyers. Throughout the 1970s and 1980s and into the 1990s a torrent of research showed that client complaints about lawyers throughout the common law world most frequently related to low-quality service (negligence, incompetence, delay, and lack of communication) and overcharging (Abel 1988*a*: 252, 1989*a*: 152, Benson 1979: ii. 254, 301, Jackson 1993, New South Wales Law Reform Commission 1980, 1993, Powell 1986: 53, Steele and Nimmer 1976, Weisbrot 1990: 210). For example, Felstiner (1997) summarizes American and British research on lawyer–client relationships showing that people complain when lawyers fail to treat clients with respect, do not consider the nature of interpersonal relations with clients to be an important part of law practice, appear to be motivated more by financial returns than professional values, are inaccessible and unresponsive, are poor communicators, and show indifference to client feelings. Aspects of billing such as excessive charges, failure to provide details of charges, and the imposition of costs in advance were also major causes of complaint for clients (e.g. New South Wales Law Reform Commission 1980, Steele & Nimmer 1976). Hourly billing, the predominant method of charging in the legal profession, was found to be particularly prone to unfair and deceptive billing practices, such as double billing for time spent travelling for one client and reading documentation for another; billing a second client for recycling relevant research or document preparation; billing extra hours for a particularly clever piece of work; billing for dubious expenses; or simply 'padding'—billing for hours that have not been worked with no attempt at justification (Lerman 1994, MacDonald 1994, Marquess 1994, Ross 1996, Selinger 1994, Simon 1994).

The most devastating critique of the profession, however, was not that some clients were dissatisfied with the quality of service offered, but that the profession did not appear concerned with consumer complaints about lawyers at all. Abel's (1988*a*) research in England and Wales showed that the grounds on which disciplinary tribunals punished solicitors—violation of accounts regulations, misappropriation of client funds, false statements in applying for a practising certificate, criminal convictions, acting as a solicitor without holding a current practising certificate, and failing to account for money—were very different from what clients complained about. Delay, which was 67 per cent of justified complaints, was the reason for punishment in only 8 per cent of cases. Seventy per cent of claims were found either to be unjustified or to concern negligence over which the Law Society disclaimed jurisdiction (1988*a*: 252). In his research on the USA, Abel (1989*a*: 152) concluded that 'Although the vast majority of client complaints involve matters of competence, professional disciplinary bodies generally reject charges of incompetence as outside their jurisdiction' (see also Powell 1986: 53).

Indeed the studies revealed that most dissatisfied clients did not bother to complain. For example the English Benson Royal Commission found that only one-third of the 11 per cent dissatisfied clients surveyed had complained either to their lawyer or to the relevant disciplinary body (Benson 1979: ii. 252). Evans's recent study of client perceptions of Victorian solicitors found that 20 per cent were dissatisfied with their solicitor (1995: 59). But only 30 per cent of these had filed a complaint with the relevant self-regulatory body (Evans 1995: 61). About half of the dissatisfied clients in a recent survey of Scottish clients did not complain to either the firm or a self-regulatory body about the service they received (MacMillan 1995: 38). Even where clients do not actually report to researchers that they are dissatisfied with the service provided, their general attitudes to lawyers suggest that many clients believe it could be better: most respondents to one survey believed that 'the legal profession is not prompt enough, do not keep clients well enough informed, and assume an air of superiority when dealing with clients' (Legal Access Marketing Group 1985: 33).

Across all the common law countries the complaints and discipline statistics show that while clients were complaining most frequently of delay, incompetence, overcharging, and discourtesy, the self-regulatory bodies were focusing 'on intraprofessional complaints (such as unfair attraction of business), practice by unauthorised persons (in breach of legal monopolies) and financial misconduct' (Weisbrot 1990: 210). In 1974 Maley analysed the ethical codes of Australian engineers, architects, and doctors, and the ethical statements and rulings of the Law Society of New South Wales. He found that the codes were primarily concerned with

> the proscription of advertising except in carefully limited and controlled ways, injunctions to maintain the established scale of professional fees, prohibition of commissions and discounts, insistence on remuneration only by fee or salary, prevention of soliciting clients, and exhortations to serve the com-

munity and uphold the dignity and honour of the profession. (Maley 1974: 393)[2]

They spent most space on the professional's 'obligations to his colleagues, to matters of etiquette between colleagues, and in carrying on his professional practice in ways which do not infringe colleague-prerogatives or give him a professional (especially an economic) advantage' (Maley 1974: 397). The policing and enforcing of the obligations was also biased towards these concerns. According to Wolfram (1978) legal professional codes in the USA were also concerned mainly with the etiquette of how lawyers attract business. Such rules were designed to prevent overt competition between practitioners and preserve the image of a profession oriented towards public service rather than allowing law to be seen as a business aimed at commercial gain (see Fennell 1982). For example, 'ambulance chasing' or touting is seen as particularly undesirable conduct in the USA and in England (Abel-Smith & Stevens 1967: 196), and has been strictly forbidden in Australia. At one stage the Chicago Bar Association even sought (unsuccessfully) to be given the power to impose prison sentences on lawyers who solicited clients (Abel 1989*a*: 145). Yet as early as 1965 Reichstein had argued that ambulance chasing is functional in a situation of inadequate legal service provision and sharp practices by insurance company assessors.

Another major area of concern for professional associations before the 1990s was pursuing those practising law without a licence. Because their professional monopoly is enshrined in law, professional associations have the power to prosecute people for practising law without a practising certificate. As the following chapter will show, the pursuit of professional monopoly through both the sanctioning of unqualified legal service providers and the maintenance of a unified professional community has been one of the main projects of the legal profession (O'Malley 1983: 76).

There was (and remains) one area of client injury which professional associations and disciplinary authorities in Britain, Australia, and Canada took particularly seriously—trust account fraud. Disciplinary authorities spend a major part of their resources on policing trust

[2] In 1993, the Trade Practices Commission found that in most Australian states and territories significant regulation on the type of advertising allowed, prohibitions on ways fees could be charged (e.g. no contingency fees), what a barrister could do, reservation of certain work to licensed legal practitioners, and regulation on the structure of legal practices continued to make up the bulk of the regulatory rules for the legal profession (Trade Practices Commission 1993: 71–7).

accounts, carrying out random audits, and ensuring that audit certificates are filed each year. Weisbrot (1990: 204) shows that almost all of the eighty-two solicitors struck off between 1968 and 1982 in New South Wales were disciplined for committing trust account breaches, a matter which accounted for only 2 per cent of complaints to the Law Society.

Certain lawyers have great opportunities to steal from clients. In the English and Australian system, solicitors hold large amounts of money on trust for clients in relation to conveyancing transactions, money from deceased estates, settlement money from litigation, and money for outgoings that the lawyer will pay on the client's behalf. Clients also leave money with solicitors for investment at higher interest rates than they might receive from a bank. There is some evidence that money left with lawyers for a long time such as estate money or long-term investments is more likely to be embezzled (Garling 1983). In many cases, this occurs where the solicitor invests the money in his or her own private finance company (Wilton 1983: 35). In Canada, Arthurs (1970: 248) found that 39 per cent of lawyers disbarred for trust account fraud had 'extra-legal' general investment or land development businesses. If this is combined with a precarious financial situation or a declining practice, embezzlement can become very tempting. This is not a problem for barristers in divided professions since they do not keep trust accounts and rarely have access to clients' money. Similarly, in the USA where lawyers do not have a conveyancing monopoly in many states and do not generally invest money for clients, it is a less important issue (Haynes 1983) and US disciplinary authorities and professional associations appear to have been much less vigilant at introducing effective compensatory and disciplinary mechanisms for dealing with it (Abel 1988*b*: 220).

One reason trust account fraud is the most frequently sanctioned offence is that it is relatively easily policed and its wrongful nature is not controversial. Compared with more subjective complaints of negligence and incompetence, a lay person can be sure they have been harmed. Thus, disciplinary authorities must act and be seen to act on trust fund problems if their legitimacy is not to be questioned. For this reason, in both England and Australia, trust fund and other financial improprieties by solicitors were a major reason for introducing significant regulation, particularly self-regulation, over solicitors in the first place (Abel-Smith & Stevens 1967: 188, Kirk 1976: 83–105, McQueen 1993: 15, 21, Paterson 1996). While fraud is clearly of major concern to clients when it occurs, their losses are generally covered by fidelity funds and problems are relatively infrequent. In contrast to what disciplinary enforcement figures suggest, clients are more commonly concerned about the quality of the service they receive and the way the bill is determined. It is unfortunate that regulatory investigation and enforcement resources have been concentrated in an area which, by definition, is likely to be of more concern to richer clients (Reasons & Chappell 1986: 40).

REFORMERS' RESPONSES

In response to these concerns about the quality of legal services for consumers, significant reforms have been made to the traditionally self-regulating arrangements of the legal professions in many jurisdictions.

First, the structural arrangements for lawyer discipline and regulation have been altered and reformed in most jurisdictions. In many places an ombudsman has been placed on top of the disciplinary process to oversee the way client complaints are handled, such as the Legal Services Ombudsman introduced in 1991 in England (James & Seneviratne 1995). Self-regulatory complaints handling, investigation, and disciplinary functions have been handed to bodies quasi-independent of professional associations (but still funded by and ultimately accountable to them) and lay representatives have been included in the process, such as the English Solicitors Complaints Bureau (now called the Office for the Supervision of Solicitors) set up in 1986. Even more radically, in some jurisdictions complaint handling functions were taken away from self-regulatory bodies and given to independent boards, commissions, or, as is frequently the case in the USA, to court-appointed bodies (Powell 1986). More radical reforms to self-regulation have occurred in places like New South Wales where the Office of the Legal Services Commissioner (OLSC), an independent statutory office, now receives all complaints about solicitors and barristers, and can either investigate them itself or pass them on to the self-regulatory disciplinary bodies of either branch of the profession. In New South Wales, even if complaints are handled by the self-regulatory bodies, the OLSC retains the power to oversee and review the profession's disciplinary functions and to direct the professional bodies as to how they should handle the complaint. Serious complaints that are found to be justified are adjudicated by an independent Legal Services Tribunal which has wide powers to discipline lawyers and grant compensation to complainants (Mark 1995, Parker 1997*b*).

As Powell's (1986: 53) research shows, however, even when disciplinary functions are handed over to an independent body the profile of matters sanctioned barely changes.[3] There must also be substantive changes in the rules and in the complaints handling process if the historical lack of attention to consumer type complaints is to be addressed. In response to this problem, the ethical and disciplinary rules governing lawyers have been changed in some jurisdictions so that regulatory bodies can deal with consumer type complaints. Regulatory processes have also been changed in some jurisdictions so that regulators can conciliate or meditate these complaints and order compensation or restitution to clients. In England, for example, delay and failure to communicate are now breaches of the solicitors' care and skill obligation to provide services which are of the quality which it is reasonable to expect. Compensation of up to £1,000 is available to clients for 'inadequate professional services'. The Office for the Supervision of Solicitors now claims to resolve over 70 per cent of consumer disputes by agreement or conciliation (James & Seneviratne 1995: 195). The Lord Chancellor's Advisory Committee on Legal Education and Conduct, with 50 per cent lay representation, also has a continuing input into professional rule-making and regulatory structures through its reports, which may ensure the complaints handling process becomes even more consumer-oriented. Similarly in New South Wales, lawyers can now be disciplined for unsatisfactory professional conduct (conduct that falls short of the standard of competence and diligence that a member of the public is entitled to expect of a reasonably competent legal practitioner), not just the more traditional professional misconduct.[4] The OLSC mediates (formally or informally) most of the consumer complaints it receives from clients, without passing them on to a self-regulatory body for investigation. In 1995/6 62 per cent of written complaints were resolved following informal and formal mediation by the OLSC. A further 14 per cent were still under mediation (Office of the Legal Services Commissioner 1997). Most of these were complaints that would have been dismissed as unsuitable for further action under the old system.

[3] See also Hansen 1994: 98–9 for the Legal Services Ombudsman's opinion that the English Solicitors Complaints Bureau still focuses too heavily on solicitor fraud and dishonesty at the expense of routine client complaints about inadequate service.

[4] s. 127 Legal Profession Act 1987 (NSW).

Professional regulators have also sought to encourage lawyers to take responsibility for delivering high-quality services even before clients take a complaint externally. In England the Law Society's 'client care' rule (rule 15) requires that all solicitors have an in-house complaints handling procedure and inform all clients about it early in the lawyer–client relationship (Greenbaum 1996: 321, Harris 1994, James & Seneviratne 1995: 198–9). In the USA, England, and Australia, professional associations have begun to enforce annual continuing legal education requirements for all practitioners as a requirement for continuing registration or licensing in the hope of improving the standard and quality of legal services (Greenbaum 1996: 319, Paterson 1996: 149). Law firms are also increasingly seeking quality assurance certification in an effort to convince potential clients, usually corporate clients who themselves need quality certification, that they will provide a good service (Dal Pont 1996: 63–8, Lockley 1993, Paterson 1996: 150). One of the major responses to evidence of lack of quality services or overservicing and overcharging among lawyers has been the corporate clients' use of 'beauty contests' and tendering processes to achieve lower costs and higher quality. In an attempt to ensure some of the same quality benefits accrue to poorer clients, the English Legal Aid Board has embarked upon a 'franchising' programme to delegate to certain legal firms the ability to be responsible for their own small portion of the legal aid budget if they meet appropriate quality criteria (see Moorhead et al. 1994, Sherr et al. 1994). Some British legal expenses insurance suppliers have also required firms on their panels to certify their quality (Paterson 1996: 156).

At a structural level, competitive reforms have been introduced to the legal professions of all common law countries particularly in the form of allowing non-lawyer conveyancers to compete with solicitors where they had not been allowed before and allowing solicitor advocates to compete with barristers in jurisdictions where the divided profession remained (e.g. Brockman 1996, Cownie 1990, Parker 1997, Powell 1985). Each of these reforms will be further discussed and evaluated in following chapters.

LAWYERS AND JUSTICE

One survey concluded that people look for commitment, integrity, competence, and fairness or reasonableness of fee in their lawyer

(Curran 1985). These are fairly prosaic standards, commonly required of service providers. Yet they hold a particular significance when the service provider is a lawyer. The self-regulatory bodies' failure to deal with consumer type complaints about lawyers did not just affect clients' appraisal of the quality of service provided to them, it also affected their perception of the justice of the legal system. As Moore's (1985: 50) survey of public attitudes to the law and legal system in Canada shows, people's dissatisfaction with the services they have personally received from a lawyer correlates well with judgments that the legal system as a whole is ineffective and unjust. Bad service from lawyers is not just another consumer issue, it makes people feel they have been denied justice. Similarly Jackson's (1993) summary of British research on the satisfaction of defendants with the criminal courts concluded that defendants felt 'let down' by lawyers when they did not give them sufficient personal contact, attention, and consultation. He concluded that spending sufficient time with their lawyer was an important factor in defendants' perceptions of the procedural fairness of the whole criminal process. Felstiner (1997: 123–4) uses evidence of people's perceptions of procedural justice to argue that in their interactions with lawyers people's self-respect and integrity is likely to be significantly affected since they see lawyers as authority figures, ministers of the justice system. But perhaps the most obvious way in which the practices of lawyers touch access to justice is the difference in the services proffered to different types of clientele.

Inequality of access to high-quality legal services

In relation to both charging and quality of services, richer and institutional clients are less at the mercy of their lawyers than poorer individual clients. Indeed people believe that lawyers will not work as hard for poor clients as for rich ones and that they are primarily interested in making money. For example, the Australian Commission of Inquiry into Poverty surveyed people in three poorer areas of Sydney and found a common impression of lawyers as capable of giving good service, but generally giving it more to the rich than the poor. A large majority of the sample agreed that: 'For a price lawyers will use every trick in the books to help their clients' (71.4 per cent); 'Lawyers are mainly interested in making money' (70.3 per cent); and 'Lawyers are not champions of the poor' (65.6 per cent) (Cass & Sackville 1975: 82; see also Legal Access Marketing Group 1985: 36). It seems likely that these perceptions are shared among the populations of common law countries. For example, Reasons, Bray, and Chappell's (1989) Canadian survey found that, while a majority of the general public accepted that lawyers' ethical standards were very high, they also thought that lawyers charged more than they were worth and disagreed that lawyers will work as hard for a poor client as for a rich one (see also Moore 1985).

The evidence suggests that people's beliefs on this score are correct. General efforts at improving the quality of consumer service meet with limited success: Jenkins's research for the English Law Society on quality management found 'a lack of enthusiasm' for the Law Society's efforts at inculcating quality among law firms (1994: 224). Only 12 per cent of the 900 firms who had actually requested a copy of the Law Society's publication *Quality: A Briefing for Solicitors* were willing to respond to a survey about it. Jenkins (1994: 224) cites evidence that the 'partnership culture' means that firms are reluctant to 'adopt procedures which concentrate on service delivery rather than on the quality of legal advice'. A survey of the client care provided by Scottish solicitors conducted for the Scottish Consumer Council also found that despite the Law Society's guidance manual on client care, the majority of solicitors still did not regularly report to clients on case developments, or tell clients what to do if they were dissatisfied with their service (MacMillan 1995: 13, 14). But large corporate clients have been able to force many of their lawyers to improve quality. The work both of Heinz and Laumann (1982) and of Spangler (1986) in the USA has shown how lawyers for business and for the rich are increasingly being forced to provide the service their clients want. Mackie's (1989: 129) study of British and Australian in-house corporate lawyers traces the rise of corporate legal departments and also the increased control that in-house lawyers are able to give their corporate employers over the conduct of cases by outside law firms. Ten years ago when Mackie did his fieldwork British in-house lawyers were already conducting 'beauty contests' (1989: 46)—demanding tenders, estimates of set fees, and presentations as to how work would be done. Similarly Galanter and Palay's (1991: 50) study of large law firms in the USA found that 'today's enlarged corporate legal departments impose budgetary restraints, exert more control over cases, demand periodic reports, and engage in comparison shopping among firms', By contrast Jenkins's 1992 survey of in-house practice management methods shows that despite the Law Society client care rule, as many as 59 per cent of sole practitioners (who are more likely to serve individual clients) had not set up in-house complaints procedures (Jenkins 1994: 233; see also Harris 1994: 9) and 36 per cent of sole practitioners and 3–4 partner firms only discussed costs with clients in response to questions, rather than disclosing them upfront as required (Jenkins 1994: 234; see also Harris 1994: 4–6).

The balance of empirical research on lawyer–client relations and communication confirms that there is a big difference between the services offered to corporate organizations and rich clients and that offered to poor, low-status, or individual ones. Research on middle-class clients is ambiguous. In the USA, Reed (1972) and Hosticka (1979), and in Australia Lawrence (1978), suggest that lawyers generally dominate their relationships with individual clients in unhelpful ways. Rosenthal (1977) also found evidence that there were breakdowns in the way lawyers deliver services to clients because of inappropriate models of lawyer-controlled decision-making. Cain (1983), on the other hand, argued that general practice lawyers do not dominate clients but faithfully translate clients' objectives into legal reality. Sarat and Felstiner's (1995) extensive project on the way lawyers and clients related in forty divorce cases shows how lawyers negotiate with, persuade, and interpret the legal system to clients who are dependent on their explanations. But they argue that neither the lawyer nor the client is consistently in control of the relationship:

> Both lawyers and clients are sometimes frustrated by feelings of powerlessness in dealing with the other . . . Often no one may be in charge. Interactions between lawyers and clients involve as much drift and uncertainty as they do direction and clarity of purpose. It may be difficult at any one moment to determine who, if anyone, is defining the objectives, determining strategy, or devising tactics. (Felstiner & Sarat 1992: 1456)

The evidence does seem clear that it is common for lawyers to dominate rather than serve low-status clients. Many studies of the criminal justice system have shown how clients are dependent on lawyers who organize and persuade them to fit in with the demands of the court system (Baldwin & McConville 1977, Blumberg 1967, Ericson & Baranek 1982: 76–110, Sudnow 1965). Similar observations have been made of lawyers who deal exclusively with low-status clients in community legal centres or legal services/legal aid offices (Spangler 1986: 144–74, Parker 1994). The level of service a client receives depends greatly on the socio-economic status of the client: '[T]he relative ease with which . . . lawyers can tell their clients what to do seems to speak more to the helplessness of the clients than to the power of the attorneys' (Spangler 1986: 171).

Relative power and status between lawyer and client may not be the only factors causing some clients to receive lesser-quality, less cost-effective service: the status of the lawyer within the profession, and the lawyer's stock of 'social capital' (Arnold & Kay 1995), also have an effect. Low-status clients are more likely to be served by solo practitioners or small firm lawyers, and there is considerable evidence that these low-status lawyers violate ethical rules aimed at promoting good-quality service more often than other lawyers. While this phenomenon was first observed in the 1960s (Carlin 1966, Handler 1967), more recent studies show that it has continued to remain true: Reasons and Chappell (1985, 1986) demonstrate that if a lawyer is engaged in solo practice, conveyancing, mortgage transactions, or general practice, he or she is more likely to be sanctioned by disciplinary authorities (see also Arnold & Hagan 1992, 1994, Arnold & Kay 1995). Weisbrot (1990: 203–4) cites evidence that solo practitioners are over-represented and large firm lawyers under-represented among solicitors against whom complaints are filed, not just those who are actually disciplined.

These results were traditionally explained by the fact that rule-making and disciplinary processes were controlled by elites who were more likely to label marginal practitioners' behaviour unethical. However, when Arnold and Hagan (1992, 1994) tried to establish this statistically in Canada, their data turned out very ambiguously. Their 1994 study gives some support for the idea that solo practitioner status and professional inexperience influence disciplinary decision-making, but legitimate factors such as offence characteristics and complaint histories were much more important. Studies such as Carlin's (1966) and Handler's (1967) relied on their own surveys of the bar and tests of unethical behaviour rather than official statistics, and Weisbrot's (1990) evidence is of complaint rather than prosecution statistics. Their conclusions are therefore not biased by official sanctioning practices. However, the ethical rules themselves are developed by elites and reflect their concerns (see e.g. Reichstein 1965). There are gaps in those concerns. As we shall see below, the whole area of distortion of justice on behalf of clients has rarely been specified beyond vague generalizations in ethical codes and discussion. Nor is it enforced in disciplinary action or informal criticism.

A more powerful explanation for decreased ethics among low-status lawyers is Arthurs's (1970) suggestion that solo practitioners are more likely to give unethical and unskilled service because they lack the collegial support of those in larger firms and are in a more financially precarious situation. Arnold and Kay's 1995 study of the statistical evidence from one Canadian law society confirms that differential 'social capital' is a significant explanatory factor in lawyer misconduct. They argue that large firms which serve high-status clients are rich in formal and informal controls on their employees. Lawyers are 'embedded within networks of social relations that provide ethical obligations, expectations . . . information channels and social norms' (Arnold & Kay 1995: 339). Their management structures, socialization processes, and, recently, quality assurance programmes mean that large firm lawyers are less likely to serve clients poorly or defraud them, and if they do, disciplinary authorities are more likely to delegate responsibility to the firm to deal with it. Their findings match Freidson's (1975) study of informal social control among medical practitioners. Where mistakes occurred within a group practice setting, other doctors spoke to the offender and were effective in influencing a change or getting them to resign. However, when solo practitioners made a mistake the main form of control was non-referral, which was too ambiguous a signal to be useful in correcting the offender. Thus informal professional control worked only in settings where individual practitioners were embedded in a local professional community.

Solo practitioners and small firm lawyers do not enjoy the social embeddedness of large firm lawyers.[5] They are less likely to have access to the network of business and management resources and contacts that lawyers in large firms have, and will generally have more financially insecure practices because of their lower-status clientele. The result is greater temptation to take on more work than they can handle, to violate ethical rules promoting good-quality service in the struggle to survive, and lesser capacity to deal with problems internally when they do arise.

Low-status lawyers are also more subject to countervailing pressures from the court system or from lack of resources. In a classic paper, Blumberg (1967: 19) shows how criminal lawyers are subject to the demands of a whole system in which their clients must be made to fit:

> Organizational goals and discipline impose a set of demands and conditions of practice on the respective professions in the criminal court, to which they

[5] However Landon's research (1985) shows that solo practitioners who practise in a close-knit community may be better advocates for clients because they are embedded in the expectations of the community.

respond by abandoning their ideological and professional commitments to the accused client, in the service of these higher claims of the court organization.

It is practice at the lower end which is more likely to be subject to these pressures. Richer clients can afford to pay lawyers who will fight the system. Poorer clients get less devoted service from lawyers who are themselves less powerful players in bigger games. As Carlin (1966: 177) concluded from his famous study of the ethics of the New York City bar thirty years ago:

> The best trained, most technically skilled, and ethically most responsible lawyers are reserved to the upper reaches of business and society. This leaves the least competent, least well-trained, and least ethical lawyers to the smaller business concerns and lower-income individuals. As a result, the most helpless clients who most need protection are least likely to get it.

Historically the professional associations exacerbated this injustice by using professional rules to prohibit innovations in services that might make lawyers more accessible and less costly. In the USA, breakthrough restrictive practices cases arose when lawyers who sought to set up new forms of legal services (that made lawyers more affordable) were prosecuted by bar associations for breaking professional rules.[6] For example, it took Jacoby and Meyers four years to be cleared of charges of breach of legal ethics over their inexpensive shopfront legal clinic which offered long opening hours and the use of paralegals to cut costs (Coleman 1985: 31). Zander (1968) discusses the British ethical rules that prevented lawyers working for the poor at that time. Even innovations to provide free legal services for no profit have been opposed: in Australia professional associations tried to use ethical rules to stop legal aid offices being set up by the federal government in 1975 (Tomsen 1992).[7]

Distorting justice for rich clients

Not only do lawyers, on the whole, perpetuate injustice by serving the rich better than the poor within the limits of the law, but majority agreement with statements such as 'For a price a lawyer will use every trick in the book to help a client' (Cass & Sackville 1975: 82) suggests

[6] See *Bates* v. *State Bar Association of Arizona* 433 US 350 (1977) and *Goldfarb* v. *Virginia State Bar Association* 421 US 773 (1975).

[7] *Ex parte Hartstein: re Bannister* (1975) ACT Supreme Court, unreported; see Disney (1975).

that people think lawyers will do anything for someone who pays well enough, regardless of ethical considerations. Not only do people complain when lawyers hinder their own access to justice, they also complain when lawyers appear to provide others with service that undermines the justice of the whole system. Large firm lawyers who serve high-status clientele are particularly susceptible to being charged with selling out to big business (see Nader & Smith 1996, Nelson 1988: 236, Smigel 1964: 294–5).

Again the evidence does seem to bear out public opinion. Kenneth Mann's 1985 study of elite white-collar crime defence lawyers in the USA presents a picture of clients who can afford lawyers so wily and well paid they can outwit prosecutors and manipulate the criminal justice system to help their clients avoid well-grounded prosecutions. In particular, he shows how lawyers are able to control the information they receive so as not actually to find out about the illegal activities of their clients and thereby conduct a defence in good faith. Compare this with the accounts of how defence lawyers for ordinary lower-class criminals persuade them to fit in with the system and accept a 'reasonable' plea bargain (Baldwin & McConville 1977, Blumberg 1967, Sudnow 1965). Both are potentially breaching the highest standards of the ethics of legal practice, but in very different ways.

Rich clients can afford lawyers who do the work of creating 'legal techniques, definitions and devices including devices which avoid state impositions and obviate other people's legal rights if they impinge on the interests of their clients' (McBarnet 1994: 83; see also Powell 1993). Galanter (1974) shows how large companies can undermine whole areas of regulation set in place to advance liberty by settling cases where an unfavourable precedent is likely to be set, using their superior access to the best legal advice to fight those cases where they are likely to achieve an interpretation in their favour. Doreen McBarnet (1994: 74) questions the way that lawyers (throughout the common law world) have been able to use their skills to help rich clients evade taxes:

> Aware that new law does not suit their interests, the owners and managers of capital may well lobby against it. But at the same time, armies of Wall Street and City lawyers will be working to construct devices which can render the law irrelevant anyway.

Levi (1988: 158–72) shows that widespread tax avoidance and evasion in Australia during the 1970s and early 1980s facilitated by accountants and lawyers, and encouraged by the Barwick-led High

Court, resulted in a public crisis of confidence in the taxation system (see also Palmer & Sampford 1994: 23). Indeed the technicalities of tax law illustrate that as lawyers spend more of their time helping achieve the goals of certain clients, so the law comes disproportionately to reflect their interests and concerns, becoming less effective than it might be for the whole community (Cain 1994). The potential injustices of lawyers' creative role in assisting the schemes of corporate capital are even further magnified in an era of globalization in which, according to Dezalay (1996: 60), 'Wall Street lawyers . . . are the modern mercenaries of [a] new brand of symbolic imperialism' through which 'the North American ruling class is giving itself the means of extending its hegemony over the whole of the planet'. Dezalay and Garth (1996) use their extensive interviews with key global players in commercial arbitration to describe the way a handful of elite North American and European lawyers have created the lex mercatoria of international commercial arbitration in which multinational corporations can settle their disputes in private according to a law of their own making with barely a thought to broader public interests.

Nelson's study of US large firm lawyers showed they felt they ought to curb their clients' unethical, unjust, or illegal behaviour, but very rarely acted on that belief: 'In the reality of practice these lawyers enthusiastically attempt to maximize the interests of clients and rarely experience serious disagreements with clients over the broader implications of a proposed course of conduct' (Nelson 1988: 232). Tomasic and Bottomley's (1993: 88) study of the running of the top 500 Australian companies in the aftermath of the financial collapses of the late 1980s found that many professional advisers thought their business clients were often unethical, but did not think it was their role to do anything about it. They also found that professional advisers including lawyers played their part in the 1980s 'decade of greed' through positive advice or failures to detect or advise against fraudulent action (Tomasic & Bottomley 1993: 185). Similar issues were raised in the US savings and loans scandals in which several law firms have been prosecuted for assisting in their clients' fraudulent schemes by failing to pass on relevant information to the regulators (see Nader & Smith 1996: 39–48).

Although it seems more likely that lawyers will be over-compliant with the pressures of client interests where the clients are rich and powerful, the temptation may also arise in relation to less glamorous clients (see Parsons 1954*b*: 371–2, 376–7). In 1966, Carlin (at 73) found that lawyers with low-status clients reported more frequent pressure from clients than lawyers with high-status clients. He concluded that where lawyers have an unstable clientele or derive the major portion of their income from a large client then they are most sensitive to pressure. On reconsidering his work in 1994 in the light of contemporary research, Carlin (1994: p. xvii) thought this had changed:

> The large firms have become more commercial, more business—and profit-oriented and very likely less ethical (evidenced most recently by the millions in settlement fees paid by Kaye Scholer and Jones Day for their roles in the Lincoln savings-and-loan mess). And given the power of the corporate clients and their greater concern with self-protection, it is more likely to be third parties who suffer from the unethical behaviour of large-firm lawyers, as in the S and L cases, rather than the clients . . . It appears then that large firm lawyers are moving closer to their colleagues at the other end of the status ladder in terms of professionalism and ethics, while at the same time moving away even further in terms of power and wealth.

The most obvious explanation for this kind of undesirable conduct is the dependence lawyers feel on their clients and the pressure to keep their business by doing whatever they want. Whether or not low-status clients can influence lawyers to act in their own interests against the public interest, rich and institutional clients will have more access to legal services and so will pose a greater threat in this regard. Increasing competitive pressures may increase the threat, and in large firms the structure of the workplace or of particular work teams may encourage individual lawyers to keep silent (see Grabosky 1990). The social capital of large firms might work to create a conscience-stifling atmosphere where such good service is expected for clients that lawyers are discouraged from taking an ethical stand against the distortion of justice.

CONCLUSION

Clients and community require lawyers to perform a subtle and complex role in facilitating access to justice in our democracies. Clients and community are concerned when lawyers fail to provide equal access to high-quality legal services and when they help their clients undermine the justice of the system to which they seek access. Disciplinary authorities seem to concern themselves with rather different matters. Historically a large percentage of the complaints that people made about their own lawyers never went any further than being scrutinized and dismissed by these authorities. Indeed legal professional disciplinary authorities disclaimed jurisdiction over many of the things that people most frequently complain about (Abel 1981*b*: 648). A number of reforms have sought to address the failure of professional regulatory bodies to respond to consumer concerns of clients. But what about the broader justice critique of the part that lawyers play in the legal system?

As the New South Wales Legal Services Commissioner has reflected in relation to the difficulties inherent in his job of dealing with client complaints about lawyers, there is a dichotomy between the perceptions of law and justice held by the profession and by consumers:

> consumers of legal services . . . are almost always seeking justice. The difficulty arises when what they receive from their legal practitioner (or the legal process) is not justice as they perceive it, but law. Common sense, or common understanding leads us to acknowledge that justice is a subjective concept unique to each member of the community seeking it . . . It has also become apparent to me that members of the community who seek justice almost exclusively consider justice in terms of outcome, while the profession, when confronting the concept of justice, almost always discuss it in terms of process. (Mark 1996: 3–4)

The argument of this book is that the profession is correct to have resisted the public belief that it should somehow be able heroically to achieve social justice in its daily work. But while the public easily confuse legal with substantive or social justice, this does not make justice irrelevant to the profession. Lawyers and legal justice are part of the processes by which we seek to institutionalize justice in our societies. As a result broader notions of justice lend lawyers their context and meaning, and will help us understand what are appropriate normative goals for the regulation or governance of the profession. In order to understand what we should expect of legal advisers, it is crucially important to understand the place of legal justice in the broader justice arrangements of the socio-polity.

3 Access to Justice

INTRODUCTION

The rhetoric of access to justice (and the reform movement associated with it) has been bringing the demands of substantive justice to bear on discussions about the legal system and on legal services over the last thirty years. The access to justice movement is a multinational, reform-oriented coalition of legal workers, government reformers, and law and society scholars. They share a common concern with making their national legal systems more accessible, and with the fact that legal processes do not necessarily lead to results that are individually or socially just. The international movement of the 1960s and 1970s was comprehensively described in the normative and empirical work of the Florence Access to Justice Project (e.g. Cappelletti & Garth 1978, Garth 1980), and the rhetoric of access to justice has remained significant in the way government policies on the legal system are marketed to and judged by their citizens. For example, in 1995 Lord Woolf published his interim 'access to justice' report for the British government which recommended the streamlining of the civil litigation system using case management and mediation options (see Zuckerman & Cranston 1995), and in 1994, the Australian federal Labor government commissioned an Access to Justice Advisory Committee to consolidate thirty years of law reform commission research and reports on access to justice and to identify key issues for action (Access to Justice Advisory Committee 1994).

Yet the term 'access to justice' has never been well defined. It has covered a wide variety of issues including the accessibility of court processes for resolving disputes over mutual rights and responsibilities,[1] the availability of adequate legal representation in criminal trials (e.g. Young & Wall 1996), access to more informal legal processes such as small claims courts and administrative tribunals (e.g. Sainsbury & Genn

[1] For example, rights to compensation in negligence or mutual rights and responsibilities in a contract or after a divorce.

1995), and the availability of legal advice[2] and public legal education. The access to justice movement has advocated more substantive reforms of law and legal procedures to ensure that the interests of the poor, minorities, and diffuse public interests can be taken into account, in addition to promoting a broad range of alternative dispute resolution methods and intra-organizational complaints handling mechanisms to avert legal processes altogether.

The reason for this extensive range of concerns is that while the term 'access to justice' has been used mainly in relation to the legal system, the 'justice' to which it refers has been taken by reformers to mean much more than legal justice. The history of the access to justice movement can be read as an ongoing struggle to overcome the discrepancy between the claims of substantive justice and the formal legal system. The term has been useful precisely because it signifies this tension between legal justice and substantive justice. Because people do see the legal profession as a major access to justice institution, much access to justice policy relies either directly or indirectly on reorganizing institutions of legal professionalism and legal service delivery. The waves of access to justice reform advocated and institutionalized by reformers over thirty or forty years therefore provide a starting point for considering whether and how the legal profession might be regulated or reformed to link it more closely to people's expectations of justice.

In the following section I outline four waves of access to justice reform that have aimed, in varying ways, at reforming or supporting legal processes to make them more just. In the second half of this chapter I move from the ways in which access to justice ideals have been institutionalized in legal reform to a conceptual examination of the access to justice ideal itself. I argue that justice should be understood as those arrangements by which people can (successfully) make claims against individuals and institutions in order to have security against being dominated by others. Secure justice implies practical deliberative democracy in which decisions and actions are easily contestable on the basis of reasons through procedures accepted as fair (see Pettit 1993, 1996, 1997). This conception of justice in deliberative democracy opens a window of understanding on the potential significance (or lack of it) of the institutions of the legal profession for access to justice.

[2] For example, where a contract is being negotiated, or to jump the administrative and legal hurdles necessary to fulfil a goal such as registering a business name or company, or to fulfil an ordinary transaction such as transferring property or administering a will.

FOUR WAVES OF REFORM

Between the mid-1960s and early 1980s access to justice researchers chronicled three waves of access to justice reform focusing in turn on (1) legal aid, (2) public interest law, and (3) informal justice (Cappelletti & Garth 1978, Sarat 1986: 532–3, Trubek 1990; see also Bottomley et al. 1994: 59–86).[3] By the 1980s, the rhetoric of access to justice had lost much of its salience among scholarly researchers while demand for justice was as insatiable as ever. The core ideal was transmogrified, perhaps cynically, into a fourth wave (4) of competition policy reform of legal service provision. These four waves may not exhaust the methods available for improving access to justice, nor do they necessarily represent a historically accurate picture of the order in which reforms have occurred in all Western countries (see Fleming 1996). But they do form a useful heuristic of the ways in which reformers and government have sought to overcome the discretion of charity by assigning responsibility to institutions of either the state (wave one), social movement politics (wave two), face-to-face community (wave three), or the market (wave four) in attempts to make access to justice secure. Moreover, in at least some parts of the world, this has been the order in which the different waves have momentarily dominated the access to justice reform stage.

Wave one: legal aid

The first wave of access to justice reform focused on increasing the availability of formal legal means of access to justice by increasing access to lawyers' services. The introduction, and in some cases reform, of legal aid emphasized the state's responsibility for delivering access to justice as a basic prerogative of citizenship (Cappelletti & Garth 1978: 22–4, Hauhart 1989). State responsibility to provide an effective, efficient and accessible court system has been recognized since Magna Carta.[4] Wave one added the obligation to ensure adequate legal representation, resulting in a massive expansion of citizens' ability to access the courts. The UK government introduced a demand-led legal aid sys-

[3] Cappelletti & Garth (1978) was written as the third wave was emerging.

[4] Magna Carta of 1215 set out the crown's responsibility to provide a forum for hearing disputes which was accessible (i.e. in a fixed place, not travelling around with the King), effective (only justices and sheriffs learned in the law should be appointed), and efficient (justice would not be delayed or denied) (McKechnie 1914, Stringham 1966).

tem in 1949 that subsidized access to certain private legal services for approximately 80 per cent of the population and greatly expanded it in 1972 (Rickman & Gray 1995: 317). In 1965 the US Office of Economic Opportunity established a legal services programme staffed by salaried attorneys in 'neighbourhood law offices' as part of the 'War on Poverty'. It was replaced by the Legal Services Corporation in 1974. France, Austria, Germany, and the Netherlands all introduced new legal aid schemes between 1972 and 1974 (Cappelletti & Garth 1978). In Australia, the Whitlam government set up federal legal aid offices in the 1970s which would provide salaried officers to both pursue cases and supervise 'judicare'-style aid for private practitioners of the parties' choice (Tomsen 1992). In recent years legal aid authorities have also experimented with franchising and block contracting (see Goriely 1995, Pleasence et al. 1996).

Legal aid massively expanded the accessibility of traditional legal justice. Yet it is increasingly limited by its expense. Since the 1970s the criteria for receiving legal aid have become incrementally narrower (Goriely & Paterson 1996: 17–18, Regan & Fleming 1994). In the Netherlands 60 per cent of the population are still eligible for some legal aid assistance (Blankenburg 1994: 805), but the figure has declined to well under half in Britain (Smith 1996: 4),[5] historically the world leader in legal aid provision.[6] Both Canadian governments and the Republican-controlled US Congress have cut legal aid spending. In Australia the means test ensures that only those close to or below the poverty line are eligible for assistance (Access to Justice Advisory Committee 1994: 225–57, Law Council of Australia 1994*b*). Around 70 per cent of those who are approved for legal aid already receive Commonwealth social security benefits (Legal Aid & Family Services 1994, 1995), suggesting that aid is only available to the very poorest sector of society. In all countries the merits tests (a determination of how likely the applicant's legal action is to succeed), matter tests (a determination of whether the issue falls into a priority area for funding), and means tests are becoming increasingly restrictive (Goriely 1995, Regan & Fleming 1994, Rickman & Gray 1995). Criminal matters are priorities while it is increasingly difficult to get legal aid for family and civil

[5] This was despite a 55% increase in funding in real terms between 1990–1 and 1993–4 (Moorhead 1998: 376).

[6] Rickman & Gray (1995: 318) cite a study that estimated that the UK devoted 0.05% of GDP to legal aid, compared with 0.04% in the Netherlands, 0.025% in Sweden, 0.02% in Germany, 0.005% in France and Ireland, and 0.002% in Belgium.

matters (Regan & Fleming 1994), an outcome that disadvantages women, who are much less likely to apply for legal aid in criminal matters than in family matters.[7] In most countries it seems that criminal cases swallow most of the funding for public legal services, followed by family cases, housing matters, and consumer and finance matters, in that order (Garth 1980: 151–6, Legal Aid & Family Services 1995: 12–13, Regan 1996, Rowley 1992: 263).[8]

As currently institutionalized, the legal aid approach to delivering access to justice is unaffordable because it aims to make formal legal justice available in wider and wider circumstances, thereby riding the tiger of costly legal professional fees and salaries (Germov 1995: 162). In Britain between 1990/1 and 1993/4 civil cases funded by legal aid increased in unit cost by 51 per cent and criminal cases by 75 per cent (Moorhead 1998: 376). Indeed the legal profession exacerbated the problem of the unaffordability of legal aid in countries like Australia by initially resisting the establishment of legal aid offices, fearing fee regulation and loss of autonomy, and then compromising on a system where two-thirds of the legal aid budget is spent on paying private practitioners on a fee-for-service basis rather than more efficiently on staff lawyers, paralegals, and social workers (Tomsen 1992, Weisbrot 1990: 239–47). In Britain the possibility of staff lawyers has barely even been considered because of the private profession's ability to co-opt the scheme to its own needs (Paterson & Nelken 1996). For Roger Smith (1997: 14), director of the English Legal Action Group, 'the origins of legal aid are buried deep in [the] enlightened self interest' of the law society: legal aid funded a massive expansion in the English legal profession in the 1970s and 1980s, making up 11 per cent of solicitors' fees and 30 per cent of barristers' fees in 1985/6 (Smith 1997: 17).

Although legal aid has significantly improved people's access, it has only marginally changed the ways legal services are provided and the legal system works. Research on publicly funded legal services agencies continually shows that despite hopes (and fears) about their radicalism, they are generally just as conservative and potentially dominating in the way they serve clients as ordinary law firms (Etheridge 1973, Kidder 1976, Mentor 1996, Parker 1994, Scheingold 1994, Spangler 1986).

[7] Australian legal aid statistics show that many more men than women apply for criminal legal aid and that applications for criminal legal aid are more likely to be successful (Legal Aid & Family Services 1994, 1995).

[8] These figures are complicated by the fact that in some countries criminal legal services are offered by different bodies from those which offer civil and family services.

Indeed as Chapter 2 showed, poor clients such as those who use legal aid services are more likely to be dominated by lawyers. Furthermore, even at its best, legal aid cannot solve the problem of the many small claims and everyday injustices that it will never be economically efficient to address using professionals.[9] While legal aid has made a huge difference to the accessibility of court processes, its access to justice significance is inevitably limited by the effectiveness of lawyers' justice in delivering the justice to which people seek access. It can do little to change law and legal processes where they do not work well, nor to challenge abuses and exploitation that continue in defiance of the legal system.

Wave two: public interest law

The second wave of access to justice reform, public interest law, addressed legal aid's limitations by seeking to change the law, court procedures, and the nature of legal practice so that access to legal justice might become more meaningful. It attempted to combat the bias law develops in favour of the rich and the organized because they are better and more regularly represented in legal processes (Galanter 1974), by emphasizing group participation in the law and the organization of under-organized interests. It also sought to solve the expensive problem of funding individuals' access to formal legal processes by aggregating claims and emphasizing diffuse, group, and public interests. The object was often to change the law or to restructure governmental agencies, rather than to win benefits for specific litigants (Selznick 1992: 466).

This meant radical changes in procedural rules of standing, fairness, and legal representation, especially in the USA (Cappelletti 1978: 35–6). The class action initiated by a public interest law firm or a consumer group became the paradigmatic wave two means of achieving justice. Procedural changes led to substantive changes and vice versa so that new areas of law and new rights began to emerge. Some lawyers also developed new and creative forms of practice. They recognized that in order to achieve substantive justice they needed to act not only in the courts but also in informal settings, such as bureaucracies and administrative agencies, and in legislatures and the political arena, and to use forms of advocacy other than litigation: 'Much of what these

[9] The English Legal Aid Board is, however, now experimenting with offering legal aid through citizens' advice bureaux that do not employ lawyers (see Steele & Bull 1996).

new lawyers did looked as much like politics as law' (Trubek 1990: 116–17).

Public interest practice relies on social movement politics to achieve justice through law. The women's, environmental, and consumer movements each used law and legal processes to achieve their goals in certain circumstances (see Abel 1985, Handler 1980). Prominent examples in the USA included the civil rights movement of the 1960s, Ralph Nader's consumer action campaigns, and the original plans for the legal services programme's contribution to the 'War on Poverty'. In Australia, Canada, and New Zealand public interest lawyers have contributed importantly to indigenous land rights movements, along with many other causes. Although particular campaigns might have been initiated by wider groups, the weight of the public interest law wave was carried by movements of sympathetic and devoted legal professionals in community legal centres and public interest law movements (Sarat & Scheingold 1998, Trubek & Trubek 1981: 133).

However the public interest law movement was limited by its focus on achieving change through the reform of legal justice. Public interest lawyers were still legalistic even when acting in non-legal arenas: They 'politicised law only by legalising politics' (Trubek 1990: 118), so that public interest law never quite lived up to its radical political promise. As Sarat & Scheingold (1998: 9) write in their introduction to an edited collection on the accomplishments of cause lawyering,

> There is some preliminary evidence suggesting that cause lawyers can overcome the defenses of formal equality. But this evidence is spotty, largely confined to the United States, and in any case, indicates that cause lawyers must both utilize and transcend law and litigation. Insofar as they confine themselves to legal processes, they remain bound to liberal institutions, values, and practices. And even if they are upon occasion able somehow to defeat the defenses of the legal process, their gains remain hostile in the face of a hostile political climate.

Yet it gestured towards the importance of social and political action in the attempt to remedy structural and group injustices.

Wave three: informal justice

The third wave drew attention to alternatives to legal justice. A range of institutions and practices were developed in an attempt to provide access to justice, not just law. These included the introduction of less formal courts and tribunals (such as small claims courts), court-based mediation and arbitration (in family and commercial matters), and private alternative dispute resolution (ADR) and community justice centres. Initiatives also included using lay persons and para-professionals both on the bench and in the bar, and modifying substantive law to avoid disputes or to facilitate their resolution. In criminal justice, the movement for restorative justice advocated family group or community accountability conferences as dialogic alternatives to the repression of court and prison (Braithwaite 1989, 1995*b*, Braithwaite & Mugford 1994, Consedine 1997, La Prairie 1995). Civil process was to be adapted and related to different types of disputes (Dezalay 1993). Some disputes should be solved quickly, while others could be negotiated over a long period of time; parties in a long-term relationship needed a different style of dispute resolution from those who barely knew each other; and disputes between parties who differed greatly in power required a different approach from disputes between equals.

The informal justice movement covered heterogeneous terrain; there were those who embraced it purely for practical reasons. There were many who saw 'in ADR the germs of a radical transformation of ideas about law and justice' (Trubek 1990: 121), one which emphasized institutions of face-to-face community for delivering justice.[10] Since law is at best a limited means of achieving justice, people sought alternative ways of achieving justice even in situations which were traditionally seen as primarily legal problems. Trubek (1990: 122) describes the community-based ideology behind their approach:

> While some who championed ADR had rather modest goals in mind, others saw in the movement for alternative forums possibilities for greater community, new sources of law, and a different understanding of self-empowerment. For these radical voices, what was wrong with traditional civil procedure was . . . the fact that it presumed that the enforcement of legally defined rights was both necessary and sufficient to ensure self-empowerment. These radical ADR proponents sought procedures that would both employ and develop community norms and values, allow the development of normative agreement through open dialogue, and be sensitive to the importance of social relationships in the maintenance and enhancement of the self.

Thus the third wave encouraged practices which rely on communal ordering as an alternative to professionalized legal justice.

[10] Some simply want more efficient ways to solve major business disputes, while others aim to divert minor cases from civil courts and others advocate a radical approach to both criminal and civil cases.

The informal justice movement, however, could not deliver what it promised (Goldberg et al. 1985: 485–501). ADR options were slow in gaining popularity and were not publicly funded. Informal justice was severely criticized for not protecting people's rights, and for privatizing justice so that domination was perpetuated rather than opened up to the scrutiny of public legal justice. It was also criticized for being private and individual and thus failing to address aggregate and widespread problems, especially consumer problems. In contrast to public interest law which emphasized using law to achieve social change, informal justice was criticized for reinforcing 'prevailing relations of power and authority by defusing conflict' (Bottomley et al. 1994: 86). Where institutions of informal justice were successfully implemented, they frequently became as rigid and technical as formal justice as time passed and especially as lawyers colonized them (Auerbach 1983, Merry 1993).

Wave four: competition policy

Much of the access to justice literature stops in the 1980s when the rhetoric of 'access to justice' seemed to lose its power until its recent revival, in Britain and Australia at least, in the 1990s. Although not necessarily labelled as such, the access to justice ideal was, however, still pursued in a fourth wave of reform to the legal system through the 1980s and into the 1990s. This wave advocated the implementation of competition policy in order to allocate access to justice resources, whether formal or informal, as efficiently as possible through market institutions.

The focus was on reforming the legal services market, which had been organized in a particularly anti-competitive way, and fitted the general priority given to micro-economic reform during that period (Perkin 1989: 472–519, Pusey 1991). The legal profession was inculpated for monopolizing the market for legal services and loading it with restrictive practices (Slayton & Trebilcock 1978, Evans & Trebilcock 1982, Albon & Lindsay 1984), leading eventually to both government- and profession-initiated reforms in the United Kingdom, Canada, and Australia. In the USA competition reform to the legal profession occurred somewhat earlier and more through private activism and the courts than threatened government reforms (Powell 1985). Globally the liberalization of the legal services market is likely to remain important as international agreements such as the World Trade Organization's

General Agreement on Trade in Services and the North American Free Trade Agreement are implemented (see Kakabadse 1996; see also Self 1985).[11]

Improving the efficiency of the legal services market was expected to render traditional services more affordable, and also to encourage a proliferation of new means of providing legal services including non-lawyer legal service provision, franchising, group legal service plans, legal insurance, partnerships with non-lawyers, advertising, price competition and contingency fees. During the 1980s such liberalization in the legal services market did occur in the commercial sector due to the operation of market forces as mentioned in Chapter 2. Companies forced their lawyers to be more competitive and used accountants and business advisers where before they might have used lawyers.[12]

There is also some evidence that the introduction of competition reforms to the legal profession improved ordinary consumers' access to justice. Much of this evidence concerns the effects of competition on the price and quality of conveyancing and other routine services, rather than litigation, which is the most expansive and inaccessible aspect of the law. In England, Domberger and Sherr (1989) found that the government's 1984 announcement that licensed conveyancers would be able to compete with lawyers was enough to cause substantial drops in conveyancing prices and some apparent increase in client satisfaction levels.[13] A later English survey (Love et al. 1992) found firms that advertised tended to have lower fees, the presence of licensed conveyancers in an area depressed fees, and that increased levels of advertising amongst some firms in an area reduced the fees of all firms in the area. Similarly in Australia, the Trade Practices Commission found that conveyancing fees tended to be lower in jurisdictions where non-lawyers were allowed to compete with lawyers (1992: 14) and that once advertising restrictions were relaxed in New South Wales advertised fees were much lower than previous scale fees (1992: 28). Another study compared small firm conveyancing fees in New South Wales between 1994 (when significant competition reforms were introduced) and 1996

[11] Paterson (1996: 147) shows that NAFTA was an important factor in the liberalization of the Canadian profession.

[12] See Chapter 6.

[13] Advertising restrictions were lifted in 1985, but licensed conveyancers were not allowed to enter the field until 1987, by which time conveyancing prices were already much more competitive. Paterson et al. (1988) produced similar results for the same time period and found that 45% of their sample of law firms began advertising after 1984 because of the perceived need to be more competitive.

and found that they had decreased in real terms by an average of 17 per cent (Baker 1996).

In the USA, advertising restrictions on lawyers began to be lifted after the 1977 case of *Bates & O'Steen* v. *State Bar of Arizona*.[14] Minimum fee schedules were struck down as restraint of trade in the 1975 case of *Goldfarb* v. *Virginia State Bar*,[15] and group legal service plans have been allowed since the late 1960s (Powell 1985: 287–8, Seron 1992: 63).[16] As Seron (1992: 63–4) writes,

> The impact of these decisions has been notable. Direct mail companies offer prepaid legal plans through credit card companies, direct sales, and telemarketing, which creates a stable client base for participating attorneys. Unions negotiate the provision of a full-time legal services unit as part of a fringe benefits package. National legal services firms open storefront offices in a variety of cities and use television advertising to market services. Local for-profit legal clinics with several branch locations in a metropolitan area advertise in *Yellow Pages*, on buses, and in newspapers.

The economic research on whether these changes have benefited US consumers is sparse, but there is evidence that the removal of advertising restrictions has led to lower prices at least for standardized less complex legal services (see Cox 1989, Schroeter et al. 1987). Cox (1989) reviewed all the literature on the effects of the liberalization of advertising restrictions up to that time and concluded that increased advertising lowered prices but its effect on quality was uncertain. Muris and McChesney (1979) compared the Los Angeles Jacoby and Meyers legal clinic with traditional firms in the area and found that the clinic's prices were lower and its quality of service higher. They conclude that advertising allowed the clinic a high enough volume of work efficiently to use specialization, paralegals, and systems management to reduce costs and improve quality. However Seron's (1996) research suggests that most small firm attorneys have not actually taken advantage of liberalized advertising and competition rules and are therefore not passing the benefits on to their consumers.

By liberalizing the market for legal services and for dispute resolution, competition reform opens up the potential for using second and third wave informal justice and public interest law which were not always possible while traditional lawyers' justice monopolized access to

[14] 433 US 350. See Cox (1989) for a description and analysis of the case.

[15] 421 US 733.

[16] Powell (1985: 288) reports that by 1979 there were already some 2,500 group legal service plans in operation in the USA covering 3.75 million people.

justice. Business was able to take advantage of the alternatives to legal justice developed in the third wave of access to justice reform by forcing the liberalization of the legal service market. As Singer (1994: 55) says,

> What began in the 1970s as a movement to settle interpersonal conflicts, racial tensions, and what the legal establishment considered 'minor' disputes was quickly seized on by important parts of corporate America as a way of keeping business conflicts out of court. To a large extent . . . corporate interest in ADR constitutes a consumer movement at the upper end of the legal market.

Breaking these monopolies and allowing a range of access to justice strategies to proliferate is not only economically more efficient but necessary since, as will be argued in the next chapter, access to justice will only ever be substantially improved by means of a comprehensive strategy that incorporates the insights of the other three waves.

It is naive to expect the market in justice ever to be organized so efficiently that the majority will be able to afford the services they need. Market solutions may well achieve significant improvements for middle-class people with some money to spend on legal services as well as increases in the speed of access to justice for commercial litigants, where substantial enough changes are made. Market reforms might also make a difference in prospective litigation where the outcome is likely to be a substantial payment out of which legal fees could later be taken. Yet even at their leanest, legal fees will never be so cheap that everyone can afford them. Those without discretionary resources will be excluded from the market and therefore from participation in the legal system.

JUSTICE AND DELIBERATIVE DEMOCRACY

Justice

In order to evaluate attempts at institutionalizing the ideal of access to justice to date, it helps to have a clear conceptualization of what 'access to justice' means. We have already seen that the term 'access to justice' has been used in many disparate ways. I will take access to justice to mean what it says; the availability of suitable arrangements or processes for people to claim justice, not just to use the law. This may be a more expansive definition of the term than customary, yet such a broad definition is necessary fully to comprehend its spirit and use in the four waves of reform ranging from legal aid to social movement politics to informal dispute resolution. Raising access to justice means asking fundamental questions about the availability of procedures for claiming social or individual justice, for securing one's place as a citizen in a good society. These are normative questions of the socio-political good which extend far beyond law and lawyers.

Selznick (1992: 431–2) points out that for most people justice 'embraces a complex set of interacting variables' including 'entitlement, justification, equality, impartiality, proportionality, reciprocity, rectification, need, desert, and participation', and different theorists may emphasize one or another. But 'the idea that justice is a matter of people getting what they deserve is perhaps the most common and tenacious conception of justice', as Campbell argues (1988: 150). Defining justice in this way—as giving to each person his or her due—means that the concept of justice is settled, but different theorists are free to disagree on what giving each person their due means in concrete terms (Campbell 1988: 4). It utilizes Rawls's concept/conception distinction to get around the problems of clarifying a term that is used in such a complex and varied way:

> The concept is then taken to provide the 'meaning' of justice, while the conceptions enunciate the evaluative criteria variously deployed to determine that certain types of situation[s] are just or unjust. Thus the concept of justice may be analysed as a set of principles for assessing social and political institutions, while conceptions of justice represent differing views on the proper content of these principles. (Campbell 1988: 3–4; see Rawls 1972: 5–6)

Thus Rawls (1972: 5) defines the concept of justice as 'a proper balance between competing claims' in relation to 'the appropriate distribution of the benefits and burdens of social cooperation'. In other words, talking about justice means talking about the social good, that is, those ideals we ought to accept for living together and governing ourselves in communities. A conception of justice is the substantive set of principles that actually set out what social and political ideals ought to be accepted; 'a set of principles for assigning basic rights and duties and for determining . . . the proper balance of the benefits and burdens of social cooperation' in Rawls's (1972: 5) terms. Rawls's own criterion of political assessment is one conception of justice, but other normative socio-political theories provide other ones.

When people want access to justice, they are concerned, like Rawls, with achieving some conception of the social good. But, like Hume (1978: 489), who saw in justice a conventional device for the regulation of disputes over limited or scarce resources, they conceive the justice to which they want access in a procedural way. The desire for access to justice is the desire for access to processes aimed at achieving some conception of the social good. Thus I will define (the concept of) justice as

> those arrangements by which people can (successfully) make claims against individuals and institutions in order to advance shared ideals of social and political life.[17]

It will yield different views (conceptions) of the required arrangements depending on what ideals are accepted as shared.

This definition makes for a very broad notion of justice. It is the means by which people seek to secure the type of social and individual relations they think are right, and to rectify them when they have gone wrong in particular circumstances. It could involve having the means to make a claim in an individual dispute about what is the correct way to solve it, or seeking to change institutional practices and culture to conform to relevant social and political ideals. Although it clearly includes legal and quasi-legal justice arrangements, my definition also embraces even the most informal methods of dispute resolution as well as a variety of forms of political participation (including informal political participation in social movements) by which people make more general claims about the way their societies should be organized and resources distributed.

Justice as deliberative democracy

A deliberative democratic ideal of justice or the socio-political good is attractive, as later chapters will show, because it opens up a theoretical strategy for reconciling the conflicting access to justice concerns of citizens and lawyers through contextual and responsive deliberation. There are many theories of what deliberative democracy requires. It is significant for understanding access to justice because it is aimed at ensuring that members of a society have security in their status and freedom as citizens. One strand of deliberative democratic theory (Dunn 1994, Manin 1994, Pettit 1993, 1997, Skinner 1984) has explained this by reference to the tradition of civic republicanism:[18]

[17] I am grateful to Philip Pettit who suggested an earlier version of this definition. The question of how a community decides on a particular set of social and political ideals will not be discussed here although clearly it is important.

[18] As Dunn (1994: 209) notes, this does not mean that modern republics have delivered much real security to citizens. Indeed, as noted in Chapter 1, Dunn suggests that

> [F]reedom was conceptualised as the social status enjoyed by someone who is not a slave and, more generally, by someone who is so protected by the law and culture of his community that he does not have to depend for the enjoyment of independent choice on the grace or favour or mercy of another . . . [Republicanism] emphasised that liberty is constituted by the support against interference, and the status of being manifestly so supported, which goes with citizenship in an appropriately governed society; in a society where the rule of law obtains and power is systematically checked. (Pettit with Braithwaite 1993: 226)

This emphasis on security against interference captures well what is at stake in the concern of access to justice reformers with the significance of secure access to procedures for achieving justice. Freedom requires the absence of interference not by accident but by design, by virtue of being secured against the powerful in an appropriately governed society. While Sunstein (1988), for example, defines his version of republicanism according to four principles or commitments with which it has been historically associated,[19] Pettit shows how institutions such as a rule of law, a constitution in which different powers serve to check and balance each other, the separation of powers, countermajoritarian entrenchment of certain laws, federalism, deliberative politics, participatory citizenship, and a regime of civic virtue in which people are disposed to serve honestly in public office, are not the foundations of republican theory but are significant purely as means by which liberty is secured against the possibility of domination.

Using this conception of social and political ideals and the procedural view of justice outlined above, justice can be defined more fully as,

> that set of arrangements that allow people to make claims against other individuals and institutions in order to secure freedom against the possibility of domination.

Justice is then about ensuring adequate arrangements and institutions to allow citizens to make claims about (1) how their freedom ought to be protected and institutionalized in the future, or (2) how their free-

republican political theory has largely failed to design institutions which will deliver real security. According to him the modern success of the republican form is due mainly to the failures of its rivals to provide a better answer to the problem of security (1994: 210).

[19] These are (1) 'deliberation in politics made possible by civic virtue'; (2) 'the equality of political actors, embodied in a desire to eliminate sharp disparities in political participation or influence among individuals or social groups'; (3) 'universalism, exemplified by the notion of a common good'; (4) 'citizenship, manifesting itself in broadly guaranteed rights of participation' (Sunstein 1988: 1541).

dom has been injured in the past and how the situation ought to be rectified.

In order to secure citizens' freedom, not only should government be constrained by checks and balances such as the rule of law and separation of powers, but citizens should have the opportunity to make their presence felt in public decision-making that offends against their interests by ensuring that

> [A]t every site of decision-making, legislative, administrative and judicial, there are procedures in place which identify the considerations relevant to the decision, thereby enabling citizens to raise the question as to whether they are the appropriate considerations to play that role. And . . . that there are procedures in place which enable citizens to make a judgment on whether the relevant considerations actually determined the outcome. (Pettit 1997: 188)

The creation of a deliberative democracy—a polity where decisions are made on the basis of dialogue and public justification accessible to all citizens—is central to a variety of recent political theories including Habermas's discourse theory of law and democracy (1996), Dryzek's discursive democracy (1990), and Young's communicative democracy (1990, 1993). It is a traditional concern of republican theory (Pettit 1997: 188–9), particularly of US republicanism (Sunstein 1988, 1993), and inspires a whole literature on active participatory citizenship inspired by the ancient Greek ideal of citizenship as 'part of the integrated life of the city-state' (Boucher & Vincent 1993: 89) and the classical civic republican tradition (Barber 1984, Oldfield 1990).

This does not necessarily require the unrealistic ideal that all public decisions originate in collective consent and universally satisfactory resolution of differences. Pettit puts forward the more practically feasible ideal of contestatory democracy as an instantiation of deliberative democracy in which decisions are legitimate if they are open to contestation in fora and through procedures that are acceptable to all concerned after they are made (Pettit 1997: 183–200). This tends to encourage decisions to be made on the basis of publicly acceptable reasons and with enough consultation and participation to ensure that all the relevant arguments and considerations are on the table. It also requires a 'republic of reasons' in which decisions that have been made are open to debate and justification, and in which citizens have access to means of contestation, and fora that adjudicate contestations fairly.

Traditionally political theorists have emphasized achieving this through formal, democratic participation in public political decision-making—the vote, the possibility of standing for election, the courts. Feminists and others have re-formed the understanding of participation in deliberative fora to include informal political participation in social movements, community groups, and the institutions of civil society (Lister 1995: 8–9). For Habermas it means the formal public political sphere must be 'porous' to the protests and contributions of individual citizens and social movements and not restricted to their involvement through elected representatives (Habermas 1996: 359–87); there must be enough participation by a wide enough diversity of citizens in a wide enough diversity of communicative styles to ensure all of the relevant considerations become part of the deliberation (Bohman 1994: 918, Young 1993).

Yet most political and democratic theory still concentrates on elaborating the institutions and arrangements by which public power is exercised. In Pettit's conception, for example, deliberation is about making sure that the public decisions of legislature, executive, and judiciary do not dominate citizens. It should equally be about ensuring that institutions of deliberation exist to secure citizens against domination by private powers.[20] As Anne Phillips (1991: 39) argues, 'it is absurd to espouse democracy at the level of the state when there is subordination in our lives elsewhere'. Advocates of participatory democracy have usually recognized that at the very least workplace democracy goes hand in hand with participation in affairs of state (Phillips 1991: 39–40). The legal profession itself is a private power that must be subject to the justice of deliberative democracy, as we have already seen. The scholarship of Foucault (e.g. Foucault 1980) should surely by now have demonstrated the radical all-pervasiveness of power as it becomes 'capillary' in the material circumstances of our everyday lives. This challenges normative political theorists to consider how ideals like deliberative democracy should be extended beyond the realm of the state.

In a strong deliberative democracy, citizens are able to use a variety of institutions and arrangements to challenge or prevent both private and public dominations, to debate whether public and private actions and decisions fit with accepted social and political ideals, and, if not, how and whether they should be rectified. They can use democratic representation in the public political sphere, recourse to courts of law, tribunals, or internal institutional dispute resolution processes. They

[20] An issue that will be discussed further in Chapter 9.

might engage in informal protest or social movement politics. They request justification for actions or decisions within a family, workplace, or community group and engage in informal dialogue aimed at promoting their conception of the good. The very existence and accessibility of these arrangements and institutions by which citizens raise their interests and concerns, in which they request justification for decisions, and argue that a decision ought to be reversed or the results of an action rectified, constitutes justice.

Access to law and access to justice

Historically, ideals of freedom, including the republican one, have been so demanding that only a socio-economic elite could attain them because only they had the resources to take advantage of all the arrangements for securing their liberty. In contemporary societies we should be happy to accept neither a lesser ideal nor an elitist conception of who is entitled to freedom. It will be crucial that all people have the means to access whatever arrangements there are for securing their liberty.

To what institutions must citizens be guaranteed access? As we have seen, access to justice rhetoric has emphasized making legal and quasi-legal justice institutions accessible to all. Political theorists, like access to justice reformers, have often concentrated on the citizen's use of institutions of law as deliberative fora in which private and public dominations can be contested and debated. Pettit and Braithwaite claim that the most obvious requirement for the promotion of freedom as non-domination is a robust system of legal protection:

> What republicans generally say is that [liberty] is exemplified by the condition of citizenship in a free society, a condition under which each is properly safeguarded by the law against predations of others. The regulative interpretation of liberty, the interpretation which guides us on what liberty requires, equates freedom not with being left alone, but with being given equal protection before a suitable law. (Braithwaite & Pettit 1990: 57)

In practice, Gordon (1985) shows that the Federalist lawyers of the early American republic saw the law over which they had guardianship as the only mechanism capable of integrating the citizens into a just and virtuous republic that reconciled commercial and self-interested activity with shared values and common purposes:

> That virtue-supplying substance, the lawyers argued, that surrogate for traditional communities and hierarchies, was law itself; or, to be more precise, was

the manifold diverse social practices of lawyers—law not as a body of rules, but as a powerful autonomous culture produced by lawyers and diffused by them. (Gordon 1985, Lecture One, 6)

It is clear that equal access to law can help make freedom or citizenship status secure by,

(*a*) providing means for individuals, groups and the state to make claims to stop, remedy, or prevent specific instances of domination and to reform dominating practices and social arrangements;
(*b*) ensuring that the rich and powerful do not have superior access to legal advice and representation that can be used to dominate the powerless;
(*c*) empowering citizens to function independently and without domination in the ordinary affairs of life, such as drafting a will, filling in a tax return, buying and selling goods, or transferring land, through access to legal information and advice; and also enabling them to lay claim to their rights in everyday situations to avoid exploitation by more knowledgeable and powerful people.

How significant is access to other procedures and arrangements for securing justice and what relationship do they bear to law and lawyers?

LAW AS JUSTICE IN A DELIBERATIVE DEMOCRACY

Limits of law as justice

There are critical limitations on the role that law can play in achieving justice. In achieving deliberative democracy, law must be supplemented and handled carefully because of its coercive potential. While it is an excellent tool for contesting decisions and actions in a reasoned manner (Sunstein 1996), generally law also attempts to restrict people's range of choice, if not the intensity of the freedom they enjoy (Pettit 1997: 24–5, 104). As Lloyd (1979: 26) comments, law as an ideal type consists of two elements, authority and force; it is legitimate coercion. This is not to deny that some law is much less coercive than other law and that much law lacks sanctions and is purely educative. We do not need to accept Austinian positivism to recognize that as an ideal type 'the force of law is and seems always to have been linked with rules which are capable of being enforced by coercion; the hangman, the gaoler, the bailiff' (Lloyd 1979: 35). Even the freedom of contract can ultimately be enforced by the court bailiff who collects damages awarded in judgment when a party defaults, although the force of civil law is generally more symbolical than physical (see Suchman & Edelman 1996). Law is a critically important method of justice in certain situations precisely because it can coerce compliance, but it is more usually effective for reasons other than its potential coerciveness.

In the liberal conceptions of liberty as non-interference, freedom is the absence of coercion, and law always represents a potential threat to freedom, even if it promotes a greater freedom (see Pettit 1993: 166–9, 1996: 595–9, 1997: 35–41). For republicans, by contrast, law is particularly suited to making freedom secure. A just law never dominates or makes people unfree (Pettit 1993: 167). However, the coercion of even a just law may still be a disadvantage because it conditions the freedom of citizens by restricting their range of choice. The advancing of freedom ultimately means having as wide a range of undominated choice as possible, and so it is preferable to avoid the making and use of unnecessarily restrictive law (see Pettit 1996: 593). If possible, an area should not be the subject of coercive law at all; it should not be the subject of prescription or proscription. If there must be law, the less coercive the better, and the way the law is enforced also ought to be as non-restricting of freedom as possible. Institutions that discourage the unnecessary use or enforcement of law should be fostered, and in any legal system enacted laws should serve the cause of freedom better than alternatives. In practice there is no reason why this republican approach should not generally lead to similar outcomes as the liberal balancing approach.

In *Not Just Deserts*, Braithwaite and Pettit (1990) call this 'the principle of parsimony'. Such a principle will be of the utmost importance in the area of criminal justice, clearly the most coercive area of legal prohibition, and so often involving radical invasions of liberty in its enforcement:

> The state should use those legislative, enforcement, and sentencing options which are minimally interventionist until the evidence is clear that more-intrusive practices are required to increase dominion. More than that, the state should actively search for alternative ways of promoting dominion to such interventionist policies as criminal punishment. (Braithwaite & Pettit 1990: 79–80; see also at 87, and Pettit 1997: 154–5)

Braithwaite & Pettit (1990: 104) go so far as to argue that there ought to be a presumption against imprisonment in any criminal statute. Although criminal justice is potentially the most coercive area of law, the coerciveness of any type of legal solution to questions of justice should be weighed against its value in advancing freedom. The use of law should be just one means of doing justice among many that include social and political action in formal and informal arenas, requests for dialogue and justification in families, clubs, workplaces, and other institutional arenas, and informal decision-making and dispute resolution fora. It will be preferable to use the most voluntary, dialogic means of achieving justice available which will mean designing law to be as minimally coercive as possible, encouraging the proliferation of non-coercive, community-based methods of social ordering, and designing institutions which encourage the use of less coercive means of doing justice before more coercive ones.

An added reason for being parsimonious about legal coercion as a means of achieving justice is that coercion may be so easily misdirected. It is easy to idealize law's ability to check domination in other areas without being stained by the taint of domination itself. Yet powerful actors will always be able to use coercive law to dominate others. They may use superior legal advice and the ability to manipulate legal technicalities to overpower the powerless and frustrate regulation put there to limit injustice. They may dominate law-making, either in the legislature or the courts, so that the law reflects their interests. The mere proliferation of law in and of itself advantages powerful organizations because they have a greater ability to hire lawyers to bend its technicalities to their own purposes. As Sutton and Wild argue, 'The more formal and complex the body of law becomes, the more it will operate in favour of formal, rational, and bureaucratic groups such as corporations. In one sense, therefore, law and justice may be fundamentally irreconcilable' (Sutton & Wild 1978: 195; see also Shils & Rheinstein 1954).

The social science of non-coercive control

If political philosophers teach us that ideally it is better to be restrained about using coercive law so that the range of citizens' freedom can be maximized, law and society research has shown that as a matter of fact non-coercive control can be a more effective means of achieving justice (e.g. Galanter 1981). Law is more just when it 'springs from the character and condition of the people' and when it is administered with regard for the integrity of social practices and people's autonomy (Selznick 1992: 469–70; see also Krygier 1997). Non-coercive social control is likely to be more effective than coercive control in achieving long-term compliance with norms that advance freedom, and coercive law is most effective when a last resort. This theme is most clearly developed in the corpus of empirical and policy-oriented work brought together by Braithwaite and colleagues in their research on criminology and business regulation.[21]

Empirical research on criminal deterrence is controversial, but the evidence does suggest that informal sanctions have a greater deterrent impact than formal legal sanctions (Ekland-Olson et al. 1984, Paternoster & Simpson 1996, Tittle 1980: 241), and that regardless of what kind of social control is attempted it is not its formal punitive features that make a difference, but its informal moralizing features (Schwartz & Orleans 1967).[22] So Braithwaite's theory of reintegrative shaming is based on the assumption that 'moralizing appeals which treat the citizen as someone with the responsibility to make the right choice are generally, though not invariably, responded to more positively than repressive social controls which deny human dignity by treating persons as amoral calculators' (Braithwaite 1989: 10). There is significant psychological evidence for a 'minimal sufficiency principle' that the less powerful the technique used to secure compliance, the more likely is long-term internalization of a desire to comply. Such internalization is discouraged by the use of rewards and punishments; reasoning and dialogue promote it (Boggiano et al. 1987, Kohn 1993).[23]

The same theory explains individual and collective responses of actors to business regulation in a variety of arenas (Ayres & Braithwaite 1992, Grabosky & Braithwaite 1986): Braithwaite and Makkai's programme of research on nursing home regulation shows that strategies of trust, reintegrative shaming, and praise are more effective at increasing business compliance with regulation than the application of formal sanctions (Braithwaite & Makkai 1991, 1994, Makkai & Braithwaite 1993, 1994*a*, 1994*b*), and Braithwaite (1985) had similar results in relation to coal mine safety. There is also much evidence that when regulators use coercive strategies to achieve compliance they break down the goodwill and motivation of those actors who are willing to be

[21] The role of law is never directly discussed in Braithwaite's work but he seems to suggest that the coercive nature of legal regulation makes it less effective than informal sanctions, community ordering, dialogue, and persuasion.

[22] See Braithwaite 1989: 69–70 for a summary of the literature.

[23] See Ayres & Braithwaite 1992: 49–51 for a summary of the psychological research.

socially responsible; resentment and defiance build up, crushing the possibility of voluntary compliance (Ayres & Braithwaite 1992: 21–7, Bardach & Kagan 1982, Kagan & Scholz 1984). Hawkins's (1984) study of the enforcement of environmental regulation in Britain suggests that this is indeed how regulators often operate in practice. Ayres and Braithwaite's (1992: 97) theory of 'responsive regulation' uses these empirical findings to propose that it is better to maximize self-regulatory possibilities for business by using less coercive, more dialogic methods of regulation first and more coercive measures only when less coercive means fail.

In relation to civil disputes, the evidence is again mixed, but the empirical studies generally show that people look more favourably on mediation than adjudication in terms of user satisfaction and perceptions of fairness (Pearson 1982), and most studies also show greater compliance with, and less relitigation of, mediated outcomes (McEwen & Maiman 1981, 1984, 1988, cf. Vidmar 1984; see Wissler 1995: 324–5 for a summary of the research). For example, in one of the most recent and most rigorous studies, Wissler (1995: 351) found that 'litigants in mediation, compared with those in adjudication, were more likely to say that the process was fair and they were satisfied with it; that the small claims court generally is fair; and that they were willing to use the same process in a future case'. She also found that mediated cases had slightly higher rates of compliance, outcomes that could not be explained by 'self-selected' differences between litigants who chose mediation and those who chose adjudication. Another study found that people were up to two times more likely to comply with mediated than adjudicated outcomes because litigants with mediated outcomes were more likely to have consented to the outcome in mediation (McEwen & Maiman 1984, 1988), a finding consistent with the evidence cited above that people are more likely to comply with less coercive, more dialogic methods of social control.

Brehm and Brehm's (1981) theory of 'reactance' provides the most refined account of the psychological phenomenon behind these findings. Their experimental evidence shows that people will resist attempts at control where their freedom is perceived to be under threat. They react against threats to their freedom by attempting to exercise precisely the freedom they feel is threatened simply to make sure they still have it, regardless of whether they would have otherwise been motivated to do so. For example, children grounded by their parents will attempt to go out when they might otherwise have been happy to stay home and watch television. Reactance will be greater depending on the intensity of the threat and how much the particular freedom means to the person. Reactance theory is helpful because it links the normative importance of freedom with the fact that restraints on freedom are empirically found to produce different effects from those intended. The implication of reactance theory is that more persuasive and even dialogic methods of changing the behaviour of social actors are more likely to be effective precisely because they respect those actors' freedom more.

Similarly when it comes to achieving broad social change in people's habits and attitudes, or in the distribution of resources and power, law is of limited use. As Rosenberg (1991) shows in his book on the social reform effect of US Supreme Court decisions, political support for social change, community pressure for change, and market conditions are all preconditions for litigation to produce reform, changes in opinions, or mobilization of citizens (1991: 31). Rosenberg argues from his data and logic that the lofty principles espoused in the courtroom are only effective in social reform if they can be implemented in the real world when 'positive incentives are offered to induce compliance or costs are imposed to induce compliance; or, court decisions allow for market implementation; or, administrators and officials crucial for implementation are willing to act and see court orders as a tool for leveraging additional resources or for hiding behind' (1991: 36). Rosenberg's data helps us see that a court decision cannot of itself produce diffuse or wide-ranging change, and that the circumstances in which it produces change are complex and dependent on interactions with many other variables (see Simon 1992). It can only accomplish change if it is effectively articulated to everyday mechanisms through markets, bureaucracies, or political, social, and personal commitment. While Rosenberg found no evidence that Supreme Court decisions mobilized the proponents of change any more than they were already active, there was, however, evidence that the perceived threat of the decisions produced resistance and strengthened the opponents of change (Rosenberg 1991: 341–2). The use of law can have a 'reactant' effect on social change to improve justice.

Effective means of producing widespread social change involve citizens participating more directly in political and economic decision-making, and also in civic education and consciousness-raising about rights, responsibilities, and issues of justice (Rosenberg 1991: 343). As Engel and Munger (1996: 48–9) show in their study of the relevance of legal rights to the life stories of two disabled women, the norms of law 'become active, not through litigation, but as part of the routines of everyday life' when they play a creative role in the transformation of internal dialogues in which people decide how to act for themselves, and in public dialogues in which they decide how to organize their workplaces, polities, and communities. This is not to advocate the replacement of the rule of law. It is to say the rule of law is meaningless without voluntary, community, and political involvement in achieving social and political ideals. Such dialogic regulation is more likely than deterrence and incapacitation to encourage 'a commitment to the rightness of the law and to the unthinkableness of breaking the law' (Ayres & Braithwaite 1992: 81).

Law in a deliberative democracy

Normative theory and empirical research both converge on the idea that while recourse to law can be one means of instituting deliberation and doing justice, it is severely limited in what it can achieve. As this chapter has shown, other arrangements and institutions for constituting deliberative democracy—such as informal means of dispute resolution, social movement politics, formal political action, and dialogic, moralizing, and persuasive means of social control—will often be preferable. The empirical social science research supports the normative concerns of deliberative democratic theory with active citizenship and civic virtue. An emphasis on deliberative participation in public life shows that the coercion of law is not enough to achieve justice without social and political action. The prominence republicans give to civic virtue, the disposition among citizens to follow routines, and take initiatives that tend towards the maximization of freedom as non-domination in society (see Pettit 1997: 241–51), means that we can and should often rely on mechanisms of a 'protective civic culture' (Pettit 1993: 167) before using law to secure freedom.

The existence and nurture of other means of justice apart from law act not only as alternatives to law's coercion but also as restraints on law's domination. Concerns with rule of law and separation of power constraints ensure that law is internally structured in such a way that it provides minimal opportunities to be subverted (Pettit 1997: 230–1). The substance of the law may also contain principles designed to shore up its own integrity. For example it might provide procedures for public interest groups to step in when diffuse interests are likely to be under threat in particular cases (Trubek & Trubek 1981). But the best checks on law's capacity to be used as a tool of domination will be external, and will rely on the existence of a strong civic culture and deliberative politics of justice. The existence of a culture that does justice spontaneously as a result of the types of communitarian and social movement alternatives to law mentioned above renders citizens more likely to follow the spirit of the law voluntarily; it becomes mostly unthinkable to use law to dominate others. When someone does the unthinkable, a strong civic culture means that there are alternative ways of doing justice available. The law itself may require the powerful to encourage a culture of justice by taking action that will undermine their own ability to subvert the law. Chapter 8 will propose that organizations be required not only to obey the law for themselves, but to develop plans for proactively doing justice to those they are in a position to dominate even before law is invoked.

Making people's ability to participate in law as equal as possible means that people can check each other's ability to use and abuse the law. Yet equalizing resources in that way may simply mean that everybody seeks to check each other's use of law by attempting to undermine the law for themselves. Such a strategy will escalate to a 'war of all against all' if there is not a supporting civic culture in which people are encouraged to comply with the spirit of the law voluntarily and not use the law to dominate others. It will be particularly important to inculcate the culture of justice in one particular group. This group is those whose job it is to help others use the law—the legal profession. If lawyers, and others who help people access the law, are willing to help clients use and subvert the law however they wish, then the law can easily be subverted. But if they challenge those who will inevitably seek to use law to undermine justice, then the law will be safer. The legal profession, in other words, ought to be there to help people access the law when they need it, but it will be crucial that the profession also sees itself, in some small way, as part of a culture of justice which encompasses much more than the law. The normative implications in this chapter therefore coincide with the empirical conclusions of Chapter 2 about what role lawyers ought to play in society.

CONCLUSION

In the republic of justice citizens have secure freedom because of their access to a variety of deliberative procedures in which they can make claims that advance their freedom as non-domination. This chapter argued that while the institutions of law are clearly central to the practice of justice, law is limited both in its effectiveness and in its desirability as a means of securing justice because of its coercive potential, and its amenability to subversion by powerful interests. Indeed community-based methods of social ordering will usually be more effective at securing freedom than law. Both theory and evidence show that coercive legal sanctions should only be used as a last resort, law should be designed and enforced as non-coercively as possible, and, most importantly, a variety of other means of doing justice including alternative dispute resolution, participation in social movement politics, democratic representation, and civic education for the respect of rights must proliferate.

In practice there are a number of problems with implementing this theory to improve justice. First, lawyers have historically been able to dominate access to justice discourse with the formalism and coercion of law. The access to justice movement itself has found it difficult to look beyond law in its attempts to improve justice. Secondly, critics of non-coercive social control show how dangerous it is to depend on community-based ordering to achieve justice. As Galanter (1981: 170) points out, such communitarian alternatives are 'not always the expression of harmonious egalitarianism. Indigenous law . . . [may be] based on relations of domination; protections that are available in public forums are absent.' De-emphasizing law may mean taking away the only resource the powerless have for achieving justice, if domination is pervasive in a culture. Similarly, the politics of democratic representation and social movements do not necessarily include all the voices that ought to be included in justice deliberation. Without rights entrenched through the coercion of law, domination within supposedly dialogic processes is all too easy. Chapter 4 uses socio-legal research to consider how we might begin to institutionalize a set of justice procedures which give law and lawyers a significant but not dominating place in the deliberative republic. Law and lawyers should not be at the periphery of a republic of justice; the challenge is how to make them central without subjugating people's justice to lawyers' justice.

4 Integrating Justice

INTERLOCKING STRATEGIES FOR ACCESS TO JUSTICE

Weaving together the four waves of reform that access to justice researchers and policy-makers have developed over the last thirty years achieves modest improvements in access to justice. The first wave focuses on helping people enforce their traditional legal rights adequately in the courts. Its strategy is to provide more state-employed lawyers in an attempt to expand the scope of formal legal services. The second wave is concerned with using social movement politics to change the law, court procedures, and ultimately society so that this access becomes more meaningful. It advocates the employment of more lawyers by institutions of civil society to reform formal legal institutions. The third wave established that much justice is and should be achieved at less formal levels. Mediators replace lawyers in fora for disputing that replace formal legal adjudication; informal community-based dispute resolution is proffered as the alternative to legal justice. The fourth wave takes efficiency to be a proxy for access, encouraging competition in order to allocate access to justice resources, whether formal or informal, through the market.

A reform that focuses on only one wave, for example ADR, can deflect policy-makers from seeing the need for other waves of reform, for example public interest law. Thus critics of ADR see proponents of face-to-face justice as failing to consider the necessity for group and political action to achieve justice through strategies such as public interest law (Abel 1981*a*, 1982*b*, Nader 1980), and therefore argue that ADR reforms often decrease rather than increase justice. Integrating at least the four waves described above is a remedy to symbolic change under the rubric of one wave which acts as a band-aid to enfeeble political prospects for radical surgery under the rubric of another. A competitive market will be more effective if the state is able to use regulation to ensure it stays competitive.[1] Where the market functions well,

[1] Thomas (1992) notes that the British Thatcher government had to be strongly pro-state in its policies, including its policies in relation to the legal profession, in order to be strongly pro-market because the state had to act to achieve the sort of market it wanted.

governments are more likely to be able to afford to take responsibility for providing a basic level of support for those who cannot afford to buy justice on the market. Where a vital community sector is providing the impetus for reform through lawyers' groups such as community legal centres, the access to justice movement, and the consumer movement, then both markets and states are more likely to stay responsive to community access to justice needs, and communitarian alternatives to legal justice are more likely to be developed.

Where the state fulfils its responsibility to support the infrastructure of legal and communitarian justice, where the institutions of community are vigorous in their attempts to improve legal justice and provide face-to-face justice, and where the market works efficiently enough for many to be able to buy their access, then there is some hope that access to justice will genuinely expand. Thus access to justice will not consist simply in access to law, but in a diversity of arrangements and institutions by which accepted social and political ideals are securely achieved. Yet despite all the efforts to date, the four waves have barely been ripples on an ocean of potential for justice. This chapter proposes that access to justice policy should now move from a focus on the four waves as separate building blocks of justice to a focus on the complex relationship between legal, informal, and social movement means of securing good social relations. The challenge is strategically and carefully to integrate legal and informal justice institutions, and to institutionalize input from public interest politics, so that access to justice policy embraces much more than lawyers' justice, and increased justice emerges from the interaction between different justice institutions.

LEGAL JUSTICE AND ITS ALTERNATIVES

Searching for an alternative to legal justice

In a well-balanced deliberative democracy, law is and should be only one of the means available to do justice. Empirical sociological and psychological research converges with normative political theory in suggesting that non-coercive and informal alternatives are likely to be more effective than coercive law in achieving long-term compliance with norms that advance justice, and coercive law is most effective when it is in reserve as a last resort (Ayres & Braithwaite 1992, Bardach & Kagan 1982, Braithwaite 1989, Kagan & Scholz 1984, Sherman 1993).

Indeed we will never have sufficient legal aid, a lean and competitive enough legal services market, nor a public-spirited enough legal profession, to do all our justice through law.

On the whole, too, people prefer to use lawyers and formal legal processes as a last resort in their attempts to achieve justice. In her ethnographic study of the way working-class Americans used lower courts and mediation, Sally Engle Merry (1990: 172) found that going to court was 'a desperate move when all else seems to have failed'. She suggests that ordinary Americans are not overwhelmingly disposed towards using litigation to solve their problems, but use court reluctantly when informal social controls fail and they need to escape the tyranny of local communities where husbands and boyfriends dominate women, and whites dominate ethnic minorities. They preferred to achieve justice by informal, dialogic, or non-coercive means, but were ready and willing to exercise their rights to use court if necessary. Similarly in Britain, the National Consumer Council (1995) found that of 1,000 people who had been involved in a civil dispute in the previous three years,[2] over one-half thought they would prefer to resolve any future dispute through mediation rather than through formal arbitration or a full trial (1995: 91).[3] Most were dissatisfied with the legal system (p. 81) and only 8 per cent thought they would like to use the legal system to resolve any future dispute (National Consumer Council 1995: 91).[4] Yet, like Merry's respondents, despite their dissatisfaction, most (59 per cent) were prepared to use the legal system if other methods did not work (National Consumer Council 1995: 105). As Lowy's (1978) famous study of court use in urban Ghana shows, despite strong social conventions against using coercive mechanisms early on, people will pursue coercive court-based disputing mechanisms, if their goal is simply money and that is the most efficient means of achieving it.

Dissatisfaction with law has been reflected in the thinking of the access to justice movement as it moved from improvements in access to formal legal justice (legal aid) to using innovative political ways to

[2] They gave the following categories (in order of frequency): damage to a vehicle, divorce, medical negligence/accident/injury, unpaid debt, faulty goods, dispute with a government agency, quarrel with a neighbour, problem at work, faulty service, custody/access, tenancy, will or estate, repossession of a home.

[3] Eighty per cent had used either a lawyer or a citizens' advice bureau to help them resolve their dispute.

[4] The percentage was higher for those who had actually used a full trial in their previous dispute, around 20%. A study by the Justice Research Centre in New South Wales produced similar results (Delaney & Wright 1997).

achieve more substantive justice (public interest law) and abandoning law altogether in an attempt to achieve justice through informal community-based means (ADR). Indeed the greatest hope of many access to justice researchers and reformers has been in the potential of informal alternatives to legal justice to nurture a civic culture of justice and avoid over-reliance on legalism.

The attractions of informal justice

The first virtue of informal alternatives to traditional formal legal justice is their (presumed) inexpensiveness.[5] Formal justice cannot be extended to everyone because of its great cost. Informal justice promises to be cheaper and quicker by abandoning technicalities, cumbersome procedure, and expensive professionals. But the attractions of informal justice run deeper than economic expedience. Merry and Milner (1993: 3) fantasize a

> popular justice . . . that is locally controlled, non professional, and procedurally informal and that envisages a renewed community and decisions made according to community norms . . . an alternative to the violence and coercion of state law.

Advocacy of informal justice is based on the belief that finding ways of resolving disputes which institutionalize community norms is more meaningful, more democratic, and ultimately more empowering for individuals than legal justice. Lawyers and court processes 'steal' disputes from the community in which they have arisen and impose alien meanings on them, risking results that have little significance to the disputants (Christie 1977: 4, Teubner 1987: 8); 'legal centralism' impairs awareness of the private orderings already extant in the communities of which we are members (Galanter 1981).

Early proponents of ADR were inspired by anthropological research into village-based means of mediation (Harrington & Merry 1988: 717). Others idealized a past small town North America which rejected legalized dispute settlement and emphasized communitarian justice based on 'mutual access, responsibility, and trust' (Auerbach 1983: 4). Formal processes abandon hope of continuing functional relationships.[6] The

[5] When settlement procedures are introduced into the litigation system in an attempt to cut delays and costs, however, the evidence suggests that neither objective is achieved (Cranston 1995*a*). Alternatives that totally bypass the traditional court system such as administrative tribunals are more likely to deliver costs savings (Sainsbury & Genn 1995).

[6] However Coglianese (1996) has found that within regulatory relationships, litigation may be consistent with an ongoing relationship.

vision of informal justice idealizes an equitable process where people communicate freely, understand each other, settle differences, and perhaps even change their behaviour rather than have a judgment (usually financial damages) imposed on them in an adversarial setting. A boss apologizes for his harassing behaviour, and his victim forgives him and receives whatever compensation fits her circumstances best; monetary damages, a public acknowledgement of wrongdoing, an overdue promotion.

The dangers of informal justice

Despite its attractions, informal justice is frequently rejected as a second-rate alternative to legal justice. Most people want to retain the option of taking their grievance to the highest court available if they wish, especially when informal justice fails, as it frequently does: 'They want the leverage of state power to obtain the redress they believe is theirs by right, not a compromise that purports to restore a social peace that never existed' (Abel 1982*a*: 8, see also Goldberg et al. 1985: 486). This is why Australian author Helen Garner's (1995) novelistic account of a real-life Melbourne University sexual harassment case was controversial: she questioned whether it was fair of two young women to press criminal charges against their college master for two comparatively minor incidents of alleged harassment. Instead she thought they should have informally asserted their rights with him straight away or at least used mediation within the college to solve their problems. The book created a public uproar when many feminists reacted angrily to her argument for informal justice by showing how it detracted from hard-fought rights to take legal action against sexual discrimination (see Parker 1997*a*).[7] Garner had failed to recognize adequately that the powerless often need to enforce their rights against the powerful in a way that consensual community-based dispute resolution does not deliver.

Critics argue that informal justice is just as likely to perpetuate the domination and oppression of everyday social life as the positive cultural values and meanings of disputants and their communities (Abel 1981*a*, Fitzgerald 1985, McEwen 1987). A woman may be at greater risk of being dominated by her husband in mediation over divorce

[7] Garner also made other arguments against which feminists reacted, especially that the young women were acting as victims when they should have recognized their own potential power in the situation.

arrangements than where the procedural safeguards of court and the presence of lawyers go some way towards putting right the structural inequalities of the everyday world.[8] The ability of transnational corporations totally to escape national legal systems when they have their disputes adjudicated in a private arbitration system created by an elitist group of French and US lawyers (Dezalay & Garth 1996) means that their private activities are rarely open to the scrutiny of public values.

Informal justice can also support structural inequality by siphoning poorer, less powerful potential litigants away from the formal justice system. It is a system of 'second class justice' reserved for the poor, the black, and women (Cain 1985). While the virtues of informality are often asserted on behalf of disadvantaged groups, the members of those groups always seem willing to use formal justice if the funding is available (Auerbach 1983: 127). The individualistic nature of informal justice tends to mean that patterns of social inequalities are not noticed: 'It thus distracts attention from, and challenges to, the status quo' (Fitzgerald 1985: 641; see also Abel 1981*a*, 1982*a*, 1982*b*, Nader 1980). It defuses conflict that might otherwise have led towards the transformation of social inequalities. Finally, institutions of informal justice may actually extend state control into areas of life which were previously not legalized by taking clients away from 'truly grass-root, community infrastructures' and encouraging them to use institutions of informal justice supported and controlled by the state (Fitzgerald 1985: 641; see also Pavlich 1996).

Overall, then, informal justice works towards creating a culture of justice very imperfectly. It often has as many features of coercive formal law as of informal community ordering. It frequently disadvantages the weak and powerless by strengthening and perpetuating the social inequalities of the real world. And it is often imposed by a state interested in saving costs, rather than evolved by community groups.[9] Yet there is still something to be said for the argument that formal profes-

[8] That is, assuming the woman does have adequate legal representation. Even where individuals do have legal representation in litigation or settlement negotiations, their unequal bargaining positions are still likely to be important. Thus Genn (1987) found that in settlement negotiations relating to personal injury actions, plaintiffs tended to hire non-specialist solicitors who were overpowered into 'cooperating' with defendant insurance company solicitors. However when plaintiffs used specialist union solicitors, defendant lawyers treated them with more respect.

[9] These are all contingent defects. It is possible to create institutions of informal justice that co-opt state power rather than the reverse (Dinnen 1996), and that attract attention to social inequalities rather than distract attention from them (see below).

sionalized legal justice is not enough. As Abel himself admits, at the end of a long critique of the informal justice movement,

> It is advocated by reformers and embraced by disputants precisely because it expresses values that deservedly elicit broad allegiance: the preference for harmony over conflict, for mechanisms that offer equal access to the many rather than unequal privilege to the few, that operate quickly and cheaply, that permit all citizens to participate in decision making rather than limiting authority to 'professionals', that are familiar rather than esoteric, and that strive for and achieve substantive justice rather than frustrating it in the name of form. (Abel 1982*b*: 310)

The limits of access to justice reform

One of Abel's strongest critiques of informal justice is that it privatizes, individualizes and neutralizes conflict, stymieing opportunities for it to be used creatively to achieve social change:

> Informal institutions control by disorganising grievants, trivialising grievances, frustrating collective responses. Their very creation proclaims the message that social problems can be resolved by fiddling with the control apparatus once more, that it is unnecessary to question basic structures. (Abel 1982*a*: 6–7; see also Abel 1981*a*, 1982*b*)

The traditional individualized processes of formal legal justice can equally be criticized for ignoring the existence of basic cleavages in society and failing to deal with fundamental structural conflict. Both formal and informal disputing are very limited means of addressing structural problems and inequalities that cause injustice.

The public interest law movement sought to address this problem. Yet on the whole, access to justice discourse has failed to comprehend the fact that access to justice means not only access to fora in which individual claims to rectify social wrongs can be addressed, but access to means by which individuals and groups can make claims to change widespread and structural features of social relations. Justice is more than access to the means to enforce certain rights once they have been established; it is also access to the means to participate in legal, political, and social life in ways that are aimed at changing law, rights, social relationships, and structures. Whether it is active participation in institutions of representative democracy or in social movements, access to justice must include political action aimed at changing the way things are structured, how other citizens think, and the rights and obligations that can be claimed through the processes of formal and informal justice. Both formal and informal justice seem desirable yet unsatisfactory means of achieving justice in individual cases. Both are weak at taking into account structural inequality or achieving the changes in social structure that are essential to securing justice. It is not sufficient simply to cumulate a variety of justice options; something more is required if they are to work together to help constitute deliberative democracy.

INTEGRATING LEGAL JUSTICE AND ITS ALTERNATIVES

A culture of justice?

The best solution that reformers and theorists have offered to the dilemma of choosing between formal and informal justice is to encourage the proliferation of both so that every potential claimant has a choice and every dispute can find its most appropriate forum (e.g. Edelman 1984). Yet this could mean continually expanding the dispute resolution system so that there are more and more avenues for people to pursue their complaints, leading to more and more disputes being brought forward for resolution (see Goldberg et al. 1985: 6), more lawyers, and more funds spent on justice, while injustice continues to be done as often as justice in a plethora of fora. Structural social inequality would remain unaddressed by access to justice initiatives and the accessibility of dispute resolution could conceivably worsen relations in society generally (Felstiner et al. 1980–1, Lieberman 1981).

Ultimately the aim of either formal or informal justice should not be to increase disputing but to facilitate a culture in which less disputing is necessary because justice is less frequently denied, a culture where claims to justice are dealt with as speedily and as well as possible. The informal justice movement appeals to our desire for informal ordering, community norms, and social relations where justice is evident as a matter of course. Yet the institutions of ADR do not of themselves achieve the type of protective civic culture where justice is instinctive and not forced. Similarly law is only effective at eliciting commitment to doing justice where it is embedded in cultural practices and informal norms that already support it. As Krygier (1997: 51) argues in the context of post-communist Eastern Europe, law must mesh with practices of everyday life if there is to be a civic culture of justice;

people must *care* about what the law says; the rules themselves must be taken seriously, and the institutions must come to matter. They must enter into the psychological economy of everyday life—to bear both on calculations of likely official responses and on those many circumstances in which one's actions are very unlikely to come to any officials' attention at all. They must mesh with, not contradict or be irrelevant to the 'intuitive law' of which Leon Petrazyci wrote, in terms of which people think about and organize their everyday lives . . . the wider social efficacy of official law requires that it enter into the normative structures which nourish, guide, inform, and coordinate the actions of good citizens; people who do not merely comply resentfully when they feel they might otherwise be punished, but who comply happily (enough) even when they are confident they will not be.

We have much evidence that law and informal norms do interpenetrate and constitute each other. Informal ordering occurs even in the most formal institutions of justice and formal ordering affects the most informal (see Galanter 1981). Henry's research (1983) on employee discipline in a number of companies showed that, regardless of the formal structure of their internal disciplinary procedures, formal state law and informal relations of private justice were inextricably interrelated in each of a variety of organizations (see also Newman 1987). Fitzpatrick (1984) uses the concept of 'integral plurality' to describe the way that law is constituted in relations of support and opposition with other semi-autonomous social fields, including community mediation (1988). Falk Moore (1978) identified a wide range of semi-autonomous social fields capable of generating rules and winning compliance, and emphasizes continuities between state law and law or quasi-law generated by group structures of society. Selznick (1992: 468) writes of the sociological doctrine of legal pluralism according to which 'The vitality of a social order comes from below, that is, from the necessities of cooperation in everyday life.' Galanter (half mocking) describes the way that those who do social research on law repeatedly discover that 'law in modern society is plural rather than monolithic . . . and that the national (public, official) legal system is often a secondary rather than a primary locus of regulation' (1981: 164).

Each of these scholars shows that law and informal forms of ordering interpenetrate. The normative policy challenge is to encourage formal and informal ordering to do more than haphazardly interpenetrate; to seek to ensure that they actually check each other's disadvantages and ultimately work together towards encouraging a culture that does more justice than injustice. When formal law facilitates and oversees indigenous ordering, there is potential for it to increase the latter's ability to do justice. Galanter (1981), writing from the legal pluralist perspective, shows how bargaining and regulatory endowments flow from the court into a world of uneven indigenous orderings. Krygier (1997) shows how formal institutions of law help support the robust institutionalization of civil society and trust in countries like Australia in contrast with the fragile attempts to develop democracy in post-communist societies such as Poland. For both Krygier and Galanter, and for others (e.g. Mnookin & Kornhauser 1979), it is possible that formal justice can oversee and improve processes of indigenous ordering and informal justice. From the other side, formal justice can also be enriched and strengthened when it is complemented by informal justice which is more likely to be complied with on a day-by-day basis. These benefits only accrue if they are integrated in such a way that they build each other up, setting justice aflow. Earlier law and society scholars such as Galanter noticed the phenomenon of the symbolic interplay of formal and informal orderings in Western as well as tribal societies. Current researchers are working in detail on the micro-institutions, practices, and systems in which attempts are made to articulate law to everyday orderings through things like corporate human resources departments (Edelman 1990, Edelman et al. 1993), professional institutions in hospitals (Heimer 1996, 1998), and community justice initiatives (Merry 1990, Marshall & Merry 1990).

A pyramid of access to justice strategies

One way to integrate formal and informal means of justice is in a hierarchy notionally prioritized according to time. In any particular dispute there are usually a variety of means or settings available for achieving justice. In Fig. 4.1, they are split into three broad categories of formality on a pyramid. Empirically, a dispute generally starts at the bottom and only moves up the options represented by the levels of the pyramid if it is not resolved and the parties have the motivation and resources to do so.[10] Normatively, the availability of a comprehensive range of justice options arranged in such a pyramid should increase access and justice overall.

[10] In their famous article on the emergence of disputes Felstiner et al. (1980–1) begin even earlier in the process of emergence of disputes by pointing out that a dispute does not even arise until someone perceives an injurious experience, *names* it as such, *blames* someone else for it, and makes a *claim* for a remedy. Many potential disputes never become claims even in the most informal fora.

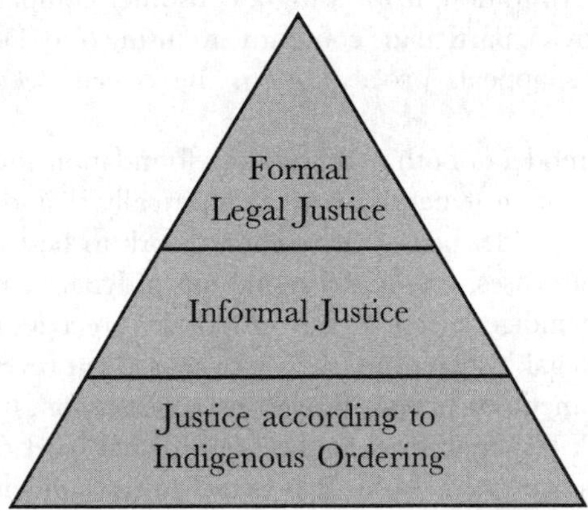

Fig. 4.1 A pyramid of access to justice options

Each level itself contains a variety of possibilities and overlaps with the next level. The first and most common level is the justice done according to 'indigenous ordering' (Galanter 1981), the ways of doing justice that spontaneously arise within everyday relationships, institutions, and settings. People are always doing justice (and injustice) among themselves in their families and workplaces and within public and private organizations. Justice according to indigenous ordering occurs where a person asserts their rights when they are in danger of being trampled within a relationship, and they are treated justly without need of recourse to any other person or body.

At the tip of the pyramid is formal legal justice to which only a few cases ever go. Even where the parties have actually invoked court procedures, most civil disputes settle by negotiation, and most criminal matters are dealt with by guilty plea, the equivalent of civil settlement, even though they could go to trial (Anleu & Mack 1995, Astor & Chinkin 1992: 25–30, Baldwin & McConville 1977, Genn 1987: 2). In the middle are a variety of more institutionalized methods of dispute resolution which fall short of formal legal proceedings, but are layered on top of spontaneous cultural means of resolving disputes and grievances. These are the institutions of 'informal justice' which are advocated as alternatives to the formal legal system. They fall on the boundary between formal state law and indigenous ordering (Merry 1993: 35). They range from neighbourhood ADR to court-based mediation and arbitration, from using a consumer complaints mechanism provided by a particular company to using the Department of Social Security's appeals process up to the Social Security Appeals Tribunal.

This simple model is both a descriptive foundation for an explanation of how disputing generally works empirically,[11] and a normative foundation for a model of how it ought to work to best deliver access to justice. In both cases, the model represents a dynamic model of justice. Empirically, indigenous ordering temporally precedes informal justice and formal legal justice more than vice versa. But reversals happen: for example, sometimes having moved up to litigation, a dispute may then move back to negotiation at the semi-formal level of arbitration. Normatively, as is argued below, it is better to try indigenous ordering before informal justice and informal justice before formal legal justice more often than the reverse. However, it will not be uncommon to decide to adjust the ordering presumption of the pyramid in particular circumstances and quickly decide to go straight to formal legal justice—a court injunction is needed now to provide the strongest protection possible against an unjust action that might threaten a human life, or a debt must be collected and the local court is the most efficient and reliable place to establish the right to the money (Lowy 1978). The pyramid is a preference ordering against rushing to formal legal justice before testing the presumption that indigenous ordering and informal justice are best tried first, maximizing access without compromising justice. It is not a rigid rule of command, designed to quash alternatives when they are required for justice.

There is evidence that a range of justice options utilized roughly according to the principles of the pyramid already work reasonably well to deliver access to justice in commercial contracting: formal justice is strong in the commercial sector because the state provides the necessary legal infrastructure and because business people can afford to use it. In recent years state-provided justice for commercial litigants has been considerably streamlined: in the USA an array of in-court settlement devices have been developed (Singer 1994: 56–7). Due to user pressures, many Australian and Canadian jurisdictions now use case flow management in commercial matters in an attempt to encourage

[11] See Hawkins (1984) for a descriptive analysis of the enforcement of environmental regulation in Britain that tends to support the theory, as well as the references in Chapter 3.

settlement and speedier decisions (Cranston 1995*a*: 48).[12] The substance of the law is also generally more responsive to the needs of the business community than to other groups.

At the most informal level, a business culture of informal dispute resolution is strong. Because many commercial players 'have a high stake in reducing the conflict costs in everyday transactions' they often prefer internal settlement to external dispute resolution and leave court processes as a last resort (Blankenburg 1994: 806). Good legal advisers have always concentrated on negotiating solutions rather than fighting to the death in court, and managers are increasingly motivated to avoid the expense of litigation if possible (Singer 1994: 56). Macaulay's classic 1963 study of the way business people used and did not use contracts shows the importance of informal negotiation and the limited role of law and legal sanctions in adjusting contracts and solving disputes. Both sides in any dispute know that threatening to use law and lawyers will cause deterioration in their relationship because, as one businessman explained, when one side threatens to bring a breach of contract suit the other feels that they are being 'treated like a criminal' and will therefore fight back (Macaulay 1963: 65). Mackie's (1989: 169–209) more recent study of the use of lawyers within British corporations tells a similar story of corporate reluctance to resort to the use of law and lawyers in resolving problems. Galanter and Rogers's (1991) research on American business disputing suggests that changes in the economy might increase disputing at particular times but that businesses will be motivated to find new forms of governance to resolve disputes privately as soon as possible. But this does not mean that legal norms have no effect: they permeate the environment of informal dispute resolution rather than dominating solutions.

Recently the demand for middle-level alternatives to litigation has increased so that private ADR options are proliferating. Riekert (1990) describes a variety of options available in Australia from the formal options of arbitration and mini-trials to mediation and conciliation, and Mackie (1989: 209) also describes an 'emerging system of "community-based justice" within the business sector' in Britain. In some areas US companies are choosing to contract in advance for a pyramid of dispute resolution options where things go wrong (Singer 1994: 80). Globally the same trend is also reflected in the worldwide movement

[12] However, as Cranston notes, the evidence on whether such mechanisms actually do decrease costs or delays is inconclusive or negative.

towards middle-level options at the most formal end, arbitration (Dezalay & Garth 1996).

The advantages of integration

Ayres and Braithwaite's (1992) theory for using both formal and informal means of regulation in the more limited context of 'responsive' business regulation shows how the careful integration of formal and informal justice can maximize cooperative solutions to injustices and the voluntary doing of justice without sacrificing the use of coercive sanctions in cases of recalcitrance. Their pyramid is a principled way of linking coercive or legal means of regulation with persuasive trust-based means of regulation (see Fig. 4.2). It is a schematic representation of the idea that instead of using their most drastic regulatory strategies first, regulators should trade on the goodwill of those they are regulating, encouraging them to comply voluntarily, using more dras-

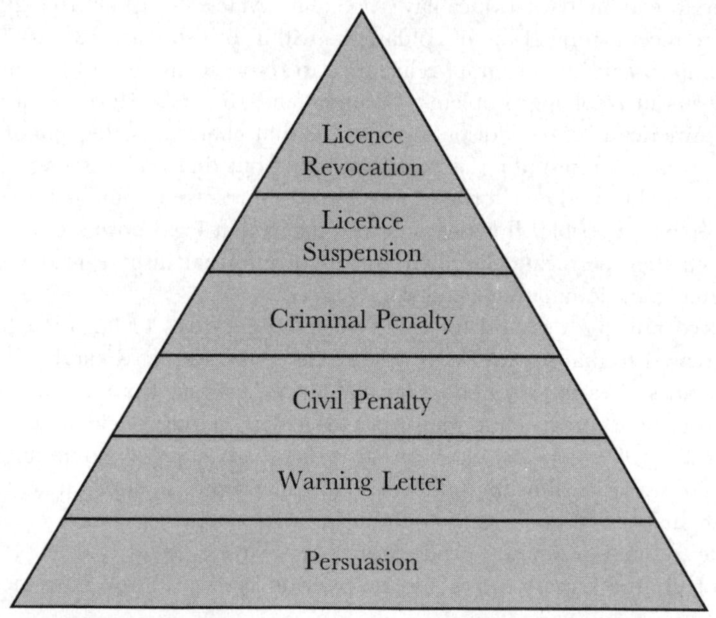

Fig. 4.2 An enforcement pyramid for business regulation (from Ayres & Braithwaite 1992: 35)

tic regulatory measures only when that fails and reverting to a trusting demeanour when these strategies achieve their goal: 'Compliance is optimised by regulation that is contingently cooperative, tough and forgiving' (Ayres & Braithwaite 1992: 51). In their model prioritizing informal means of regulation in time ensures that cooperative measures are used more frequently without compromising the possibility of using more formal measures where necessary.

It is the argument of this chapter that Ayres and Braithwaite's model is timid in restricting its relevance to state regulation of business. The same model could also provide a normative foundation for solving general problems of doing justice in democratic societies. It is not only state regulators who generally do and ought to follow the presumptions of the pyramid it is also mothers, lovers, bosses, creditors, unions, and generals struggling for justice in child-rearing, relationships, employee management, finance, industrial relations, international trade, and warfare. Where the formal legal act is as elevated as a declaration of war or initiation of a formal trade dispute under the GATT, or as mundane as sexual harassment litigation, this model generally describes the disputing preferences of most actors. Because all of these actors ought to be concerned to be just, the presumptions of the pyramid also have a normative relevance that ought to bear on their decision-making.

Doing justice deliberatively according to the pyramid has obvious economic advantages. Encouraging people to utilize less expensive strategies for achieving justice first means that the resources of formal justice processes can be more efficiently allocated to those who really need them to assert their citizenship. Taking this principle seriously might mean arranging things so that rich litigants cannot clog the courts with litigation designed purely as tactics in bigger corporate battles (Tomasic 1990). We might channel those who are rich enough into a truly user-pays system of formal justice and keep state resources for those who cannot afford the full price of formal adjudication. It also means that where it is more important to people that a problem is resolved quickly than resolved right, they can opt for informal justice. Where it is more important that it be resolved right than resolved quickly, they can keep moving up the pyramid until all avenues of checking that the outcome is right have been exhausted.

Using economic arguments to justify the imposition of an access to justice strategy in which people are discouraged (perhaps even disabled) from using the resources of law to make their claims until they have exhausted informal alternatives is itself unjust. It is open to the criticism that ordinary people will be forced to lesser (informal) justice in the interests of economic expedience, while the rich will still be able to buy full access to the law. The careful integration of formal and informal justice need not deny people formal justice where they require it. It does suggest that keeping access to formal justice available as a second (or third resort) can make less formal justice work better in the first instance. The more middle-level options there are, the more opportunities there are to resolve disputes without the disadvantages of a formal process. Ensuring that people can always escalate to formal justice means that their rights are more likely to be protected earlier, more cheaply, and with less emotional pain, and that if they are not, they will get relief.

Doing justice according to the pyramid also addresses the ADR movement's concern about the 'maintenance and enhancement of the self' (Trubek 1990: 122). Emotional pain is too often neglected in both economic and lawyerly analyses of justice. Yet as the ADR movement indicated, a fundamental fact about injustice is that it hurts and a fundamental fact about justice that satisfies consumers is that it heals. So much so that there is virtue in crossing over empirical and normative claims of the theory: empirically injustice hurts, therefore normatively justice should heal. Restorative justice theory, research, and praxis show that justice needs many anterooms before one reaches the courtroom if it is to be given a chance to heal (Cragg 1992, Galaway & Hudson 1990, Marshall 1985, Messmer & Otto 1992, Van Ness 1986). The pyramid leaves plenty of space for healing.

Checking injustice

In this model integrating formal and informal justice makes each more efficacious not only because it improves their efficiency but because it checks some of the dominations and injustices involved in the other. External legal norms increase the value of informal orderings for access to justice by checking the tyranny of the majority. Law and formal legal processes, at their best, are designed to protect people's rights and safeguard due process. When formal justice is layered over other forms of justice then it is not only an alternative to them, but also a regulator of them. We have already seen that Sally Engle Merry (1990) found that working-class Americans used courts for just this purpose, to escape the tyrannies of community.

As Habermas (1996: 122–6) has comprehensively argued, law as a form embodies a few basic principles that create the conditions in which the justice of deliberative democracy can be established. It is these basic principles that law ought to enforce in informal justice in local communities, organizations, informal tribunals, and all other places where justice is attempted. First, is the threshold right of someone to be treated as a member of the relevant group to whom justice must be done, and who should be afforded the maximum level of individual liberty consistent with the other procedures laid out below. Secondly, one of the most valuable achievements of the law is the development of the notion of procedural fairness or natural justice which is capable of contextual variation in application to many situations from clubs to courts. At the most basic level, it involves the right for someone to be informed of decision-making that may affect them, the right to be heard, and the right to have the decision made by an unbiased decision-maker. The law should be used to ensure that due process rights are followed in contextually appropriate forms all the way down the pyramid. Thirdly, law can enforce the basic right of all members of the relevant group to participate in the processes by which the group defines further rights—a meta-right to participation to define further procedural and substantive rights. This should include the right not only of individuals to participate, but of groups or social movements to input into justice procedures. Fourthly, the law should enforce in the micro-institutions of any society those substantive individual or group rights that have been deliberatively adopted by the whole society, such as the rights set out in a nation's constitutionally entrenched bill of rights or internationally ratified rights documents. These are the four basic principles that the law should enforce in all places where justice is attempted: the three procedural guarantees of membership, procedural fairness, and the right to participation that institutionalize deliberative democracy, and the fourth right to all those rights promulgated at a national level.

The law is also a fertile source of basic values and principles such as conscionability in contracts, self-defence in criminal law, proportionality in administrative and government action, which may be utilized and enforced as important considerations in particular circumstances in informal justice. The courts have had to learn to become quite adept at balancing competing considerations in determining whether an otherwise legal contract is being relied upon in unconscionable circumstances (conscionability), or whether proposed government actions impose a burden on some section of the community disproportional to the good to be achieved (proportionality). In the case of both these doctrines, formal legal doctrines have been formulated partially in response to justice demands coming from below. These legal doctrines can now be used downwards through the pyramid to provide resources for formal law to condition the justice of informal orderings.[13]

If an informal justice mechanism completely ignored some consideration that the law has traditionally seen as fundamental in determining the remedies due to a complainant or the penalty or restitution due from an offender, then a court should be able to step in and re-decide the case on the basis of more conventional considerations. For example, if an informal justice conference completely ignored evidence that an assault occurred in self-defence, or did not even give the alleged offender the chance to put that side of the story, the offender should be encouraged to appeal to a traditional legal tribunal to have his or her case heard. Conference convenors would soon learn to be sensitive to the basic issues that a court would be likely to criticize in informal justice orderings, such as lack of consideration to intent, self-defence, or diminished responsibility due to age or intellectual disability. To preserve the integrity of informal justice orderings, however, the conference convenor should simply ensure that these issues are being actively considered, discussed, and understood by participants, not lead the conference into a thicket of complex legal reasoning. The conference convenor's skill lies in being able to make fundamental legal considerations concrete in the individual circumstances and troubles of people's lives by ensuring that everybody gets a chance to tell their side of the story (procedural fairness) and explain their motivations and reasons for their actions (e.g. self-defence), and then help people come to a concrete decision on what they think would be a just way to repair the damage from there, rather than abstract the decision to a finding of guilt or innocence and a 'sentence' that is substantively unrelated to the original problem.

While recourse to formal legal processes might help solve the tyranny of majority in community, it exposes citizens to the risk of tyranny by formalistic and professional procedures. The danger of formal legal processes is that they are often dominated by professionals and unresponsive to the values and norms of others. Legal supervision of informal justice expands institutions of the law into 'supervision and governance of [the] intimate world of neighbourhood and family' (Merry 1990: 182). As Merry (1990: 181) notes,

[13] See Chapter 8 for an example of how considerations of conscionability might apply to a bank's internal customer dispute resolution scheme.

To return to court again is to offer the court the opportunity to shape the problem in *its* discourses, to name it, and to point towards its solution. As the average person returns to court with new demands, he strengthens the power of the law over his life, both its direct coercive power and its ideological domination, its capacity to interpret and make sense of his problems. The use of the law challenges existing social hierarchies, but the discourses of the courthouse continue to constrain and restrict the way these problems are understood. Plaintiffs rebel against the social order, but their complaints are held within a framework established by the law, by traditions of social relationships, and by the language of therapy and help.

Even where informal or democratized means of justice are successfully introduced they can easily be colonized and stultified by lawyers.[14] Reforms based on integrating formal and informal justice will only be successful if the relationship between legal justice and more communal processes of justice is such that they both check the dominations involved in the other. Integrating formal and informal justice means not only that formal justice can be an alternative and regulator of informal justice, but that informal justice can be used persistently to critique professional models of justice and challenge it to become more collaborative, personal, and based in community norms and power:

Popular justice subverts state law by constructing a cultural space—an alternative justice that is more responsive to community desires—even if this alternative is phrased within the language and structure of state law itself. It creates an oppositional discourse within state law that insists on the possibility of managing conflict without violence and asserts a model of community ordering. By constructing a vision of an alternative justice, it confronts the legal system with a persistent critique. (Merry & Milner 1993: 9)

Informal justice options that utilize communal relations can enrich legal justice by checking the domination of unaccountable professional judgment but ought not to oust its concern with due process and the protection of people's rights: in restorative justice conferences being trialed in the Reintegrative Shaming Experiment at the Australian National University, mothers do sometimes tackle the police on abuses such as excessive use of force against their children.[15] Ideally the pyramid of access to justice strategies would look something like Fig. 4.3, where formal law goes down the pyramid to facilitate and oversee

[14] This problem will be addressed in Chapter 8.

[15] Fieldwork notes from the Reintegrative Shaming Experiment, Australian National University, Canberra, conducted by Heather Strang, Larry Sherman, and John Braithwaite.

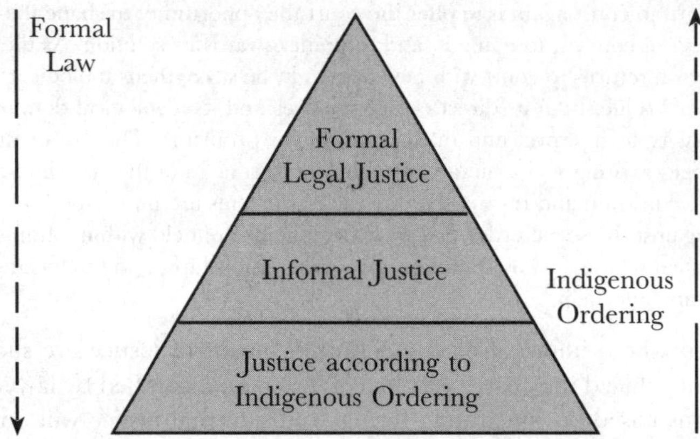

Fig. 4.3 The checking of injustice in a pyramid of access to justice options

informal justice so that problems of oppression and domination are weeded out. But indigenous ordering goes up the pyramid so that people are developing for themselves an increasing number of options to resolve their own disputes meaningfully. Such mutual interpenetration would set the conditions for a comprehensive culture of access to justice in which legal and other strategies are able to contribute.

Most justice and injustice that already occurs does so at the most informal level. Therefore the aim of this strategy is to create incentives for people to do justice at the lowest level possible at the same time as their sensibilities are sharpened by the need to protect rights through improving formal legal justice. As informal justice was made more accountable to public justice, the base of the pyramid would get larger because people would prefer to settle matters lower down when they found that matters could be settled in a way that protected their rights at that level. Such institutions of dispute resolution would maximize the effect of law in encouraging voluntary aversion to injustice, and provide means and techniques to restore justice quickly at the most informal level. Formal justice would remain (or rather become) available whenever necessary. Thus integrating formal and informal justice challenges the 'intellectual cliche that communal relations deteriorate with the increase of formal, impersonal and technical social regulations' (Galanter 1981: 166). In an integrated pyramid of access to justice options, communal relations of justice are enhanced by formal justice and vice versa.

Integrated access to justice strategies: an example

Workable access to justice reform would thus use state-, market- and community-based initiatives (the four waves) not just as complementary justice alternatives but as an integrated range of formal and informal strategies for access to justice. Blankenburg's (1994) comparative study of litigation rates in the Netherlands and a neighbouring region in West Germany shows how this might work in practice.

The German state of Northrhine-Westphalia has litigation rates from thirteen to twenty times higher than the Netherlands, according to Blankenburg's analysis, but no significant difference in adversariness and other relevant aspects of culture or in the number of potentially litigious social relationships. Legal aid is much more widely available in the Netherlands than in West Germany, as are legal advisers. So formal justice is stronger in the Netherlands, but at the same time, according to Blankenburg, there are many more alternatives to litigation, pre-court conflict institutions and also alternatives to formal legal services (since there is no lawyers' monopoly). So there are a variety of ways both of avoiding conflicts in the first place and of resolving them without court explaining the Netherlands' much lower litigation rates. Nevertheless since legal aid is available to approximately 60 per cent of households the courts are free to hear important cases. As Blankenburg (1994: 806) explains, this means more people get access to justice overall:

> In a number of conflict constellations where the law protects the socially weaker parties against the more powerful ones (like consumer protection, tenants rights, and employment protection), 'alternative' institutions attract a high number of cases that would not find a forum in a more litigious culture. At the same time that they effectively filter out recurrent routine cases, thus relieving the court dockets, the infrastructure of legal aid nevertheless offers an opportunity for strategic test litigation.

In Blankenburg's example, institutions of state, market, and civil society each contribute to establishing the pyramid of options that give people access to justice. A strong state provides substantial legal aid and therefore supports the availability of formal justice but also legitimizes a variety of less formal means of dispute resolution. The fact that anyone is entitled to give legal advice and to represent people in the lower courts and that fees are not strictly controlled means that there is a strong market in legal services which makes formal justice more affordable and encourages a variety of means of delivering justice services.

Strong institutions of civil society support a variety of informal and semi-formal means of justice. For example, Blankenburg (1994: 801) argues that better funded and more active Dutch consumer organizations set up complaints boards which handle a higher caseload than those set up by the comparatively weaker German consumer organizations. But what of the need to have access to procedures by which people can change more fundamental and structural injustices?

Achieving justice where structural inequality reigns

If both formal and informal justice fail to deal comprehensively with structural inequality, then a strategy that integrates them is not likely to do much better. Pyramids of access to justice strategies, however, need not be completely useless at dealing with structural inequalities or achieving social change. In the case of both formal and informal justice, significant gains can be made when procedures are changed to empower communities and groups to take part, and to take account of patterns of domination and oppression. The public interest law movement was an attempt to deal with precisely this sort of criticism of formal justice. The courts can also be the locus of liberating conflict in certain circumstances (Abel 1981*a*: 251). For example, a decision that a company is vicariously liable for the sexual harassment of one of its employees will frequently encourage it (and other firms) to put in place programmes and policies aimed at discouraging such behaviour from occurring in the future, and providing grievance mechanisms if it does occur, thus improving the lot of women in the firm (Parker 1999). A decision granting a particular indigenous group land rights might force the government to enact legislation giving more general indigenous land rights, and start a public debate in which indigenous claims to justice are taken (at least a little) more seriously than before.[16] Anti-tobacco litigation can reveal damaging information about the tobacco industry, cause an increase in media coverage, and constitute new ways for policy-makers to address tobacco regulation and preventive health care (Mather 1998).

Just as there are ways of empowering groups to take part in formal justice processes instead of simply pitting powerless individuals against powerful organized interests, there are ways of organizing groups to even up the power inequalities in institutions of informal justice. There

[16] But see Rosenberg (1991) who argues that such decisions rarely achieve the social change enthusiasts claim for them, and may even cause a backlash.

is no reason why Abel's (1982*b*: 288–9) criticism of informal justice fora should always apply:

> Although neighbourhood institutions constantly speak about community, what they actually require (and reproduce) is a collection of isolated individuals . . . Informalism appropriates the socialist ideal of collectivity but robs it of its content. The individual grievant must appear alone before the informal institution, deprived of the support of such natural allies as family, friends, work mates, even neighbours.

Community accountability conferencing in criminal justice is one attempt to turn institutions of informal justice into fora where individuals are empowered through the presence and support of their most trusted friends to confront and receive an apology and compensation from those who have wronged them, even when the offender is much more powerful than themselves. Rather than seeing the restorative justice event as a dyadic mediation between two individuals, in 'community accountability' or 'family group' conferences both parties bring along friends, family, and supporters: 'It is a meeting of two communities of care, both of which contain men and women, children and adults, the cool and the uncool, the organised (like the Aboriginal Community Council) and the unorganized' (Braithwaite 1995*c*: 7; see also 1995*b*: 198). This approach de-individualizes informal justice and muddies individual imbalances of power. There is no reason why it cannot be applied to informal dispute resolution of civil disputes or internal dispute resolution in organizations. Indeed one of the basic principles law could enforce in informal justice is the right of parties to involve communities of support in the resolution of disputes as an element of procedural fairness and rights to participation.

A further way of addressing issues of structural inequality in institutions of informal justice is through ensuring social movement politics percolate into the deliberation of conferences, to defend minorities against tyrannies of the majority and connect private concerns to campaigns for public transformation. This could mean state funding of advocacy groups to receive copies of all conference agreements, to watch for agreements that are oppressive or worse than a court would have done by one of the parties, and to watch for structural injustices for which there are large classes of additional victims whom the advocates should apprise of their access to a remedy. This is actually a potentially more efficient way of publicizing access to remedies than the haphazard publicity of the court. A similar strategy could be used in other areas where dyadic ADR has been the norm, such as divorce and custody disputes. Giving responsibility to organized community and interest groups, such as consumer or feminist NGOs, to monitor informal dispute resolution fora, such as industry consumer complaint schemes, divorce mediation centres, and even complaints mechanisms for the legal profession, can also help ensure that patterns of exploitation and oppression are noticed and dealt with. The NGO monitoring of a telecommunications ombudsman might note that a number of recent complaints have concerned speakers of English as a second language who were pressured to buy extra services they could not afford, and lobby the phone companies to change the disclosure practices and sales tactics of their sales agents.

Neither the processes of informal nor formal justice can go far towards achieving justice by themselves if they are not embedded in a context in which groups and individuals are striving for social change using processes of representative democracy and social movement politics external to the law. Conversely, the potential for change when political and restorative justice are intertwined is great:

> But if the assertion of authority to resolve disputes and control behaviour has the potential to contribute to the creation of a countervailing power that can oppose both state and capital, it can do so only as part of a broad social movement . . . Such a movement is essential to informal institutions in two ways: First, it alone can create the community base that allows informal institutions to function by giving people incentives to resolve conflicts rather than sever relations and by conferring authority to examine behaviour, intervene in conflict, and enforce decisions. Second, legal institutions can gain broad significance only if they are integrated in the pursuit of social, economic, and political objectives. Informalism, thus, is not an end in itself, but it can be a very important means in the struggle for justice. (Abel 1982*a*: 12–13)

In addition to formal legal means and informal face-to-face means of achieving justice, the politics of social movements and active citizenship are necessary to achieve the sort of social change that justice requires. Access to justice for women, aborigines, or gays mainly involves working outside either the legal system or ADR fora to change people's conceptions of what is right and to redistribute power, wealth, or status. But it will also be important for these groups to know that they can effectively utilize the legal system and ADR fora as groups and individuals when strategic to achieve their goals. Often the outcomes of political and social struggles will be rights which themselves become institutionalized in legal processes and eventually in pyramids of formal and informal options of enforcement. When women fought for equality, the result was not only changed consciousnesses and practices, but changed laws on voting, pay and access to the workforce, property rights, and so on (e.g. Burgmann 1993: 98–100).[17] The policy challenge here is to imagine ways of ensuring that the pyramid of formal and informal justice options are always embedded within a politics where different groups can put their ideas about the social good onto the agenda and there are processes by which it is decided how they should be able to enforce their rights. The political must be continually acting on all levels of the pyramid to change both the rights and the processes it institutionalizes. The gains of the public interest movement in terms of procedural changes that allow group input into formal legal processes should be extended and enforced into informal dispute resolution, as well as formal legal processes. The law may have to enforce group rights of participation or input into decision-making under the pyramid and decisions that have had the benefit of group input to identify patterns of domination and oppression should filter into the law.

CONCLUSION

While the institutions of law are clearly central to the practice of justice, law is limited both in its effectiveness and in its desirability as a means of securing justice because of its coercive potential, and its amenability to subversion by powerful interests. Improvements in access to justice could be made when we free access to justice policy-making from legalistic over-reliance on the processes of law. This does not mean severing issues of justice from law, but seeking out the potential for interdependence between legal and non-legal means of justice set within a broader context of participation in social movement politics, democratic representation, and civic education for the respect of rights. The aim is a culture which maximizes both the doing of justice spontaneously and informally under the shadow of the law, and the accessibility of legal and semi-legal remedies when injustice is done.

This chapter has argued that layering formal and informal injustice means that both have a chance to check the disadvantages and

[17] But also note Burgmann's (1993: 98) description of the way the women activists in the Australian Equal Pay Case hearings of 1969 felt disenfranchised by the formality of the legal process dominated by men in contrast with their liberated involvement in the social movement politics of protest.

injustices of the other. Prioritizing informal justice in time encourages the development of communal means of resolving problems. It can avoid the escalation of conflict and imposition of alien values which frequently occur in court. It can free up formal law for important disputes and develop new models for empowering individuals and communities in justice processes which might eventually be applied to law. The ready availability of more formal justice when informal justice fails means that people might be more likely to do justice earlier to avoid the sanctions of more formal processes. The value of the four waves of access to justice reform has been in showing the importance of institutions of state, market, and civil society in building up the range of strategies necessary to improve access to justice.

We saw that in the commercial sector a sufficient range of alternatives has almost spontaneously developed for inter-firm disputes. This is only because two conditions are fulfilled in that sector. First, many firms can afford to go to the apex when they need to protect their rights and can make credible threats to invoke it so that they really do bargain 'under the shadow of the law'. Secondly, there is already a strong business culture in place which provides the basis for informal and middle-level means of justice. The pyramid strategy works best between equals who can bargain and negotiate freely at the most informal level and who are motivated to get on not only because of the threat of court, but because they want a continuing relationship.

These two conditions are not necessarily met in those areas where improving access to justice is most crucial. They are not likely to be satisfied when an individual cries injustice against the large company where they work or the government department on whom they depend for benefits: access to justice reform must concentrate on proactively ensuring that an integrated range of justice options are available even to those who cannot afford to buy legal justice on the market or are liable to being dominated by those more powerful than themselves. People most frequently experience injustice within the institutional loci of their everyday lives, the organizations where they work, shop, and spend their leisure time, the government bodies which make important decisions on their behalf, and family groups where men can dominate women, adults can dominate children, and the able can dominate the old and disabled. Building up integrated sets of access to justice options for individuals and groups within these powerful institutional structures ought to be the priority of any fifth wave of access reform. Such a fifth wave will be the topic of Chapter 8.

An even more difficult problem is ensuring that in practice legal and indigenous regulation do check each other's dominations rather than multiplying them. It is possible to have pyramids in which the injustice of each level fails to check the injustice of the other. For example McConville and Mirsky's research in New York City criminal courts showed that reliance on guilty pleas by public defenders meant that courts could not adequately fulfil their function of protecting people's procedural rights and checking informal police culture. The domination of police at the level of arrest affected the way court cases were decided:

> Our research shows that guilty pleas in New York City are a part of a vertical process: What will happen later at the court stage influences what happens earlier at the police stage. Routine processing in court, through guilty pleas, reinforces the actions and expectations of the police and defendants, thereby encouraging sweeps, dragnets and other non-individuated arrests. This integral feedback loop, in which facts are of little consequence and in which witnesses are not called at either hearings or trials (and the propriety of policing and the reliability of police evidence are untested), institutionalizes domination. (McConville & Mirsky 1995: 229)

The ideal is for formal law to go down the pyramid to facilitate and oversee informal justice so that problems of oppression and domination are weeded out; and for indigenous ordering to go up the pyramid so that people are developing for themselves an increasing number of options to resolve their own disputes meaningfully. Whether this occurs will depend on the way institutions of formal and informal justice are designed, interlocked, and regulated. But the one institution which could have the greatest effect on the success or otherwise of any access to justice pyramid is the legal profession.

Lawyers may either help or hinder the flow of formal and informal justice between the layers of the pyramid depending on their attitudes and organization. Each of the four waves of access to reform has historically relied heavily on reforming and reorganizing the legal profession to achieve its goals. Claimants will usually believe that in each of their individual cases the services of a high-quality lawyer are the best way to secure justice. Yet overall access to justice reform that is feasible and desirable means nurturing ways of providing access to justice that do not ride on the back of professional fees and adversarialism, and encouraging a culture in which justice is done at the most informal level. In this context access to justice reform conceived purely as reform to lawyers' justice is not sufficient. At the same time it will be crucial to ensure that lawyers are reformed and regulated to be suited to a world in which justice is a cultural and political practice, not just a legal one.

5 The Ethics of Justice

INTRODUCTION

While the community sees the legal profession's problems in terms of specific complaints of overcharging, low-quality service, and the distortion of justice for the highest bidder, the most serious potential pathology of the legal profession is its failure to comprehend its role in a broader access to justice agenda. The primary significance of the legal profession for access to justice lies not in how well or badly they perform the technical task of providing legal services to a range of citizens, but in the culture or ideology of justice lawyers carry and support. It may be so narrow that it colonizes and corrupts non-legal forms of justice, denying the breadth of processes by which citizens may gain access to justice. It may be so unfocused that lawyers disclaim responsibility for helping people gain access to the justice of law, which facilitates, complements, and oversees other means of justice. The previous two chapters established the broad contours of an access to justice agenda grounded in theory and evidence which puts citizens and justice—not lawyers—first. This chapter and the following two consider how lawyers might best be regulated and organized to contribute to the practice of justice.

Chapter 2 mined the evidence for people's concerns about lawyers. In this chapter I focus on the positive ideals that might assist them in performing their part of the task of contributing to just democracies. The purpose is not to prove that all lawyers in fact follow these ideals; far from it, as we saw in Chapter 2. It is to determine what ideals, however dimly understood and practised, might already have some life in legal professional culture and be capable of reconstruction and reinvigoration to serve as normative goals for the regulation and governance of the profession. Despite their serious potential for domination and injustice, lawyers do not lack aspirations towards assisting in the achievement of access to justice. This chapter argues that the normative ethical traditions (and ideologies) of the profession can be read as a statement of what the lawyer's role in facilitating access to justice ought to be. The first part of this chapter presents lawyers' claims that their ethical self-regulation accomplishes the institutionalization of four main ethical ideals. The following sections discuss and reconstruct each of these ethical ideals in turn, indicating how each can address the potential lawyer injustices that have been identified in earlier chapters. The chapter concludes by considering the idea that a self-regulating professional community can help constitute these ideals.

THE ETHICS OF LAWYERS

An important support for the profession's attempts to elevate its own status and to preserve its self-government has been the creation and enforcement of a set of ethics that can address public concerns about the role of lawyers in the justice system. The self-regulatory tradition has spawned a group of ethical ideals which have attempted to articulate (both to the public and to the profession) a conception of what it is that lawyers do and how they should do it. Writers like Abel (1981*b*) argue that the promulgation of ethical rules does not promote ethical conduct but serves the latent function of furthering professional market control and the symbolic function of legitimization—they 'create a myth about what lawyers might be in order to disguise what they are' (Abel 1981*b*: 668). This need not mean that rhetoric and traditions arising out of the struggle to achieve and maintain self-regulation are worthless. Ideals and norms developed by the profession to appeal to public sensibilities can be appropriated to a theory of the regulation of the legal profession regardless of whether they have actually been implemented in practice. Indeed such norms can be a more powerful tool of persuasion and change than norms imposed from the outside because they carry the power of self-critique.

In contrast to Abel, many commentators from within the profession itself look nostalgically back to a past age in which certain ethical ideals were accepted and practised. Two recent books by prominent US law professors adopt this perspective (Kronman 1993, Glendon 1994), and it can be frequently found in the speeches of older judges and professional patriarchs. A realistic look at the history of self-regulation suggests that there never was an idyllic age in which lawyers held ideals they are now losing. Now and in the past ethics have been a matter of struggle, conflict, and public rhetoric (Paterson 1996, Pue 1995). Ethical norms are likely to be as relevant (and irrelevant) now as they ever were.

What then are the ideals of lawyering that the tradition of self-regulation has claimed to nurture and institutionalize? Four interwoven ethics or conceptions of what it is that lawyers ought to do can be discovered in lawyers' ethical debates, treatises, and codes:

1. The ideal of devoted service to clients in a legal system where citizens need advice and representation to use the legal system (the advocacy ideal).
2. The ideal of fidelity to law and justice if the system is not to be sabotaged by clients who will pay a lawyer to do anything (the social responsibility ideal).
3. An ideal of willingness to work for people and causes that are usually excluded from the legal system (the justice ideal).
4. The ideal of courtesy, collegiality, and mutual self-regulation amongst members of the profession (the ideal of collegiality).

These four basic traditions or ideals can be found in most treatments of legal ethics. For example, Croft's (1992) description of the English ideology of lawyering which he argues was easily transplanted to early republican America included:

> an overriding commitment to public service (with compensation as a byproduct), a duty, as an 'officer of the court,' to the judicial system and to the institution of law itself, a strong fiduciary and agency relationship with clients, and a professional relationship with colleagues marked by fair play, collegiality and candor. (1992: 1281–2)

Croft's summary covers (in order) the justice ideal, the social responsibility ideal, the advocacy ideal, and the ideal of collegiality. The American Bar Association's 1983 *Model Rules of Professional Conduct* (Morgan & Rotunda 1993: 1–142) include (1) rules to ensure that lawyers zealously serve and represent their clients (the advocacy ideal), (2) rules to ensure that they show candour to tribunals, fairness to opposing parties, and are allowed to reveal information to prevent a client committing a criminal act (the social responsibility ideal), (3) rules regulating the way public service is given and encouraging lawyers to do pro bono work (the justice ideal), and (4) rules governing relationships between lawyers within firms and upholding the integrity of the profession as a whole by reporting misconduct (the ideal of collegiality). The code of conduct developed by the Comité Consultatif des Barreaux Européens, a consultative body linking all the legal professional associations of the European Community, recognizes that lawyers have duties

(1) to serve clients, (2) to remain independent enough to not derogate from standards of professionalism and justice to please clients, courts, or third parties, and (3) to maintain the corporate spirit of the profession (Godfrey 1995: 269–95). It does not contain an encouragement to voluntary public service.

Ethics textbooks from North America, Australia, and Britain also tend to propagate the same sets of traditions, but concentrate on duties to clients (the advocacy ideal), with some material on duties to uphold the integrity of the legal system (the social responsibility ideal) and to a lesser extent duties to maintain collegiality within the profession and to engage in justice-oriented, public interest work (e.g. Bayles 1989, Dal Pont 1996, Disney et al. 1986, Drinker 1980, Inns of Court School of Law 1989, Rhode 1994, Ross 1998). A number of recent books by academics and practitioners on the ethics of the legal profession seek to remedy a perceived lack of emphasis in contemporary discourse on the independence of lawyers, especially their need to remain independent of clients so that the social responsibility ideal can be fulfilled (Glendon 1994, Gordon 1988, 1990, Kronman 1993, Linowitz 1994, Luban 1988), and the need of lawyers to do more pro bono work and take the justice ideal more seriously (Galanter & Palay 1995*b*, Katzmann 1995, Lopez 1992, Stover 1989).

It seems that these four broad categories of ethical ideals command at least some agreement among the profession about what it is that lawyers ought to do. While each has been criticized, they have enough historical sway and contemporary resonance to be used to anchor debate on the role of the legal profession. The following sections outline the meaning of each of these ethics, the ways in which they can be criticized as misguided or incomplete, and a reconstruction of the ideals for the contemporary role of lawyers in access to justice.

ADVOCACY IDEAL

The ethic of zealous advocacy

The 'Liberal Advocacy Ideal' (Gordon 1988: 10) is the predominant conception of what lawyers' role and ethics ought to be in most common law countries. It emphasizes a duty of zealous advocacy to advance client ends and relies on the principle that the lawyer is not morally responsible for the client's cause, but must act as his or her agent in aggressively advancing it, regardless of the lawyer's own opinion (Luban 1994: p. xiv). It is most obviously based on the role of trial lawyers, especially criminal defence advocates who must vigorously assert the rights of the accused against the superior power and resources of the state. But it is applied equally to all situations in which a lawyer represents and acts for a client in court, in negotiations, or for any other purpose.

Lord Brougham's 1820 defence of Queen Caroline before the House of Lords is a favourite example of the ideal in action. King George IV was trying to rid himself of Caroline by alleging that she had committed adultery, but it was well known that the King himself had been unfaithful. Lord Brougham implied that although he did not yet need to defend the Queen by attacking her husband, if such a defence did become necessary neither he nor,

> even the youngest member in the profession, would hesitate to resort to such a course and fearlessly perform his duty . . . [A]n advocate, in the discharge of his duty, knows but one person in all the world, and that person is his client. To save that client by all means and expedients, and at all hazards and costs to other persons, and, amongst them, to himself, is his first and only duty; and in performing this duty he must not regard the alarm, the torments, the destruction which he may bring upon others. Separating the duty of a patriot from that of an advocate, he must go on reckless of consequences, though it should be his unhappy fate to involve his country in confusion. (Quoted in Mellinkoff 1973: 188–9)

These words were controversial at the time they were stated (see Mellinkoff 1973: 189 ff.), but are still used as inspiration for the advocacy ideal today (Alexander 1984: 15, Pannick 1992: 105). Numerous less exaggerated versions of this argument can be found in the official and 'after dinner' speeches of judges and senior practitioners (e.g. Mason 1993: 3).

The advocacy ideal teaches that a lawyer has a supreme duty to serve his or her client by faithfully achieving the client's goals. Because the lawyer rather than the client tends to become the effective participant in many legal matters (Sarat 1986: 547), it is crucial that lawyers do for their clients whatever the client would do for themselves. In the case of barristers it is taken as far as the 'cab rank' rule which requires that a barrister take on and vigorously defend a brief in any area in which he or she practises if he or she is available and the client can pay (see *Rondel* v. *Worsley* [1967] 3 WLR 1666; Inns of Court School of Law 1989: 17). While solicitors have not had such an onerous duty to take on clients, once they do have a client they, like barristers, owe duties of loyalty, to pursue the clients' cases vigorously, to keep them fully informed, and to take instructions from the client (see Disney et al. 1986: 597–827). Indeed most of the rules of law and ethics governing lawyers taught in legal ethics and professional responsibility courses relate to the lawyer's duty of advocacy. For example Cranston (1995*b*: 6) traces the duties of confidentiality, diligence, and fidelity or loyalty (all principles deriving from the lawyer's role of agent or fiduciary in relation to the client) back as far as an address to new serjeants at law in England in 1648:

> The general consist in three things, secrecy, diligence and fidelity.
> 1. For secrecy, advocates are a kind of confessors, and ought to be such to whom the client may with confidence lay open his evidences, and the naked truth of his case, sub sigillo, and he ought not to discover them to his client's prejudices, nor will the law compel him to do it.
> 2. For diligence, much is required in an advocate . . . in giving a constant and careful attendance and endeavour in his clients' causes.
> 3. For fidelity, it is accounted vinculum societas, the name of unfaithfulness is hateful in all, and more in advocates than others, whom the client trusts with his livelihood, without which his life is irksome, and the unfaithfulness or fraud of the one is the ruin of the other.

These duties to clients are limited only by the general requirements of the law: a lawyer must represent his or her client to the full extent of the law.

Historically, the advocacy ideal was essentially liberal, motivating lawyers to pursue client interests primarily against the power of the state. It was dependent on a conception of the rule of law which puts the courts between citizens and governments, and required lawyers independent of the state and available to help those who want to use the law to challenge or defend themselves against the government (Halliday & Karpik 1997).[1] The argument that the profession must be completely independent of government control so that individual lawyers are free to serve their clients' interests is raised whenever regulatory reforms to the legal profession are suggested (see Gordon 1988). In using this argument, lawyers are saying that structural independence from government is necessary to achieve the deeper good—empowerment of clients.

[1] Indeed Halliday & Karpik (1997) show how legal professions in different countries have historically been important in constituting the independence of the judiciary, the rule of law, and hence the conditions of liberal democracy in Western countries.

The ideal is also extended beyond representing client interests against state interests to representing client interests against other private interests. For example Speiser (1993) sees the class action negligence lawyer as living out the American dream of earning a good living while enhancing justice by helping individual plaintiffs vindicate their rights against powerful and rich companies on a contingency fee basis.

Client empowerment in the contemporary market

The advocacy ideal encourages lawyers to advance access to justice by empowering those who need to use the law to organize their affairs, settle a dispute, defend themselves against the powers of the state, or establish a right against some private interest. This counters the potential injustice of lawyers failing to take their duty to vigorously pursue client interests seriously, and dominating clients with expensive and bad service.

While it is sometimes suggested that ethics are irrelevant to the contemporary business orientation of the legal profession, the ethic of zealous advocacy is consistent with a market model of legal service delivery. According to both, one should make money by devotion to achieving justice for (paying) clients (Speiser 1993: 13). Indeed a well-functioning market assumes a strong advocacy ideal. Private contracts for justice services will be most efficient when the lawyer follows an advocacy ideal so that the client gets what he or she bargains for. When the market fails because clients lack bargaining power or knowledge, intervention may be justified to ensure that lawyers still fulfil the advocacy ideal. In practice, that will most often be necessary in low-status and poorly paid areas such as criminal defence and welfare work, where people most need lawyers to empower them for access to justice.

If the market model assumes a strong advocacy ideal, the advocacy ideal assumes a perfectly functioning market. The partisan nature of the advocacy ideal means that the market must function in such a way that both sides to any dispute can afford legal representation. If one side cannot afford services of the same quality as the other then their interests will not be taken into account and the 'justice' the system gives will be skewed in favour of those who can afford it (see Luban 1988). Even the state frequently spends fewer resources on legal services than wealthy individuals and companies who want to avoid tax or liability for white-collar or company offences. The liberal advocacy ideal's assumption that everyone will have adequate access to legal services through the market is also compromised by the restrictive practices that lawyers have seen as another part of their traditions (see the discussion of the collegiality ideal below). Emphasizing the business side of legal practice means abolishing traditional restrictive practices, but its focus on consumer choice and service is completely at one with the tradition of making zealous advocacy available for paying clients.

The incompleteness of the advocacy ideal

As Gordon (1988: 20) points out, the fact that the liberal advocacy ideal prescribes only the barest obligations to the legal framework is a recipe for sabotage. While the legal system works on the basis that people will generally internalize norms and comply voluntarily, under the advocacy ideal,

> [lawyers] are expected and even encouraged to exploit every loophole in the rules, take advantage of every one of their opponents' tactical mistakes or oversights, and stretch every legal or factual interpretation to favour their clients. The guiding premise of the entire system is that maintaining the integrity of rights-guarding procedures is more important than obtaining convictions or enforcing the substantive law against its violators. (Gordon 1988: 10)

Some of the most notorious examples of lawyers helping to sabotage the legal framework in the interests of client advocacy have occurred in the area of tax evasion and corporate law practice. One example is currently emerging evidence of the practices of US attorneys acting for major tobacco companies who helped their clients conceal scientific evidence of the harmful nature of smoking by abusing the rules of lawyer–client privilege. Tobacco companies established the Council for Tobacco Research ostensibly to commission and publish credible data on the health effects of smoking. But in fact any unfavourable research was assigned to the 'special projects' section of the Council which was directed by lawyers purely for the purposes of claiming privilege on those data to keep them out of the public domain and any future lawsuits (Nader & Smith 1996: 18–31).

The advocacy ideal shares 'the blindness of classical liberalism toward the domination and exploitation exercised by capital, including that which occurs through lawyers' (Abel 1981*b*: 670). There has been little room for the idea that the power of the state and the law might make legitimate claims on a client, that people might have responsibilities as well as rights under the law, that a democratic state might 'have a role as guarantor of freedom where liberty is most at peril from the actions of individuals or private institutions' (Weisbrot 1990: 44–5). Its compatibility with the market underscores and exaggerates the potential problems of the ideal: the business model of the lawyer–client relationship is a private contract for services, in which the lawyer does what the client wants without regard to public considerations of justice or the public interest. The fact the advocacy ideal prescribes devoted service to clients' ends, whatever they may be, is problematic where the market functions so that the rich can buy up most legal services. It is also problematic when it creates a culture in which good advocacy means a culture of excessive adversarialism that raises the costs and length of litigation, making it more and more unaffordable (S. Parker 1996).[2] The advocacy ideal needs to be limited in what it motivates lawyers to do for well-paying clients. This is the role of the second ideal, the social responsibility ideal.

SOCIAL RESPONSIBILITY IDEAL

The social responsibility ideal

The 'regulatory' (Simon 1988) or social responsibility ideal balances the advocacy ideal. While the advocacy ideal emphasizes the lawyer's duty to pursue client goals and interests vigorously, the social responsibility ideal emphasizes the lawyer's duty to maintain the justice and integrity of the legal system even against client interests. It comes from the ethical tradition of duty to the court, the law, and considerations of justice. It sees the lawyer as contributing to the effectiveness and enforcement of substantive law and forbids him or her using loopholes and procedural rules to frustrate the substance and spirit of the law. It requires lawyers to transmit information about the law in such a way that the client makes a responsible decision, rather than one that manipulates the law in the interests of the client's goals (Simon 1988: 1086). It does not necessarily make the lawyer responsible for positively pursuing substantive justice in his or her relationships with clients, but it does require the lawyer to refrain from helping the client to use the legal system or legal advice to do injustice.

It is beyond contention that no matter how much it may be in the interests of his or her client, a lawyer must not break the law to further

[2] Stephen Parker's research suggests that family lawyers engage in a variety of adversarial practices that unnecessarily lengthen and complicate the resolution of disputes.

a client's case. If a lawyer knowingly assists or advises a client in breaking the law then the lawyer will be liable for the breach like any accomplice or co-conspirator. In some cases the lawyer may even become a 'criminal entrepreneur'—the architect of an illegal course of action, such as an illegal scheme to evade tax. In the USA lawyers and accountants have been convicted of complicity in fraud in such circumstances (Haynes 1983: 48–9, 53). There are also a variety of ethical rules designed to ensure that lawyers do not abuse the court process on behalf of their clients—including rules against misleading the court, going back on undertakings to the court, bringing vexatious or frivolous cases and intimidating or insulting witnesses (Disney et al. 1986: 831–936). At the least, it can be said that a lawyer has an overriding duty to obey the law and maintain the effectiveness of the court system. However, the social responsibility ethic goes further than that—it suggests that lawyers have some sort of duty to justice, to the integrity of the law.

Lord Brougham's statements extolling the ideology of advocacy were still controversial forty-four years later when Brougham restated his belief in what he had said. The *Law Times* reported a speech in which he praised a French advocate, M. Berryer, and the great English advocate Erskine. Lord Chief Justice Cockburn spoke on the same occasion and at the conclusion of his speech he tried to balance Lord Brougham's view of advocacy by reference to the duty of lawyers to uphold the integrity of legal justice:

> Much as I admire the great abilities of M. Berryer, to my mind his crowning virtue—as it ought to be that of every advocate—is, that he has throughout his career conducted his cases with untarnished honour. The arms which an advocate wields he ought to use as a warrior, not as an assassin. He ought to uphold the interests of his clients per fas [through what is lawful], but not per nefas [through what is criminal]. He ought to know how to reconcile the interests of his client with the eternal interests of truth and justice. (Quoted by Mellinkoff 1973: 215)

According to this ideal not only is it desirable for lawyers to be independent of the state, but also to show some autonomy from clients and powerful private interests (Gordon 1988: 13). As Nelson (1988: 234) argues, 'If lawyers do not moderate their [corporate] clients' tendency to extract the maximum advantage from the legal system, we can expect legal outcomes to become increasingly skewed in favour of resourceful parties, thus undermining the legitimacy of legal institutions.'

This conception of independence has been discussed in the USA more than in Commonwealth countries (Gordon 1985, 1988, 1990, Linowitz 1994), perhaps because, as writers like Gordon have shown, it fits well with America's republican heritage. Thus Gordon (1988: 14) refers to Louis Brandeis and other lawyers 'nourished on the political theory of Montesquieu' as exemplars of the idea of a regulatory ideal as a constraint on the advocacy ideal:

> Lawyers were to be the guardians, in the face of threats posed by transitory political and economic powers, of the long-term values of legalism. Performing their positive functions entails the assumption of a special responsibility beyond that of ordinary citizens. They are to repair defects in the framework of legality, to serve as a policy intelligentsia, recommending improvements in the law to adapt it to changing conditions, and to use the authority and influence deriving from their public prominence and professional skill to create and disseminate, both within and without the context of advising clients, a culture of respect for and compliance with the purposes of the laws.

So Brandeis invented 'public interest' law to complement his commercial practice. Similarly, according to Gordon (1985: Lecture One, 10), many of the founders of the Association of the Bar of the City of New York were railroad lawyers disillusioned with the commercial task of exploiting loopholes in legislation enacted for public purposes. They got together to define their role and 'cartelise practice standards' to 'reclaim law-making institutions from corruption by special interests and to strengthen the capacity of the profession to supervise neutral rights-definition and impartial administration' (Gordon 1985: Lecture Two, 1). Although it is less prominent, the ideal also exists in British and Australian legal ethics (Cranston 1995*b*: 19–27, Dal Pont 1996: 384–96, Disney et al. 1986: 918–36, Nosworthy 1995, Pannick 1992: 105–6). It has been called the 'regulatory' ideal because lawyers are given a role in helping (or at least not hindering) the state (or more precisely the rule of law) to regulate clients. It can also be named the 'social responsibility' ideal because it gives lawyers the role of guarding the integrity of the legal system for the whole community by seeking to ensure that clients do not abuse the law

The practical relevance of the social responsibility ideal

The social responsibility ideal clearly addresses the problem of lawyers helping clients to escape, manipulate, or abuse the legal system, described in Chapter 2. Yet emphasizing the social responsibility ideal puts lawyers in danger of simply becoming governments' 'yes men and women', and not adequately serving clients' goals and interests. Probably for this reason there is no strong tradition in Anglo-American legal systems which emphasizes the social responsibility ideal of duty to the justice of law without also emphasizing the advocacy ideal of duty to client. This is as is it should be. The two ideals are clearly complementary.

The tradition which sees both ideals as important sees law as a 'public profession' in which lawyers have a mediating function, between the client and the law (Gordon 1988, 1990, Kagan & Rosen 1985, Luban 1987: 11, 1988, Parsons 1954*a*). Lawyers represent clients' interests to judges and law-makers, and help reform the law to cope with the realities of which clients are aware. They communicate the justice of law to clients by counselling against socially pernicious schemes that subvert the rule of law. At the same time they help clients who wish to take a stand against laws which they view as unjust for public-regarding reasons. Nelson's sample from four large law firms suggests that, at least in the USA, large firm corporate lawyers do adhere to a broad conception of their role as involving social responsibilities as well as advocacy responsibilities: 'More than three-quarters of the sample (seventy-six per cent) responded that it was appropriate to act as the conscience of a client when the opportunity presented itself—a consensus that did not vary by age, firm, or field of practice' (Nelson 1988: 255).[3] Another US survey found that 90 per cent of corporate lawyers would seek to persuade a corporate client to cease violating a law, if they were doing so, and would also consider resigning if the client did not follow their advice. Fifty per cent might take the matter to the firm's shareholders or the relevant regulatory authority (Sloter & Sorensen 1983: 704). In both studies, however, the corporate lawyers admitted they had rarely if ever put these beliefs or intentions into action.

The whole way an in-house legal department or law firm is oriented towards offering its services may have a profound effect on the capacity of lawyers to fulfil the social responsibility ideal. Empirical research (Rosen 1989) tells us that there are two main postures available to corporate lawyers: the reactive and the preventive:

> Legal departments adopting the narrow view sharply distinguish legal from business advice and confine the lawyer's role to the strictly legal; their advice is

[3] See Nelson (1988: 235) for his defence of why his sample is useful even though it only comes from four firms.

reactive, neutral risk analysis, given only when sought, accepting as the 'client' whatever manager at whatever level consults it, and accepting the 'problem' and the corporation's 'interest' as defined by the manager. They don't ask what happens when the 'client' leaves their office—unless required to perform monitoring or auditing functions, in which case they will confine themselves to formal questions and formal responses. Under attack by regulators or civil adversaries, they will see their function as simply minimising liability in every case . . .

Legal departments adopting the broader view see their role as that of building compliance goals and prevention-and-monitoring mechanisms to reach those goals into the company's own strategies and routine operations, so that compliance becomes not a grudging response to a lawyer-policemen muttering vague threats of state terror, but company policy, implemented through its regular divisions. (Gordon & Simon 1992: 252–3)[4]

While the reactive posture is not unethical, the preventive posture of lawyering presents more opportunities for a corporate lawyer to engage in ethically reflective and responsible practice. It is also more attractive to best practice businesses who recognize the dynamism of law and community attitudes and prefer to be leaders than followers (Silverstein 1987). While writers like Gordon (1985, 1988, 1990) and Luban (1987, 1988) refer to a past age in which American lawyers like Louis Brandeis exemplified the practice of law as a public profession, their conception is also relevant to the modern corporate lawyer. In a context of increased regulatory scrutiny and of a 'neo-liberal' state in which increasing reliance is placed on enforced self-regulation (Burchell et al. 1991, Grabosky 1995, Majone 1994), the need for lawyers to play this type of role is likely to become greater.[5] The expansion of business regulation in areas like environmental, anti-discrimination, consumer protection, and prudential regulation have actually created a market for corporate advisers on 'socially responsible' law. Thus in their book on 'interactive corporate compliance' Sigler and Murphy (1988: 95–6) write,

The tasks of corporate lawyers are changing from those of reacting and responding to outside pressures to the construction of plans for preventive maintenance. These new tasks involve corporate lawyers in weighing whether the firm is under or over-complying with laws and regulations. But it also

[4] Gordon & Simon are summarizing Rosen's (1989) research.

[5] There is a growing literature on the practice of preventive law (Brown 1986, Brown & Kandel 1995), and on the importance of lawyers and auditors as gatekeepers in helping corporations comply with their legal and social responsibilities (Halliday & Carruthers 1996, Kraakman 1985, Wilkins 1993).

means that corporate lawyers will increasingly serve as educators of the corporation, as monitors and auditors of corporate activities, and as lines of communication between regulators and the firm. The American private enterprise system and the American corporation have had social responsibilities thrust upon them. The corporate lawyer must serve as translator (not merely as advocate) of those public responsibilities and also convey to government the point of view of his corporation regarding those responsibilities.

The distinction between narrow and broader corporate lawyering quoted above was drawn from Rosen's research on US in-house legal departments. Mackie (1989) conducted similar research on British and Australian companies and found the same two concepts of reactive and preventive lawyering at play. He defined preventive lawyering as translating law into business practice with a capacity to guide and influence practical business behaviour. Unlike Rosen, however, Mackie's respondents did not see them as alternative conceptions of lawyering. Rather, the ability to engage skilfully in reactive lawyering, when necessary, was an essential component of best practice preventive lawyering. The importance of both these postures fits well with the tradition which sees the practice of law as a 'public profession' in which lawyers have a mediating function, between the client and the law (Gordon 1980, Kagan & Rosen 1985, Luban 1987, Parsons 1954*b*).

Keeping the advocacy and social responsibility ideals together could deal with many of the objections to the liberal advocacy ideal, while affirming its general desirability as the first duty of lawyers. Perhaps the liberal advocacy ideal should be more emphasized where lawyers serve ordinary people in order to combat the problem of lawyer domination of clients, but the social responsibility ideal should be more emphasized to those serving powerful private interests.[6] One way of doing this would be to concentrate regulatory intervention aimed at improving the quality of lawyers' services on lawyers for individual clients, while increasing corporate lawyers' gatekeeper and reporting responsibilities in relation to their clients in particular regulatory regimes such as duties

[6] However the tradition of the social responsibility ideal must be carefully handled. The liberal advocacy ideal and the social responsibility ideal have often been used together negatively to say that lawyers should be absolutely independent from everyone (clients, communities, and governments), rather than to affirm that they owe positive duties to both their clients and the law. This rhetoric has been used by barristers to justify their arrogant detachment from clients as well as their independence from government. It has also been used by judges to say that they ought not to listen to concerns about gender and racial bias and other community values (see Wilkins 1992 for a general discussion of the way lawyers use independence arguments and their validity).

to deal honestly and fairly with securities regulators and to report suspected client frauds.

The existence of a social responsibility ethic is also essential in a competitive market for legal services in order to preserve the integrity of the legal system against the temptation to 'buy' injustice under the guise of buying justice. Since the market will always be such that some people will be able to buy more than others, there must be some limits to what they can buy. An ethical and regulatory system that delivers lawyers who can say no to those who are prepared to use their economic power to compromise the integrity of the justice system is necessary for access to justice. This need not mean lawyers who self-righteously force rigid interpretations of the law on unwilling clients. As Gordon (1990: 277) argues, it means lawyers who creatively combine technical skill, a lively sense of social responsibility, and the vigorous pursuit of clients' interests; lawyers who do not demand 'dumb, literal obedience to every rule but creative forms of compliance that, although aiming to minimise cost and disruption to the company, effectively still realise the regulation's basic purposes'.[7] Lawyers of this type do not confine themselves to being 'the ministry for stopping [suspect] business'.[8] They also engage in the creative task of designing systems for ensuring legal compliance and public legitimacy that add value to corporate products and services, improve business efficiency, and enhance corporate image.

JUSTICE IDEAL

The justice ideal

The justice or public interest ideal has traditionally enriched the basic conceptions of the lawyer's workaday role provided by the advocacy and social responsibility ideals. It is a tradition of active citizenship by lawyers to solve the problems in access to justice that simply doing their duty by clients and the legal system leaves untouched. It encourages lawyers to have their own convictions about what would be justice and to seek out ways to act out those convictions as lawyers.

At an extreme this might mean 'cause lawyering' where lawyers seek out those whose interests they wish to represent. But the predominant

[7] See Shaffer & Cochran (1994) for a theory of lawyer–client relations that might instantiate this ideal.

[8] This phrase was used by compliance counsel for an insurance company in an interview with the author, 7 January 1998.

outworking of the public interest ideal has been giving up time to do voluntary work for the poor.[9] The American Bar Association's 1983 *Model Rules of Professional Conduct* state that 'a lawyer should render public interest legal service' (rule 6.1, Morgan & Rotunda 1993: 84). In 1993 this rule was amended to say that every lawyer should aspire to devote fifty hours a year to pro bono service (Galanter & Palay 1995*b*: 197). The duty can be discharged by

> providing professional services at no fee or reduced fee to persons of limited means or to public service or charitable groups or organisations, by service in activities for improving the law, the legal system or the legal profession, and by financial support for organisations that provide legal services to persons of limited means. (Morgan & Rotunda 1993: 84)

Some have seriously hoped that this ideal might support rules setting mandatory pro bono requirements (see Luban 1988, Eldred & Schoenherr 1993–4), and several (voluntary) local bar associations in the USA have indeed imposed pro bono requirements as a condition of membership (Galanter & Palay 1995*b*: 197). Doing legal aid work for a reduced fee and becoming involved in the community legal centre movement have been more common instances of the justice ideal in action in Britain and Australia. It seems likely that many lawyers hold a latent belief in the value of justice-oriented, public interest work, even if they do not act on it. Studies of law students and their socialization show that many students as they enter law school have strong commitments to using law to achieve goals of justice, social change and public interest ideals which they continue to hold even after their commitment to pursue them actively is dissipated by law school socialization and the allure of corporate practice (Goldsmith 1995, Granfield 1992, Stover 1989).

Eldred and Schoenherr (1993–4: 369) articulate the notion of *noblesse oblige* that lies behind many lawyers' acceptance of the ideal: '[L]awyers do possess a fundamental duty of public service, which emanates from the monopoly that the bar retains over the provision and distribution of legal services' and the 'legitimacy of the system of justice depends upon the legal profession recognising that lawyers have a fundamental duty to perform legal services for those who are too poor to retain private counsel'. Thus large firms in the USA (where legal aid is weaker

[9] The justice ideal can also motivate work towards improving the effectiveness and efficiency of the law (Halliday 1987) or the perfection of legal science (Gordon 1984) through public-regarding law reform.

than Britain and Australia) have taken pro bono obligations upon themselves in the interests of maintaining good public relations, and often at the insistence of idealistic younger lawyers (Galanter & Palay 1995*a*, 1995*b*: 198–200). Galanter and Palay's data (1995*a*) showed that pro bono activity increased as an absolute amount and per lawyer between 1990 and 1993 in large American law firms and that as firms grow they do more rather than less pro bono work (against pessimistic views of the effects of large firm practice on pro bono work). In Melbourne, the Public Interest Law Clearinghouse was set up jointly by community legal centres, private law firms, and barristers to receive requests for pro bono legal assistance and to determine which come from needy clients (non-profit associations or those unable to obtain legal aid or unable to afford legal services) with legal matters of sufficient 'public interest' to refer on to private law firm and barrister members of the scheme. In 1995/6, 367 requests were received and almost 100 were referred on to a member for action. The scheme has been instrumental in involving private lawyers in important community interest cases that would not otherwise have been heard, such as challenges to gambling in local shopping centres and representation of hundreds of consumers who lost money to hearing loss companies (Public Interest Law Clearing House 1996).

This tradition of justice-oriented public service has some resonance with the idea of ethical discretion in lawyering advocated by Simon (1988), that lawyers should only ever act for those whose causes they personally believe in. But such an approach neglects the wisdom of the liberal advocacy ideal which ensures anyone who can afford it can get representation and the chance to argue their case in court rather than first having to persuade a lawyer that their case is worthwhile. The ideal of ethical discretion can also run the risk of ignoring the social responsibility ideal by encouraging lawyers to act without any regard to law and justice when they do find a client they believe in.

Taking the justice ideal beyond *noblesse oblige*

Even though the justice ideal as traditionally exhorted by professional associations and leaders has encouraged little more than a *noblesse oblige* mentality, it has been of great significance in increasing people's access to legal services. We are dependent on legal service providers who are willing to work for reduced fees or voluntarily, ones who will be committed to a cause, who will fight battles no one else will fight, and who will seek to reform their own profession in the interests of achieving access to justice. The justice ideal goes beyond the advocacy ideal which only sees an obligation to give paying clients access to justice. It goes beyond the social responsibility ideal which does not envision lawyers proactively finding causes in the public interest in which to act. It also contains the seeds of an ideal which encourages lawyers to look beyond legalism and beyond *noblesse oblige* in seeking to help people claim justice.

In recent times the justice ideal has motivated some lawyers to find and pursue more political agendas for interests which have been excluded from participation in the system, whether oppressed groups such as women or Australian Aborigines, or diffuse interests such as consumer or environmental interests. The justice ideal shows potential for bringing non-legal perspectives and concerns into lawyers' views of themselves—to be an ideal which encourages lawyers to learn not to dominate the justice agenda with narrow legalism. Thus Luban (1988: 238–40) includes not only providing legal services to the have-nots in his conception of lawyer public interest obligations, but also politicizing the representation of poor clients by seeking to reform laws, advance the aims of social movements, or change the social landscape. He concludes that 'politicised public interest practice on behalf of have-nots helps to perfect the democratic process by overcoming barriers to their political mobilisation and participation' (1988: 240).

For some lawyers, their commitment to looking beyond legalism to other ways of achieving justice has involved them in setting up and encouraging participation in community mediation and alternative approaches to securing justice. It has meant becoming more concerned with the whole person of the client and his or her community, and becoming interested in nurturing alternative means of doing justice that empower clients and communities to solve problems for themselves without law and lawyers. Their justice commitment therefore motivates some lawyers' involvement in not only the second (public interest) but the third (ADR) wave of access to justice reform. Nurturing political and cultural means of justice outside the legal profession, through initiatives such as the fifth wave of access to justice reform described in Chapter 8, will be the most fruitful way to ensure a diverse and full access to justice agenda. Yet the justice ideal is a promising means of encouraging lawyers to take into account more than just the law when they attempt to ensure justice is done. It combats lawyers' domination of the access to justice agenda from within.

THE IDEAL OF COLLEGIALITY

The collegiality ideal

Together the advocacy, social responsibility, and public interest ideals provide broad norms which can help orient lawyers towards fulfilling their external responsibilities for access to justice. According to the fourth ethical tradition of duty to the profession, the 'ideal of collegiality', practitioners must show 'confidence, mutual respect and cooperation' (Dal Pont 1996: 427) to one another and seek to uphold the integrity and honour of their profession. This means that young lawyers are taught rules of courtesy, etiquette, and respect for other practitioners. It also means that all lawyers have some responsibility to ensure that self-regulation works well. For example, the final section of the 1983 American Bar Association *Model Rules of Professional Conduct* (rules 8.1–8.5), which is concerned with maintaining the integrity of the profession, requires lawyers to be honest in their statements to bar associations and disciplinary bodies, and to report professional misconduct in order to sustain a self-regulating profession (Morgan & Rotunda 1995: 98).

The sinister side of collegiality

The more sinister side of the ideal of collegiality is the traditional 'ethical' rules which lie behind certain restrictive practices of the profession such as rules against advertising, undercharging, and other overt forms of competition (Disney et al. 1986: 355–96, Rhode 1994: 101–22). Although these rules have been justified as necessary to protect clients because of imperfections in the market for legal services, they were also seen as necessary to preserve the unified image of the professional community and its reputation as being wholly above business tactics:

> In order to promote a professional community professions attempt to limit potentially divisive economic competition among their members by promulgating rules designed both to temper the spirit and substance of intraprofessional competition and to establish a basic income floor for all its members. (Freidson 1992: 221)

Breach of these rules was a breach of professional unity.

The self-regulatory collegiality of professional community has, however, in the past been constructed at the expense of minorities who were excluded from the profession or experienced discrimination within it, and low-status lawyers who were prevented from competing and advertising to gain fee paying clients (Abel 1981*b*: 654, Pue 1995, Rhode 1994: 53–63, Ross 1995: 97–112). As Pue shows, legal professional associations in Canada, Britain, and the USA have been historically 'xenophobic, elitist and generally aligned with capital interests': They have been guilty of 'pervasive racism, anti-Semitism and class bias' and their disciplinary powers have often been used for the purposes of political suppression (Pue 1995: 762–3). The legal profession throughout the common law world remains constituted by a socio-economic elite. King and Israel's (1989) research suggests that commercial solicitors' firms in Britain still discriminate on the basis of race in their recruitment practices, while the most notorious basis for discrimination within the profession is gender. Despite massive numerical gains in the profession in all common law countries, women are still disadvantaged in terms of career advancement and flexibility to manage family care responsibilities (Canadian Bar Association Task Force on Gender Equality in the Legal Profession 1993, Dixon & Serron 1995, Epstein 1993, Gatfield & Gray 1993, Hagan & Kay 1995, Keys Young 1995, Lentz & Laband 1995, Thornton 1996).

Far from idyllic unified community, many employee lawyers also feel exploited by other members of their own profession. Employee lawyers are often pressured to work long hours to achieve a minimum requirement of billable hours. Yet they earn only a fraction of the gross amounts they bill out. The rest goes in expensive overheads, and profits for partners. Galanter and Palay (1991) describe the dynamic of the 'promotion-to-partner tournament' that has forced large law firms to adopt this structural exploitation. The large law firm makes profits for its partners only on the basis that much of its work is done by junior lawyers who will work hard for a lesser salary than they charge out to clients in return for the institutional backing of the firm and the hope of one day making partner. However it is increasingly the case that only a small proportion of salaried junior lawyers will make partner. With the growing number of salaried lawyers, who are likely to remain salaried for life, industrial relations have become relevant to law firms and some employed lawyers have even joined unions (see Anleu 1992: 197–8, Spangler 1986).

Finally, individual lawyers and groups of lawyers often feel that they are excluded from or victimized by the self-regulatory practices of their professional associations. Lawyers point out that finicky trust account regulations and Law Society audits overburden honest practitioners while barely contributing to solving serious problems of fraud.[10] Such attitudes are present amongst segments of the profession in England and Wales who are dissatisfied with the Law Society's failure to act strongly against government reforms (Ames 1996), and also in Canada where Ontario lawyers responded to a survey by complaining that their professional organization failed to represent their interests (Mew 1989: 229). There is certainly evidence that self-regulation has led to practices such as 'scape-goating' individual practitioners for failures of the whole profession (Daniel 1998).[11]

Turning the collegiality ideal inside out

Since many of the ethical rules that traditionally relied on the ideal of collegiality are now discredited, the ideal of collegiality is given little prominence in contemporary works on legal ethics. However, the ideal of collegiality could be rehabilitated to serve a more useful purpose: it might be turned inside out so that instead of using the ideal to exclude some and exploit others (creating a narrow community of similar people), it would be an inclusive ideal calling for all legal service providers to treat each other with respect and honour (creating a broad community embracing difference). It would ask lawyers to take some responsibility for remedying problems of discrimination and exploitation of those already in the profession and also those seeking to enter it.

Professional associations have already begun to see this as important, as evidenced by the institution of race relations committees by British legal professional associations (Inns of Court School of Law 1989: 34–8) and initiatives to understand and remedy gender discrimination in the profession in a variety of countries (e.g. Attorney General's Department and Department for Women 1996, Canadian Bar Association Task Force on Gender Equality in the Legal Profession 1993). Thus there is some grounds for hoping that the ideal of collegiality might be reconstructed to combat the problem of lawyers' domination and injustice

[10] A number of Australian lawyers in my interviews for Chapter 3 expressed these views and, in some jurisdictions, groups of lawyers with these views had challenged the law societies in professional politics and public meetings.

[11] However, as Brockman and McEwen (1990: 33) point out, whenever formal disciplinary action is taken against lawyers there is potential for trust and goodwill to break down within the professional community and particularly between the individual lawyer and the professional association.

towards each other. As we shall see, the ideal of collegiality remains an important ideal for lawyers if they are to nurture the ethics of justice.

CONSTITUTING THE ETHICS OF JUSTICE

If law is a means of claiming justice, and if lawyers are often our means of accessing law, then it is logical that the legal profession should claim to have some aspiration toward justice. This chapter has argued that lawyers indeed do hold themselves out as following a set of ethical ideals which have substantial relevance for access to justice. Yet ethical ideals are impotent without effective regulatory methods to bring them to life. Traditionally the ideal of collegiality has itself been relied upon to bring legal ethics into effect. Collegiality has been thought to support a professional community in which professional ideals are discussed, passed on, and enforced. On this view, legal professional ethics are constituted by the collegiality of legal professional community and enforced by institutions of professional self-regulation. It is true that in order to preserve and transmit ethical traditions lawyers need a strong professional community. However, this need not (should not) mean a unitary profession which accepts only one perspective on things. It could mean a group of people who accept that they have similar goals and aspirations because of their occupation and will accept discussion and debate on how those goals and aspirations should be achieved.

An ethical regime of communal self-regulation on its own is clearly an insufficient means of operationalizing justice norms. Both this chapter and Chapter 2 have already foreshadowed the fact that communal self-regulation can be criticized for not being good enough at ensuring that lawyers act on the advocacy, social responsibility, and justice ideals, and indeed that it has sometimes been aimed at more nefarious purposes such as market control, exclusion of minorities, and status enhancement. In recent times a variety of alternative methods of regulating the profession have been suggested and implemented. Chapters 6 and 7 consider these criticisms of self-regulation in some detail, evaluate the alternatives, and outline a new deliberative democratic theory for the regulation of the legal profession. While the set of ethics outlined in this chapter may not be self-implementing, they do define access to justice norms by which we might judge the effectiveness and outcomes of any proposed regulatory scheme for the legal profession. The attempt to weave the waves of access to justice reform of Chapters

3 and 4 into the fabric of deliberative democracy would be bound to unravel for impracticality if these four ideals had no vitality among lawyers. The following chapters consider the techniques by which that vitality might be strengthened.

6 Competing Images of the Legal Profession: Competing Regulatory Strategies

INTRODUCTION

Policy arguments for reform to the regulation and organization of the legal profession often take place within the framework of two basic paradigms. Traditionalists prefer the ideal type of an independent, self-regulating profession, while reformers lean towards a model of forcible deregulation to meet requirements for a competitive market. Normative policy arguments reflect the underlying and inchoate theories of the empirical nature of the profession their proponents hold. Corresponding theories can also be found in the scholarly literature on the professions: sociological functionalism portrays lawyers as a learned, independent community of specialists who must be trusted to govern themselves (Goode 1957, Parsons 1954*a*), while the market control approach sees the profession as an inherently self-serving monopoly protected by ideology and a lack of accountability, which should be distrusted (Abel 1988*b*, 1989*a*, Larson 1977).

These two competing images may be useful reminders of the good and evil potentials of the profession, but they are artificial. The bulk of recent sociological evidence problematizes the dichotomy, and shows that a more effective interpretation of the legal profession draws on both images. This can also ground a more sophisticated understanding of normative regulatory issues. The first two sections of this chapter clarify and criticize the descriptive theories on which prescriptive arguments are based, using empirical and theoretical evidence on the nature and potential of the profession. They conclude that the legal profession is an ambiguous target of regulation—segmented, fractured, diffuse. It has a power of special knowledge and trained competence in the crucial institutions of the law that warrants trust. It has a power from cartelization that warrants distrust. The final part of the chapter uses a case study in regulatory reform of the Australian legal profession to examine how this complexity can affect regulatory practice and processes of reform. The theoretical, empirical, and experiential evidence together suggest that only a regulatory strategy that flows from the kind of deliberation that enables it to be contextually flexible is likely to comprehend the ambiguity of the profession.

COMPETING POLICIES; COMPETING THEORIES

The legal profession as conspiratorial cartel

Critiques of the legal profession from both the left and the right have relied heavily on competition reform to improve the regulation of legal professions. In Britain, the Office of Fair Trading (and its predecessor the Monopolies and Merger Commission) had pursued reforms for twenty years, but it was only when reform of the profession became part of the market reforms of the Thatcher government that significant change occurred (Paterson 1996: 146; see Benson 1979, Brazier et al. 1993, Cownie 1990, Hughes Commission 1980, Partington 1991, Perkin 1989: 472–519, Smith 1989).[1] In Canada the interpretation of the Charter of Rights and Freedoms by the Supreme Court contributed to 'the abolition of minimum fee schedules, the relaxation of the rules on advertising, the sweeping away of citizenship requirements for admission to the profession and the permitting of inter-provincial firms' (Paterson 1996: 147) and was supplemented by government- and profession-initiated reforms in particular provinces (see Arthurs et al. 1988: 138, Brockman 1996, Trebilcock et al. 1979). Within the European Community the mutual recognition directive and introduction of the single market in 1992 have begun to force competition reform in national legal professions (Paterson 1996: 147). In the USA, competition reforms to the legal profession occurred earlier than in other

[1] In the United Kingdom, the Monopolies Commission had already reported on professional practices in general and the practices of the legal profession in particular in 1975 and 1976 when the Thatcher government introduced legislation breaking down solicitors' conveyancing monopoly in 1983. In 1988, the Marre Report, which was the result of an inquiry into the future of the legal profession, recommended that rights of audience be extended to individual solicitors with appropriate qualifications. Then in 1989 the Lord Chancellor released three green papers on the *Work and Organisation of the Legal Profession*, *Conveyancing*, and *Contingency Fees*, advocating a substantial restructuring of the legal practice. These reforms were welcomed by the Law Society but the bar's reaction was more mixed (see Weisbrot 1990: 186–7). The Courts and Legal Services Act (1990) further broke down the conveyancing monopoly as well as the probate monopoly and barristers' previously exclusive audience rights in higher courts.

common law countries and often at the instigation of segments of the profession itself rather than government reformers (see Powell 1985, 1986), for example when lawyers brought antitrust cases against their own professional associations (Freidson 1983, Rose 1983).

Competition reformers see the legal profession as a cartel which has managed to achieve monopoly rents and privileges by self-over-regulation. Lawyers are not free to compete with each other or with members of other occupations because of restrictive rules and practices which erect barriers to entry, restrict the structure of legal work, prohibit normal competitive conduct such as advertising, and institutionalize anti-competitive practices such as price-fixing. At its most extreme, the picture of the legal profession as cartel is justified by the neoclassical economics of Milton Friedman. In his theory special regulation always becomes 'a tool in the hands of a special producer group to obtain a monopoly position at the expense of the rest of the public' (Friedman 1962: 148; see also Gellhorn 1956). Other economists recognize the force of arguments for deregulation of the legal services industry but seek to balance the demands of competition and protection. They argue that consumers would benefit from price competition, more advertising, and opening the market to non-lawyers, but do not necessarily accept that there should be no licensing at all (Albon & Lindsay 1984, Curran 1993, Dorsey 1983, Evans & Trebilcock 1982).

A dominant perspective in the sociology of the professions over the last twenty years complements this economic critique.[2] Since Johnson, sociologists have seen professions as occupational groups organized to maximize their power by claiming the status of 'profession' and the privileges that go with it (Johnson 1972: 45). For Larson the 'professional project' is to use claims of special knowledge and skills to strive both for market control (economic power) through monopolization, and social status (social power) through a collective mobility project (Larson 1977: p. xvi). The most important strategy in the struggle is to control professional education so that the profession holds a collective monopoly on knowledge or expertise itself, as well as on the supply of producers:

> In a perfect market situation, the sovereignty resides, theoretically, in the consumer. The professions ultimately depend on the public's willingness to accept and legitimize the superiority of their knowledge and skills. The singular char-

[2] See Begun (1986) for a discussion of how sociological and economic views of professions fit together. See Macdonald (1995) for an example of how the market control approach dominates the sociology of the professions.

> acteristic of professional power is, however, that the profession has the exclusive privilege of defining *both* the content of its knowledge and the legitimate conditions of access to it, while the unequal distribution of knowledge protects and enhances this power. (Larson 1977: 48; italics in original)

This theory sees traditional self-regulation as aimed at ensuring that competition between members is minimized and the profession acts in solidarity to advance its collective goals. Traditional professional claims of disinterested public service and of a social bargain mandating self-regulation form part of an ideology which justifies and obscures the social structural inequalities caused by professionalism. The profession provides a clear path for individual members to achieve power and prestige within its tightly regulated structure so that they remain committed to a unified profession and contribute, deliberately or not, to its collective project (Larson 1977: 70–4).

Considerable empirical evidence supports the application of Larson's theory to the legal profession: Abel shows how this theory explains the history and behaviour of the legal profession in the United Kingdom (1988*a*) and the USA (1989*a*). Thus he writes that the American Bar Association's model code of ethical rules

> sets forth criteria of 'moral character' sufficiently rigorous and, more importantly, sufficiently vague that they can be used to restrict the number of entrants or to exclude certain categories from the profession. It cautions the laity against self-help and discourages lawyers from helping lay persons represent themselves. And it devotes an entire Canon, nine Ethical Considerations, and three Disciplinary Rules to protecting the professional monopoly against the threat of 'unauthorised practice'. (Abel 1981*b*: 654–5)

Weisbrot (1990) and O'Malley (1983) tell the story of the Australian legal profession from the same perspective. It is a 'conspiracy against the laity' inherently unworthy of trust.

It is true that institutions of professional community often fail to live up to their own rhetoric of effective self-regulation. In addition to the material outlined in previous chapters on the failures of self-regulation, there is also compelling evidence that self-regulatory professional communities encourage 'in-group solidarity of occupational incumbents, who frown on revealing to the public any unsavoury activities of an individual worker unless they become so blatant as to harm the whole group' (Haug 1980: 66):[3] Less than 10 per cent of complaints to

[3] See also Freidson's (1975) research on the regulatory process in the day-to-day work life of medical practitioners. He shows that practitioners worked on the assumption their

disciplinary tribunals come from other lawyers and judges (Brockman & McEwen 1990: 12–13).[4] There is also evidence that many workers might be capable of providing competent legal services if unauthorized practice rules which hedge lawyers' professional monopolies did not prevent them from doing so. Thus Zemans (1982) shows that in Canada, England, and the USA there are already many paralegals, operating under the direct control of lawyers, who could conceivably take more responsibility for themselves and competently provide unique contributions to access to justice services if lawyers would let them (see also Brockman 1996, Trebilcock and Reiter 1982: 95).

It is ironic 'that much of the criticism of professionalism by radicals seems to advance the implicit alternative of the individualistic free market that underlies capitalism' (Freidson 1992: 219). The policy consequence of accepting the market control theory of the profession is to reform lawyers by breaking down professional organization and self-regulation and forcing more competition. As Abel (1989*b*: 302) argues at one point, 'though more stringent regulation of incompetence and discourtesy surely is needed . . . the profession consistently opposes the most effective cure—free competition, particularly with non-lawyers'.

The legal profession as community of competence

On the other hand, lawyers, like other professionals, have asserted a right to self-regulate without institutionalized accountability to anyone else, and to be immune from reforms of either a competition or consumer protection perspective enforced from outside. Underlying their arguments is an image of the profession as qualitatively different from business in the expertise of the services it provides, in its communal organization, service ethic, and therefore in the type of regulation appropriate to it.

For Parsons (1954*b*: 381), the sociological functionalist, professionals are different from members of other occupations or markets because they are 'trained in and integrated with, a distinctive part of our cultural tradition, having a fiduciary responsibility for its maintenance, development and implementation'. They must therefore be specially regulated to ensure they are suitably trained and certified to interpret, develop, improve and practically apply this tradition for the benefit of

colleagues were trustworthy, honest, and competent, that internal social control worked, and that it was bad form to criticize them.

[4] Most come from clients.

others (Parsons 1954*b*: 372). Goode (1957: 196) argued that unusually restrictive rules were necessary to protect individual clients from being dominated by expert professionals:

> The problems brought to the professional are usually those the client cannot solve, and only the professional can solve. The client does not usually choose his professional by a measurable criterion of competence, and after the work is done, the client is not usually competent to judge if it was properly done.

Economists have also shown that failure occurs in the market for professional services because of 'informational asymmetry, in which the seller knows the quality of his service or product, but the buyer does not' (Leland 1979: 1329). Intervention in the market to ensure minimum quality standards is thus necessary (Akerlof 1970, Arrow 1963, Horowitz 1980, Leland 1979). The functionalists argued that since unqualified persons are not competent to meddle in professional affairs, professionals must be trusted to do this special regulation themselves: 'Professionals *profess*. They profess to know better than others the nature of certain matters, and to know better than their clients what ails them or their affairs . . . Since the professional does profess, he asks that he be trusted' (Hughes 1963: 656; italics in original).

Self-regulatory communities which socialize lawyers into ethical behaviour and discipline undesirable conduct therefore make sense as a way to achieve necessary regulation. Indeed Durkheim (1992) proposed that the professional genre of ethics be extended to the whole of economic life as a solution to the evils of unrestrained capitalism. His thesis was that we can trust neither market forces nor state regulation to inculcate ethics (1992: 12). They must be the concern of sufficiently coherent self-regulating occupations which teach each member to look away from their self-interest and towards the whole community, and thus develop the general disinterestedness on which moral activity is based (1992: 23–4).[5] The more protection given these groups the better their ethics will be (1992: 13).

The regulation of the profession can thus be seen as a social bargain characterized by trust. The legal professional community takes on the burden of specially regulating itself since it alone is competent to do so. In return society at large and clients trust legal professionals and protect them from interference, supervision, and competition, as well as

[5] Similarly Goode (1957) argued that as an occupation professionalizes, it becomes more like a community, and it is through its community aspects that social control over individual members is exercised.

giving them higher remuneration and social status.[6] But these privileges can be withdrawn if the profession fails to regulate itself in the public interest:

> [T]he larger society has obtained an *indirect* social control by yielding *direct* social control to the professional community, which thus can make judgments according to its own norms . . . the social control of the professional community over its members may be seen as a response to the threat of the larger lay society to control it. Failure to discipline would mean both a loss of prestige in the society, and a loss of community autonomy. (Goode 1957: 198, emphasis in original)

Of itself this social bargain may not be sufficient to make every individual professional altruistic, but it means that the profession as a whole will be motivated to organize, regulate, and socialize individual lawyers to serve and not exploit clients (see also Rueschemeyer 1983: 41). This theory of a social bargain between the profession and the community has also received contemporary support from Barber (1983), Dingwall & Fenn (1987), Halliday (1987), and Paterson (1995, 1996).[7]

The evidence of social psychological research tends to support the assumptions of this theory. When people identify with a group or accept its values then their sense of self is linked to acting in compliance with group norms including norms about ethical behaviour. The motivation is internal: it is not linked to judgments of risk in the environment (Tyler 1998, Tyler & Dawes 1993; see also May 1996). Thus, where a practitioner identifies sufficiently with his or her professional community, he or she is likely naturally to follow professional ethical norms. The issues are whether professional community does in fact exist; if so, what type of norms it instils in its members; and whether the social bargain is sufficient to ensure self-regulation occurs in the public rather than the profession's interest.

COMPREHENDING AMBIGUITY

The empirical work of sociologists and economists based on Larson and Friedman has demonstrated that the legal profession has not acted in

[6] There are parallels between this sociological view of professions and human capital theory in economics which sees individual professionals as receiving the privileges of professionalism as a reasonable return on their investment in education, and overwork (Becker 1975, Schultz 1961).

[7] These theories will be discussed and evaluated in more detail in Chapter 7.

conformity with the image of trusted self-regulatory community of competence. Critics of the profession often see even apparent gains as trivial or subverted to the profession's own interests. For example, at one point Abel (1989*b*: 292) writes that the opening of the legal services market in Britain to licensed conveyancers is too insignificant to pose any real danger to legal professional domination. According to his 'hermeneutics of suspicion' attempts at reform are futile, unless they totally destroy the monopoly power of the profession.[8] The evidence adduced by proponents of the traditional image of the profession (as above), however, shows that the critical view is too simplistic a basis for responding adequately to the complexity of the profession. Indeed it is clear from the bulk of research on lawyers that at least three ambiguities confound dual approaches to comprehending the profession (discussed in turn below); its segmentation, its complex culture, and the ambiguity of its use of claims to special knowledge. Regulatory policies for the profession ought to respond explicitly to the ambiguities that scholarly theorizing describes; normative discourses that rely on either self-regulation or enforced competition and accountability reform alone are generally too blunt to address such complexity.

A segmented profession

Both the market control and the professional self-regulation approaches assume that internal socialization processes will keep lawyers more or less unified in ethics and goals. The market control perspective assumes that the profession will adequately control its members so that it can act as a unified whole in its own economic self-interest. The professional self-regulation approach assumes that the legal professional community will effectively discipline and socialize individual lawyers into a professional community which serves the interests of the public and clients. Yet the profession is unified as neither self-regarding cartel nor other-regarding community; it is profoundly segmented. Different segments have different interests and concerns, some of which may accord more closely with the views of reformers than others, and some of which may be more public-regarding than others.

That barristers and solicitors have different interests became clear in England when they squabbled over the nature of reforms to the profession allowing solicitors to appear as advocates in court (Belloni 1996,

[8] See Hopkins (1978: 5–13) for other examples of the way critical legal studies scholars apply this hermeneutics of suspicion to reforms.

Cownie 1990: 214–15). Similarly in Australia the two branches of the profession have frequently disagreed over the desirability of reform to division of the profession (Disney et al. 1986: 22–36, 92–122). More recently large firms of solicitors have begun to challenge the bar's monopoly and to complain of unacceptable and inefficient bar practices (Weisbrot 1993: 4, 11). Urban and rural lawyers or city and suburban solicitors also conflict, especially over allowing licensed non-lawyer conveyancers (McQueen 1993: 18), and other competition reforms. In the USA differences in ethical and regulatory matters have led to splits between plaintiffs' lawyers and lawyers who defend insurance companies and corporate clients (Powell 1985: 283) and between in-house corporate counsel and other members of the American Bar Association (Schneyer 1992). Many small firm lawyers feel left out of professional self-governance and would prefer disciplinary issues to be dealt with by an independent body rather than professional associations which they see as elitist.[9] Women lawyers have their own demands for reform in the profession to make it less discriminatory and more inclusive, while employee lawyers are beginning to form and join unions (Anleu 1992: 197–8).

Heinz and Laumann's (1982: 319) study of Chicago lawyers found that the legal profession could be split into two 'hemispheres' according to 'one fundamental distinction—the distinction between lawyers who represent large organisations (corporations, labour unions or government) and those who represent individuals'. This segmentation is likely to have significant effects on acceptance of competition reform: Heinz and Laumann (1982: 322) infer that organizational clients will exercise much more control over their lawyers than individual clients and there is much evidence to suggest that commercial clients have forced their lawyers to become more competitive.[10] Evidence from Britain shows that acceptance of competition reform varies greatly by geographical locality (Love et al. 1992, Paterson et al. 1988).

Recent more sophisticated, competition-based theories of the profession inspired by Bourdieu's analysis of social 'fields' show that competition occurs between factions of legal workers who use their social capital and appeals to the symbolism of autonomous law in their attempts to dominate the legal field. For Dezalay and Garth (1996) it is the competition of elite groups of lawyers for the global business of

[9] See Chapter 5 for further discussion of these internal criticisms of 'professional community'.

[10] See below.

commercial arbitration, while for Shamir (1995) it was the shape and future of the US regulatory state which was at stake for competing academic and commercial lawyers in the New Deal period.

Powell (1985) shows that developments in the regulation of lawyers in the USA were initiated or facilitated by segments of the bar seeking to further their own interests. For example, legal clinic entrepreneurs allied themselves with consumer activists to challenge minimum fee schedules and prohibitions on advertising. Paterson (1996: 149) argues that the British profession gave way to reforms because factions within it supported certain government and consumer concerns. In Australia in the 1970s 'radical' lawyers clashed with professional associations over professional regulatory rules which were hindering the development of legal aid and of community legal centres (Bell 1985, Chesterman 1996, Tomsen 1992).

It would be wrong then to see reform as imposed from outside on an unwilling profession united against change. The profession has a variety of interests and concerns, some of which accord more with the traditional professional model and some with reformers' views of how things should be done. Forces for change and for stagnation can be found among different segments of the profession. At different times different segments gain ascendancy to champion reform or resistance to reform.

The ambiguous culture of legal professionalism

Not only do differences in interest, concerns, and ideology occur among different segments of the legal profession, the culture of legal professionalism, into which all lawyers are socialized to a greater or lesser extent, is itself profoundly ambiguous. The market control approach saw the culture or ideology of professionalism purely as the tool of economic interest; a false or distorted set of beliefs propagated as justification for the self-interest of the profession. The traditional view sees the institutions of self-regulation as adequate to sustain a culture of public regard. The culture of legal professionalism, however, is aimed neither solely at justifying economic self-interest nor at inculcating public-regarding ethics. It does contain elements of professional arrogance, and self-justificatory ideology, but there is also a strong tradition of public service and responsibility, even if it is sometimes paternalistic or misguided.

Theories that see the profession as motivated by wider cultural forces and institutional concerns explain how legal professional culture can play this more ambiguous role. For example, Halliday (1987) argues that the status and power of the profession does not depend solely on economic power and an associated mobility project, but on the ability of the profession to convince society that it has legitimate expert and moral authority in certain areas. So while the project of attaining monopolies might be the focus of legal professional ideology as long as its concern is self-preservation, once the profession becomes established it moves 'beyond monopoly' and can afford to concern itself with a broader range of functions and actions, including contributing to an 'efficient and effective legal system'.[11] Similarly, Kritzer (1991: 539) argues that the professional project can be more usefully seen as one of institutionalization than market control: '[I]nstitutionalisation involves two primary components: (1) establishing boundaries between the emerging institution and other organisations, entities, etc; and (2) rationalising the internal form and operation of the emerging institution.'

According to these conceptions the profession will be perfectly willing to reform itself by shedding restrictive practices and becoming concerned with the public interest in order to maintain legitimacy. Pue goes further and argues that the culture of legal professionalism must be seen as part of the larger culture of modernization and rationalization, not just an artefact of economic forces. The market control approach is unable to

> accommodate a sophisticated appreciation of professional 'ideology'. Like all variations of economism it tends to reduce ideology to little more than a mystification trick deliberately designed to dupe outsiders into acquiescence in their own exploitation. Professional ideology is not taken seriously on its own terms, and the relationship of professional ideology to larger currents of intellectual thought is under-emphasised. (Pue 1990*b*: 406)

Powell's (1986) study of why and how the Chicago Bar Association gave up their disciplinary powers over attorneys in that state to a court-controlled commission lends some support to Pue's argument. Powell suggests that the Chicago Bar Association faced a crisis of legitimacy at the time and that the reason they voluntarily ceded responsibility for disciplinary functions was their concern to restore the reputation of the legal profession, and indeed the legal system. Their reaction was not simply the pragmatic acceptance of a reform that would otherwise have

[11] Halliday's work was based on extensive study of the historical records of the Chicago Bar Association. McQueen (1993) shows how the Law Institute of Victoria moved through similar stages between 1885 and 1930.

been forced upon them; there was no imminent threat to the Bar Association's control of disciplinary functions (Powell 1986: 40–1). Rather, Powell suggests that the maintenance of self-regulation was not as important in their culture and ideology as the maintenance of a good reputation for the profession and the legal system, and since it would have been expensive to reform the disciplinary system adequately, the Bar Association handed control over to the court, which now (in Powell's judgment) runs a much better system.

By giving the culture of legal professionalism recognition, we could understand actions of the profession and individual professionals as based on the logic of the legal ideology, which like all ideologies contains public-regarding elements and self-interested elements. For Croft (1992: 1278),

> that ideology can both inspire and obfuscate. In certain circumstances, ideology may help move professionals beyond purely economic or political interests to serve genuine aspirational/inspirational goals, such as promoting a professional tradition of autonomy and responsibility in professional work . . . However, to the extent a given professional ideology deviates from the actual institutions and structural foundations of the profession, it may also obfuscate.

As we have seen, the culture of lawyers may also differ from segment to segment, emphasizing different elements of an ambiguous legal professional ideology. Indeed Chapter 7 will argue that the access to justice aspirations of the whole profession can be maximized by capitalizing on exposure to the public-regarding elements in the ideology of specific movements within the profession such as community legal centre lawyers, women lawyers, or black lawyers.

The power of knowledge

Finally, a normative theory for regulating the profession should take the knowledge and expertise of the profession seriously without accepting that it justifies professional domination. The conspiratorial cartel image sees the profession's claims to special knowledge as ephemeral: they are a fake support for the profession's economic self-interest. The traditional view sees the claim to special knowledge as unassailable: it justifies the complete unaccountability of the profession. A more appropriate view sees their claims to knowledge as defeasible, open to the challenge that they are often not capable of carrying the weight of trust the profession claims. Professional power does come from knowledge—

albeit carefully manipulated claims about knowledge—not merely from the ordinary power of vested economic, political, and bureaucratic interests (see Sterett 1990: 366).[12] The knowledge the legal profession holds is of great importance and value to society. But the profession also has great opportunity to exaggerate and exploit its special knowledge so as to dominate individual clients and also the community as a whole.

Freidson (1986) shows how, in the Anglo-American world at least, professions are the place where formal knowledge is institutionalized. He demonstrates how professionals in the USA use formal knowledge to gain influence and power in various institutions. He concludes that professions and professionals gain power 'in policy-making and administration, power to define public needs and problems, power in resource-allocation, power over clients, and power to control work' through claims to knowledge that are accepted as legitimate by society as a whole (1986: 213). Brint (1994) sees modern professionalism as based solely on applied formal knowledge and expertise, unlike traditional professionalism which was based on both expert authority and community orientation. Abbott (1988) also places claims to knowledge as central in his analysis of 'the system of professions'. He sees professions primarily as competitors for contestable jurisdictions, the basic sets of problems that conceptual knowledge is developed to deal with. The extent of each profession's jurisdiction will depend on the success of its claims to expertise. Shamir (1995: 6), following Bourdieu, sees legal knowledge and lawyers' work as so inseparably linked that the legal field of work can only be described by reference to the 'interaction of ideas with [the] differential positions [of legal workers]'. While Dezalay and Garth's (1996) analysis of global commercial arbitration (also inspired by Bourdieu) is still embedded within an economic heuristic which ultimately explains the representations and actions of groups and individuals 'in terms of self-interested maximisation of their position within the field' (Buchanan 1997: 370), Shamir follows Bourdieu more closely by seeing the legal field not purely as the site for a crass contest for economic self-interest. It is a struggle for the right to define legal knowledge, especially the symbolic meaning of law's autonomy, in which ideas are as important as economics.

As long as there are specialist legal workers, they will have the potential to exercise at least some power derived from their special, symbolically laden legal knowledge. This may be worked out in a variety of

[12] See Macdonald (1995: 157–6) for an overview of different sociological approaches to knowledge and the professions.

ways, including developing restrictive practices, dominating individual clients, or taking over areas of policy development. In economic terms it implies that the information asymmetry between lawyers and clients should not be underemphasized. A perfect market in legal services will never be possible: some restrictive regulation, even licensing, will be necessary to protect some clients from the special power of knowledge. On the other hand, since lawyers do have special experience and knowledge of their own area, it will be desirable for them to be involved in the regulation of their own profession to some extent.

DYNAMICS OF REGULATORY REFORM

Both the images of the legal profession as conspiratorial cartel and as community of competence fail to comprehend the ambiguity of the profession evident in its segmentations of interest, its ambivalent culture, and the defeasibility of its claims to knowledge. Regulatory stances based on the assumption the profession conforms to either image are therefore also likely to be unsuccessful in practice. Strategies based totally on self-regulation will be exploited when lawyers are motivated by self-interest. While acting on an image of the profession as self-interested conspiracy might break the cartel, it will not encourage lawyers to behave in a public-regarding way.

While critiques of the profession often assume that the profession's self-interest will never allow it to give up self-regulation, the evidence suggests that lawyers can and will respond constructively to reasonable proposals for change in certain circumstances. Surprisingly both competition and accountability reforms have been voluntarily embraced by much of the legal profession in many countries. For example, Paterson et al. (1988) found that English and Welsh solicitors' notions of professionalism had changed considerably in just five years (since the government announced reforms) to come to accept the propriety of advertising and competition. Powell (1986) describes the way that US bar associations voluntarily embraced accountability reforms in the early 1980s by ceding responsibility for lawyer discipline to independent court-appointed bodies. It seems that traditional notions of self-regulation are a 'historically contingent' part of lawyers' notion of professionalism (Powell 1986: 54). Given the complexity of the profession, the way that reform proposals are introduced and pursued may have a great effect on whether reforms build on public-regarding aspects of legal professionalism and stifle self-interest, or whether they meet resistance that confirms the less public-regarding institutions of the profession. The following section uses empirical evidence on the process of reform of the Australian legal profession in the early 1990s to examine this issue.

In Australia, throughout the 1970s and 1980s traditional self-regulatory practices were scrutinized and attacked by reformers seeking to introduce competition and accountability reforms (Clarkson Committee 1983, New South Wales Law Reform Commission 1982).[13] Although many piecemeal reforms were implemented during the 1970s and 1980s (Weisbrot 1990: 164–222, 1993), public debate on the legal profession only reached a peak around 1994 when more far-reaching competition and accountability reforms were proposed than ever before. The Trade Practices Commission (TPC, Australia's antitrust regulator; 1992, 1993, 1994), state law reform commissions (Law Reform Commission of Victoria 1991, 1992*a*, 1992*b*, New South Wales Law Reform Commission 1993), federal and state governments (Government of South Australia 1992, Wade 1994), and independent committees of inquiry (Access to Justice Advisory Committee (AJAC) 1994, Hilmer et al. 1993) all focused attention on anti-competitive and unaccountable professional practices and sought regulatory reform. Competition policy was the focus of the debate, but it was not the only basis for change. Reforms to make the legal profession more accountable to the community, most notably by giving independent boards or commissioners responsibility for overseeing self-regulatory disciplinary practices, were also prominent (AJAC 1994: 195–212, Mark 1995, Wade 1994, Craven 1995).[14] By the end of 1996 the competition principles of the Trade Practices Act 1974 (Cth.) had been made applicable to all Australian lawyers (Corones 1996), and self-regulatory discipline and complaints handling in the two largest states, New South Wales and Victoria, had been completely restructured (Craven 1995, Dal Pont 1996: 11–12, Legal Profession Reform Act 1993 (NSW), Legal Practice Bill 1996 (Vic.), Mark 1995, Parker 1997*b*).

At first many Australian lawyers reacted angrily and defensively to proposals for reform by appealing to the social bargain traditionally governing the relations between lawyers, the state, and the community

[13] The New South Wales Law Reform Commission in particular undertook an extensive inquiry into the legal profession between 1977 and 1984 which went largely unimplemented until the 1990s (see Disney et al. 1986: 210–27, Parker 1997).

[14] This had already occurred in Western Australia during the 1980s.

and arguing that self-regulation was still the best way to assure the quality of legal services and professional independence from government. It was 'shallow and simplistic' to see lawyers as 'providers of services' rather than members of a profession (Phelps 1995: 3; see also Farmer 1994: 297, Kirk 1994). Proposed new schemes requiring lawyers to be licensed and regulated by government-appointed bodies would 'destroy the independence of the legal profession and the independence of the courts' (Rayner 1995).

By and large, however, Australian legal professional associations had officially adopted competition as a goal by the middle of 1994 (see Parker 1997*b*: 43–5). The Law Council of Australia (LCA, the peak body of Australian legal professional associations) produced its *Blueprint for the Structure of the Legal Profession: A National Market for Legal Services* (LCA 1994*a*) in July 1994, setting out how it thought competition goals should be achieved. The executive committee of the Law Institute of Victoria (LIV, the self-regulating legal professional association in Victoria) wrote in a policy paper that it 'supports the proposition that the legal profession, along with other providers of goods and services, should be subject to general competition policy principles' (LIV 1994: 1); and the New South Wales Law Society endorsed the introduction of an Act in that state which implemented many of the TPC's proposals even before the TPC's final report (Fairlie 1994, Fife-Yeomans et al. 1994, Legal Profession Reform Act 1993 (NSW)).

It was accountability reforms that ultimately met with more hostility (Callick 1995, Conroy & Wilson 1995, Green 1995, McGuinness 1995, Wilson 1995), particularly Victorian Attorney General Jan Wade's proposals (Wade 1994, Craven 1995) to introduce an independent legal practice board to issue practising certificates and make rules of professional conduct, and an ombudsman to receive and act on complaints about lawyers. Newspapers reported that lawyers said her proposals would contravene United Nations human rights principles which required lawyers to be a self-governing profession (Conroy 1995) and the president of the Law Council of Australia wrote that they would 'severely' erode 'the independence that underpins the integrity of the legal profession' (Fowler 1995: 14; see also Wilson 1995).

In order to understand when Australian lawyers accepted reform and when they resisted it, my interview-based research pursued a diversity of views using the difference discovery method of sampling (a variation on snowball sampling). The resulting in-depth interview data were analysed using Glaser and Strauss's constant comparative method. The methodology used is detailed in the Appendix. The focus of enquiry was not on reviewing substantive arguments for and against the application of competition and accountability policies to the legal profession; rather it was on understanding the process of reform. Two broad dynamics can be discerned from the diverse experiences of reform that these lawyers described; one of persuasion and dialogue resulting in conversion and acceptance of reform, and one of imposition and disrespect engendering resistance.

Dynamics of conversion

Many interviewees told their own or other people's stories of conversion to the desirability of competition or accountability reforms prompted by public debate and the insistence of reformers. Their experiences (as described below) ranged from spontaneous responses to community concerns in order to preserve their profession's legitimacy, through response to persuasive reasons, to the pragmatic acceptance of fate in the face of inevitable reform, and the persuasive effect of market forces which made government reform either irrelevant or within their self-interest. While these motivations might vary in moral praiseworthiness, each could result in genuine commitment to change and reform in the public interest.

Preservation of legitimacy

Some lawyers attributed their support for reform proposals simply to the need to be responsive to community concerns. They thought it was vital to listen to and accept reasonable community expectations of change in order to preserve or restore their profession's legitimacy:

> I think the main challenge to the legal profession is to make itself a credible profession. Society is more consumer-oriented. Society demands a greater level of accountability and the profession isn't giving it. Lawyers have always been smelly but they're getting smellier. (FSG6)

Certainly the instinct to act to preserve or restore legitimacy in the eyes of the public can be a powerful motivation for legal professions to reform themselves. Giffen's (1961: 121, 130) research on Canadian lawyers suggested that the profession's voluntary introduction of legal aid and reimbursement funds was prompted by a 'high level of sensibility' to negative public attitudes. Powell (1986: 40–1) concluded from his study of the voluntary cession of lawyer discipline by the Chicago

Bar Association to court bodies that they were motivated by a perceived legitimacy crisis to restore their reputation rather than feeling the coercive threat of a new system being imposed from outside. The mere mobilization of public opinion against a legal profession may be enough to encourage it to reform itself in order to restore its reputation. The Australian lawyers interviewed described the way in which their own attitudes to professional issues had to change over the years to keep up with changing community attitudes:

> [W]e used to think it was unethical to advertise, but that was changed years ago in the ACT [Australian Capital Territory]. We used to think it was unethical to take someone else's client, now we openly compete with each other. We used to think it was unethical to charge less than the set fee. All those things have changed. Ideas about ethics change. The change lags a bit behind community attitudes but so do all laws. (MSL18)

Some thought that even though they were not personally convinced there were problems with the present regulation of the profession, they ought to be open to change if the community perceived a problem. Even though she did not see a need for increased lay representation in disciplinary processes, for example, FSL22 supported such reforms in order to avoid negative public debate about accountability: 'I tend to think if it's not broke you shouldn't fix it. But if there is a perception of a problem, then that might be the same as having a problem.' Similarly another senior lawyer thought the profession ought to reform its self-regulation so that the public would give it the legitimacy it deserved:

> I think the legal profession is an honourable, dignified, caring profession. But the public perception is stereotyped in a different direction and one way to overcome that is to make the profession transparent and involve the community in what it does so that they can see what the profession does . . . There is no duty to the public at large, but there is a public element in what lawyers do and for that reason lay participation is important . . . So I think there should be self-regulation but in a transparent way with lay input. We shouldn't regulate ourselves in a way the public can't see and can't understand. (FJ1)

Persuasive dialogue

A more active process of persuasion and dialogue had convinced other lawyers and leaders of legal professional associations that they should support reforms. One woman changed her mind through the process of dialogue with a friend she respected even though she had at first rejected the TPC report:

When I first heard Alan Fels [Chair of the TPC] talking about regulation of the legal profession I felt professionally horrified. Then I was at lunch with a good friend from the Industry Commission, who is a lawyer who specializes in business deregulation, and I've always respected his opinion, and he asked me why? I went away and I thought about it and I realized my professional training has led me to believe that the legal profession is some kind of sacred cow. We think that regulation by professional bodies makes us better. There is something different and better about lawyers than the customer service section at a manufacturing company. I really agonized about this. I realized that opinion conflicted with my own personal philosophy of life and my approach to being a lawyer . . . So I faced those presumptions and assumptions and I really just turned around. (FSG6)

A leading male solicitor also rejected the TPC but was persuaded by what he saw as a more credible economic argument: 'The document that really hit home for me was the *Hilmer Report* [Hilmer et al. 1993]. It was not just lawyer-bashing. It had a proper economic basis and talked about every sector of the economy not just the professions' (MSL9).

This was a widespread phenomenon, at least among the elite professional decision-makers who counted. Officers of the TPC were able to describe the way they saw lawyers change their minds through the TPC's attempts to engage them in dialogue:

We had a lot of debate and discussion with the legal profession which was pretty constructive. Then there were submissions from them, then the draft report, further discussions and further submissions. There was also debate in the press and the governments. During this debate we believe we could see the legal profession broadening its perspective. They had to address things in our terms . . . Increasingly they were thinking about our arguments and their public interest arguments. They had some very clever justifications reworking their arguments within our framework. So we moved the debate. In some states the whole profession has changed. (MR3)

In their final report they noted that while the legal profession had already been reforming itself before they started their study, 'the pace of reform accelerated markedly during the course of the study' (TPC 1994: p. x). This perspective on how the reform process progressed is supported by newspaper reports at the time of the release of the TPC's final report:

Compared with the fierce opposition from certain quarters of the legal profession which greeted the draft report, yesterday's reaction was mainly conciliatory. The traditionally staid profession has acknowledged not only that most of the reforms are inevitable in an increasingly competitive market but also that some, albeit grudgingly, are welcome. (Fife-Yeomans et al. 1994: 3)

Thus active dialogue encouraged some lawyers to examine their beliefs and presumptions, in the light of public opinion and reformers' arguments and to give up views they found they could no longer rationally defend. Public debate and a politics of deliberation about legal professional reform utilized what Sunstein calls 'the civilising force of hypocrisy'[15] to bring the culture of professionalism more in line with community concerns and desires:

Without making heroic assumptions about the human capacity for virtue and the transcendence of self-interest, we might observe that a system of public discussion requires people to speak in public-regarding terms. Policies must always be justified on the basis of reasons, or on the ground that they promote the public good. In a deliberative politics, even the most venal or self-interested participants in politics must invoke public justifications in their support. If 'hypocrisy is the tribute that vice pays to virtue,' at least we can say that in a system of public deliberation, everyone must speak as if he were virtuous even if he is not in fact.

The requirement for justification in public-regarding terms—the civilising force of hypocrisy—might well contribute to public-regarding outcomes. It may 'launder' preferences by foreclosing certain arguments in the public domain . . . It might even bring about a transformation in preferences and values, simply by making venal or self-regarding justifications seem off-limits. (Sunstein 1993: 243–4)

Pragmatic acceptance of fate

The 'civilising force of hypocrisy' was even more evident in the way that as lawyers became convinced that significant reform was imminent—whether they liked it or not—many decided voluntarily to join the dialogue about what changes would take place, and even to preempt government reforms: 'I think it comes down to looking over our shoulder. We could see that people were going to do things and the profession decided to do it first and do it better' (MSL9). One commentator on reforms in Victoria noted that the determination of the Attorney General's stance 'has impressed LIV leaders if not with admiration, at least with the recognition that regulation as an issue could not be moved to the backburner. The decision was taken to let go what was lost' (Evans 1994: 292). Similarly in Britain the status quo persisted only until the strength of the government's commitment to laissez-faire

[15] He attributes the term to Jon Elster.

ideology meant that the profession could no longer ignore proposed changes, but had to accommodate them (Weisbrot 1990: 186). In Australia, a TPC officer described how a prominent bar leader changed his mind about supporting reform by a combination of moral suasion and a growing realization that change would occur whether he wanted it or not. Since change was going to occur anyway he decided it would be better to enter the dialogue about how it would occur:

> When I first met him he was a complete opponent and now he is the most reformist president of the bar association. After I spoke at a seminar . . . one time he berated me for over an hour in the corridor about how I didn't understand anything. Now maybe he's in damage control. He says we have to accept that there will be reforms. Let's do them ourselves in the spirit of the government's reforms but the way we want them. He turned 180 degrees partly because he engaged in dialogue. As long as you have genuine debate then you have to move a bit in dialogue, *as long as the arguments have something to them.* But it was also a survival issue. Now the bar will be there to fight another day. (MR3; italics added)

Even though the lawyers in this category originally accepted change only because they felt they must, consistent with Sunstein's theory of the 'civilising force of hypocrisy', their entry into the dialogue meant that they could later become positively committed to the idea that 'the arguments have something to them' (see MR3 above). They were able to adapt voluntarily to reform and even accept its desirability under the shadow of the axe of reform before it fell:

> I think some good will come out of the debate . . . It has forced us to look at some of our rules and we have made some dramatic changes . . . For example advertising. We argued with the bodies that said we should change the rule against restraints and said why we thought there should be restraints. But when we came and looked at the rules we saw we didn't really need them . . . Our initial reaction was this is ridiculous that you're coming in and telling us what to do, but when we sat down and looked at it we realized we could make some changes. The changes give more freedom instead of just petty restraints. (MB4)

This change in attitude was confirmed by the comments of a prominent solicitor:

> The bar cleaned up their act quite markedly. Before that they thought the world would never change. But then they accommodated changes . . . They realized the game was about to be up. But it was not just self-interested: when they focused on their service they realized there was a better way to do it. (MSL13)

Surrender to market forces

An important impetus for competition reform was the fact that market forces, especially consumer power in the commercial sector, had already forced segments of the legal profession to accept the reality of a more competitive legal services market (see Clifton-Steele 1994). This was particularly true of lawyers in large commercial firms who had been forced to become more cost-efficient by powerful clients even before the TPC's reports (Ackland 1994, Stretton 1994):

> Partners were charging a particular bank $300, $315, $350 an hour, and last year that bank told them $200 an hour, take it or leave it. (MSL5)

> At the top end it is absolutely cut-throat. They have been tendering for business and a while ago I heard that firms were tendering below cost. The competition is absolutely intense . . . Practitioners are working too hard. They're literally killing themselves. Last week one of our leading superannuation lawyers died. She was only thirty-seven. (MA2)

The renegotiation of the legal professional self-regulatory bargain was not just being played out between profession and state; powerful third parties in the form of corporate consumers and competitors added considerable leverage to the reform debate. Lawyers believed they no longer had any monopoly on 'legal' work: 'Accountants have been giving legal advice in breach of the Act for years especially in the tax area. It's a joke to think that the Act gives me competition protection. It is a purely theoretical monopoly' (MSM24; see also Pengilley 1994, Tabakoff 1994*b*, TPC 1993: 122–3).

The market for individual legal services in areas like personal injuries and family law had also become much more competitive:

> I only know of two firms in the suburbs who have put their prices up in the last four years. (FR1)

> All of a sudden solicitors are actually selling their services. We are capturing and chasing clientele. Lawyers are having to back their own judgments by means of contingency fee arrangements . . . Changes are occurring not because of the government reforms, but because of competitive forces. (MSM11)

> You like to take clients from other solicitors and find superiority in that. (MSL23)

Indeed during the process of the debate some lawyers came to the opinion that the application of competition policy to their profession might actually be in their self-interest. One partner in a large law firm and a leader of his state's professional association attributed much of the support for competition reform to the fact that lawyers realized their firms must become more competitive to survive in the future:

> Every individual lawyer had a scary financial situation a few years ago. There was the 1987 crash and we thought it would never affect us but in three years we all had a really hard time. Then when the politicians and others talked about competition, we thought that maybe there was something in it for our benefit. (MSL9)

Others thought that reforms might help them compete more effectively with accountants: 'Part of the reason accountants have been taking over our work is because they're less regulated than we are' (MSS16). For the large firms, restrictive state-based rules stood in the way of creating national firms which could compete more efficiently locally and in global markets. For example state rules requiring all partners of a firm to hold practising certificates in any state where the firm conducted business were expensive and inconvenient. Brazier et al. (1993: 210) suggest that the desire to compete in global markets was also an important factor encouraging British large firm solicitors to adopt competition reforms.

As a result, legal professional associations were already motivated to abolish many of the restrictive rules attacked by competition reformers: 'I don't know what else the TPC will do. The LIV has already gone through all its rules and regulations and taken out the anti-competitive ones' (FR1). It seems likely that many leaders of the profession were ready to accept the application of competition policy to professional regulation by the time the TPC made its final report in 1994. Certainly once government determination to reform the profession to make it more competitive was combined with credible dialogue calling for further change, lawyers who had already felt the pressure of market forces were willing to join the competition reform process voluntarily. Similarly many lawyers accepted the desirability of accountability reform because of public debate and the perceived lack of legitimacy in existing self-regulatory processes. Deliberative processes enabled reformers to capitalize on public-regarding elements in the profession and on professional leaders' need to appeal publicly to legitimate reasons to defend themselves and were able to convince the profession to accept many reforms.

Dynamics of resistance

While some lawyers told of conversion and responsiveness to reform agendas, others' stories were of defiance and resistance. Other areas of regulatory research suggest that the processes and strategies by which people attempt to influence and control the behaviour of individuals are crucial in determining whether they voluntarily consider the desirability of change and reform themselves, or resist. Thus Sherman (1993), a criminologist, explains varied sanction effects by hypothesizing that offenders will react 'defiantly' to sanctions and threats, regardless of their substantive merits, where they believe they have been applied in an unfair, stigmatizing, and disrespectful way. Their proud and self-righteous reaction entrenches them in deviant behaviour and makes them more likely to re-offend (Sherman 1993: 459). Sherman's theory is based in part on Lind and Tyler's (1988) social psychology of procedural justice. It also finds empirical support in the recent research of Paternoster et al. (1997), who found that when police treated domestic violence suspects fairly when arrested, the rate of subsequent domestic violence was significantly lower than when they did not. Consistent with Sherman's theory, when lawyers saw reformers as uninterested in cooperative dialogue or in listening to legitimate concerns about reforms, what will there was for change in the public interest was stifled by the desire to defend themselves against critics. Where lawyers perceived they were being discredited and disrespected by the views of reformers (as discussed below), the opportunity for constructive debate and cooperative reform was lost, or at least attenuated. A speech from a past president of the Law Council of Australia illustrates the potential for lawyers to feel unfairly imposed upon by a disrespectful reform process:

> The Cost of Justice inquiry was politically motivated, where some members of the committee openly set out to blame all of the ills of the justice system on the legal profession and those responsible for administering it. The TPC report was, I suggest, very much influenced by the TPC's imperialist ambition to have the professions and especially the legal profession brought under the umbrella of the *Trade Practices Act 1974* and the TPC itself. The *Hilmer Report* was predicated on the sacred cow 'competition' and the premise that a national competition policy would be a good thing . . . These reports are replete with statements of economic theory . . . On the other hand, notions such as the maintenance of professional standards in the public interest, which are of some moment to the profession, are glossed over and dismissed with apparent disdain. (Meadows 1994: 85)

Discredit

When lawyers perceived reformers as unwilling to give them credit for having reformed themselves in the past and being prepared to do so in the future, the will to cooperate dissipated. Michael Baumann, then president of the Queensland Law Society, was quoted criticizing the draft TPC report and claiming that the Queensland legal profession was already competitive, 'A lot of people see the legal profession as this type of institution which they want to have the credit for reforming without appropriately giving credit to the profession for reforming itself' (Woods 1993).

A barrister in Adelaide felt that government reformers were not even aware that the South Australian profession had governed itself in a more progressive manner than lawyers in the eastern states for many years, let alone given credit for it:

> A few years ago, Chris Sumner, the old Attorney General, had a white paper and a green paper and there was a debate about the organization of the legal profession. He was advised by people from interstate and there was a fuss about restrictive practices at the bar but those rules were not applicable here. . . A lot of criticisms were directed at the restrictive practices of the bar—the two counsel rule, the chambers rule, direct access, having conferences only at barristers' chambers, even the two-thirds rule. None of these things applied to Adelaide [capital of the state of South Australia]. (MB2)

Another barrister was frustrated with hearing the profession attacked when he knew that suggested reforms had already been implemented by the profession some time before: 'I have talked to consumer groups who just don't know the facts. They don't recognize that we don't regulate ourselves' (MB5). Because he felt that the reforms the profession had already made were discredited and discounted by reformers, he was unwilling to countenance further demands for reform.

Disrespect

Similarly when reformers did not seem to take seriously lawyers' own perspectives on how their profession operated and how best to reform it, lawyers found it difficult to trust those who had not respected them enough to listen:

> If you look at the section of the TPC *Final Report* on barriers to entry there were a number of questions that the LCA raised from that in the *Draft Report* that they didn't answer. Our comments were ignored. We sent a submission with experts in trade practices law making points. They just ignored it . . . That didn't go down well with the legal profession at all. It's dishonest. It's indifferent . . . The way they treated us, it doesn't make us want to be subject to them. (MA2)

One leader of the national profession described the reform process as one of 'governments wanting to be seen to be doing something—bullying'. His response was defiant, 'Now we are in the position of having made all the changes and we are going to fight back. We have been suckers, easy hits. We've made enough changes and we're not going to just get hit any more' (MB5). Another lawyer felt that the TPC had treated the profession so disrespectfully that he would make the head of the Commission his personal enemy:

> The TPC is a bunch of turkeys. I have written a letter to Professor Fels [chair of the TPC] saying he is a liar. I asked Fels a few years ago how he was going to approach the inquiry into the legal profession. He said they would do it diligently and with proper consultation. Well we went along to the consultations. They didn't know what they were talking about and then they came out with the conveyancing report. It was released to the press before the president of the LCA got it and on the same day that the presidents of the Law Societies got it. It contained quite a few factual errors. It was a great big political exercise . . . Also there was an innuendo that SA [South Australian] solicitors are worse at conveyancing than the [land] brokers. I haven't forgiven him for that. I'm younger than him so I'm going to outlive him. (MSM15)

Lawyers were particularly apt to feel disaffected when reformers failed to listen to arguments that the profession had already become very competitive. Those who continued to suggest competition-type reforms were considered 'doctrinaire', and not interested in listening to lawyers to find out what was already happening in the real world:

> The [Australian Capital Territory] government is threatening to license conveyancers. The Law Society's position is that is a doctrinaire reaction. It can only have a basis in doctrine not reason. In Canberra, lawyers have been allowed to advertise since 1974 so fees are very competitive. So it is not anti-competitive and the government won't achieve anything because conveyancers can't do the work any more cheaply and effectively. The government is just doing it because other states are doing it. (MSL5)

When lawyers feel that their profession has been treated with such discredit and disrespect, it is not surprising that they might 'defiantly' resist reform and entrench themselves in defence of traditional self-regulation.

The significance of self-regulation

Ayres and Braithwaite have found that similar principles apply to the collective responses of actors to business regulation. Thus when regulators use strategies of 'dialogue, communal judgment, reciprocal wooing, and persuasion, which is minimally coerced by power relations', constructive regulatory outcomes can be negotiated (Ayres & Braithwaite 1992: 97). In contrast when regulators use coercive strategies they often break down the goodwill and motivation of actors who might otherwise have been responsive:

> When punishment rather than dialogue is in the foreground of regulatory encounters, it is basic to human psychology that people will find this humiliating, will resent and resist in ways that include abandoning self-regulation. (Ayres & Braithwaite 1992: 25)

These principles apply not only to individual regulatory encounters, but also to the development and imposition of regulatory schemes for whole industries. Thus governments are more successful in achieving their goals of regulatory reform if they allow an industry the discretion and responsibility to implement self-regulatory reform first rather than moving straight to imposed command regulation. The place given to self-regulation is often the crux of the difference between strategies of persuasion and dialogue and dynamics of discredit and disrespect. Where reformers allow the profession to have a role in reforming and regulating themselves, lawyers are more likely to cooperate with reform than where self-regulation is totally impugned. Attacking the legitimacy of self-regulation is a powerful way of communicating discredit and disrespect to the profession, because it denies lawyers a continuing role in their own regulation and is critical of their historical accomplishments in creating a comparatively ethical profession. The idea that as a profession they ought to be able to be trusted to be responsible enough to self-regulate is imprinted in many lawyers' minds: It is 'part of being a profession, being responsible for your own ethics and rules' (FL1), 'taking responsibility for the standards that are set' (MJ2). If self-regulation is abolished, 'you lose that key sense of professionalism, your own obligation and it becomes just rules' (MSL13). These lawyers see a dignity in having a profession which is able to exercise the disciplinary tasks of self-government, with the responsibility collectively to ensure that the profession as a whole is of a high standard:

> There are waves [of opinion] in different places saying we ought to be a trade union but that is not what the profession is about . . . Some practitioners say the Law Society is a policeman and it is prosecuting me and it should look after me. The Dental Association doesn't prosecute dentists. It is the Dental Board and the Dental Association gets in and stands up for the dentist. But I think the

Dental Association is a moribund, hopeless group because it is not concerned about the whole man. (FJ1)

When the idea of competition reform was first introduced, much of the profession reacted defiantly because it seemed that competition policy was going to be imposed on it by the TPC, which would then become the legal profession's main regulator (see Colebatch 1995). As the profession realized that it would be able to implement competition reform for itself, it became more compliant with reformers' wishes.[16] Thus the LCA's *Blueprint* (1994*a*: 2) states both that national competition principles should apply to the legal profession and also that 'the independence of the legal profession is dependent upon the profession's right to self-regulation'. The profession is happy to accept competition reform, as long as it can be introduced within the bounds of self-regulation.

Accountability reforms are also acceptable to the profession as long as they do not completely abrogate self-regulation.[17] Having achieved the major objective of self-regulatory competition reform, the LCA was willing to concede that this self-regulation could then be 'subject to an external and transparent process of accountability' (1994: 2). President of the New South Wales Law Society David Fairlie (1994*a*: 2) could contrast accountability reforms in his own state which did not threaten self-regulation with those proposed in other states:

Although there remain imperfections, I believe we should support the introduction of the Act as it is now framed. While there is now non-lawyer participation in all aspects of our regulation, the fundamental point is that we remain at the core a profession which is self-regulated. This is in stark contrast to the proposals for change to the legal profession released by the Victorian and Queensland Governments.

The New South Wales reforms were made only after extensive consultation with the profession, and gave the new Legal Services Commissioner power to receive and investigate all client complaints, and to either refer them to the profession's own disciplinary bodies under the Commissioner's monitoring and direction, or to investigate them him- or herself (Legal Profession Reform Act 1993 (NSW), Mark 1995, Parker 1997*b*).

[16] This was confirmed by an interview with a Trade Practices Commissioner.

[17] Of course, for some lawyers the total abolition of self-regulation is desirable. But by and large the profession is more likely to accept reform if it does not completely abolish self-regulation.

In contrast, the Victorian Attorney General's initial proposals for reform (Wade 1994) were made without significant consultation with the profession, and changed very little before being enshrined in legislation. Interviews in Victoria with a prominent member of the LIV (MSL27) and an officer of the Justice Department (MG4) showed that the Attorney General put out her initial paper (Wade 1994) without consulting with the profession. She proposed that a Legal Practice Board be appointed which would oversee the regulation of the legal profession, issue practising certificates, and administer the solicitors' guarantee fund and professional indemnity insurance. It would accredit 'Recognised Professional Associations' to make rules and perform disciplinary functions. Although the Attorney General's working party on the legal profession consulted widely and thoroughly before issuing their report on her initial proposals (Craven 1995), only one significant change was made at the behest of the legal profession as a result of this consultation before the Bill was drafted (Legal Practice Bill 1996 (Vic.)).[18] By this stage the profession had largely accepted the inevitability of the changes, but this was not evidence of a successful reform process. Rather, according to one prominent member, the LIV felt that it had little chance of influencing the Attorney's reforms which had already been largely decided before any consultation occurred:

> We're not unhappy with the changes. But if they had come to us at the outset and said, 'These are our political objectives, how would you like us to achieve our goals?' there is a good chance we could have together come up with something less bureaucratic and less costly. (MSL27)

Indeed the process by which reforms had been introduced made the LIV executive feel that their ability to self-regulate had been completely impugned, and that it would be better if the government took over their self-regulatory disciplinary functions entirely (Meadows 1996).[19] By the end of the reform process, they felt so discredited as a self-regulator that they thought it might have been better if they had been asked to give up any pretence of public-regarding professionalism:

[18] That the whole Legal Practice Board would not be appointed by the government but some members be elected by the profession.

[19] Indeed the LIV had some reason to feel that they had been doing the best they could under difficult circumstances. Interviewees described the government's reforms as coming in a context in which members who were disciplined had been vocal in their criticisms of the LIV for continuing its involvement in self-regulation, while the Professional Standards department of the LIV had implemented an accredited quality assurance programme to ensure it dealt with client complaints well.

What happened was that the government wanted to reform our regulation . . . We said why don't you come and look and whatever functions you think we're not doing well, you just take them over. We're very tough on our own members. It's hard to discipline your own members and they don't like it . . . We said why doesn't the government take over our disciplinary functions entirely . . . if we're not going to be completely self-regulating, then the government should take it on. But they're just doing this halfway house. (MSL27)

CONCLUSION

In the Australian case study, engaging the legal profession in dialogue proved effective in converting lawyers through debates where their view was heard, but where it was not necessarily the predominant one. Some lawyers were responsive to such dialogue simply to maintain legitimacy in the eyes of the community. Others opened their minds to the ideas of reformers and were persuaded by their merits. Yet voluntary change was most common where persuasive dialogue was accompanied by a perception of the inexorability of the reform process. For some, inexorability was about the power of commercial consumers to force competition. For others it was about the determination of reformers who had power in a climate of micro-economic reform to introduce change. Conversely, attempts to force change without dialogue produced unnecessary resistance to reform and entrenched conservatism among lawyers. When reformers seemed to assume that the profession had not and would not reform itself, or where reformers seemed to refuse to listen to lawyers' perspectives on their own profession, lawyers experienced reform proposals as illegitimate insult. The apparent inexorability of reform became a goad to defiance and reactance.

Given the empirical reality of conversion stories based on productive dialogue reported here, self-regulation and dialogue must be taken seriously as normative ideals for lawyers' regulation. Yet it is foolish to trust lawyers to self-regulate in the public interest, and to reform themselves when necessary simply in response to public dialogue. Strategies based totally on self-regulation are exploited when lawyers are motivated by self-interest. While acting on an image of the profession as self-interested conspiracy might break the cartel, it does not encourage lawyers to behave in a public-regarding way. As Barber (1983: 140) argues, 'The public must both trust and distrust professionals, as it must trust and distrust all wielders of social and political power.' A sophisticated image of the legal profession which sees it as capable of effective self-regulation and self-reform (and of unhelpful conservatism and self-interest) is necessary in order to develop a useful regulatory strategy. The challenge for theorists and policy-makers is to reconcile trusting and distrusting strategies in flexible regulatory reform, which recognizes the commonsense view that the profession is complex and ambiguous. The evidence outlined here suggests that utilizing a politics of deliberation to renegotiate the social bargain might be most effective.

In practice, the application of the deliberative model might mean that an independent or government regulator and public interest groups would maximize the opportunities for voluntary cooperative reform by examining the legal profession, engaging it in dialogue, and giving it a chance to reform its own regulation before going any further. Reformers will acknowledge reforms that have been made by the profession before exercising the authority to make further reforms in negotiation with the profession, and impose change only where the profession is recalcitrant. Adopting a deliberative process of regulatory reform would mean leaving a variety of different substantive regulatory policy options open. For example, if reformers want to adopt a posture of dialogue, they will probably not begin by proposing the complete abolition of self-regulation because to do so would be to communicate distrust towards the profession by discrediting its efforts at regulation in the past and disrespecting the value of its opinion and experience for the future. In a process of persuasion and cooperative reform, the content of reforms is decided by that process and cannot be set beforehand. Thus in relation to competition policy in Australia, a mixture of debate, dialogue, and the realization that some change was unavoidable meant that the profession came to the negotiating table, with the result that the content of reforms varied from state to state and was rather different from what the TPC had originally envisioned. The availability of an element of self-regulated reform was an important contributor to the viability of cooperative change. A result of pursuing such a dynamic approach to the whole of legal professional regulatory reform might be that self-regulation with minimal accountability would be appropriate for trust account regulation since the profession as a whole is keen to have a good public image in this area, but a more coercive strategy, perhaps giving regulatory powers to third parties such as tax office investigators, would be desirable to prevent lawyers assisting outrageous tax evasion schemes. Detailed empirical work from sociologists of the legal profession will be helpful in making these decisions.

The responsive approach would promote deliberative democratic participation in the regulatory institutions surrounding the legal profession, while simultaneously affirming a Durkheimian vision of the legal profession's privilege and responsibility in playing a part in its own regulation and reform. Neither of the dominant paradigms of professional regulation envisages the profession playing such a role: one treats lawyers as incapable of contributing to their own regulation except as economically self-interested players in a competitive market place. The other sees them as under no responsibility to negotiate, deliberate, or make themselves accountable to the rest of the community for their self-regulation in any but the most general way. The theory of access to justice outlined in Chapters 2, 3, 4, and 5 saw lawyers as integral to democracy, yet also capable of great mischief. The conclusion of this chapter is similar: the profession is complex, and in order to comprehend its ambiguity, lawyers must have the privilege and responsibility of deliberation with and accountability to government regulators and community groups.

7 Renegotiating the Regulation of the Legal Profession

A NEW SOCIAL BARGAIN?

Chapter 6 used empirical evidence to argue that the best way to make the profession sufficiently accountable without crushing the possibility of public-regarding professionalism is through a responsive contextual strategy of professional regulation. Normatively this would require that regulatory regimes be developed as part of a deliberative process and remain subject to deliberative contestation. The dynamic, contextual nature of the regulation advocated is well suited to capitalizing on the public-regarding elements of a complex and ambiguous profession, without sacrificing the ability to deal with its self-interested elements. Making the legal profession an active citizen in a dynamic, communicative regulatory process (Sunstein 1993: 241) gives lawyers a chance to live up to their conventional ideology of serving the community by a process of deliberation with community and state which ensures they really do so, rather than just saying that they do.

Does this simply mean readjusting the social bargain between profession and state for the contemporary context, maintaining the basic structure of regulation described by Durkheim (1992) and Goode (1957)? The bargain between the profession and the state would authorize self-regulation, but institutionalize distrust by contemplating that the state could withdraw the profession's privileges where it did not live up to its trust. The terms of the contract might be renegotiated to require more competition and more accountability than before, but the profession would retain its basic privileges. Paterson (1995: 175; see also 1996: 149) argues that reform to the British profession in the 1970s and 1990s did successfully renegotiate 'the tacit contract placing a greater emphasis on the consumers' side of the equation, while leaving the essential elements of professionalism intact'. It remains, of course, open for the profession to regain lost ground in the bargaining process if the state does not remain strong and watchful. Dingwall and Fenn (1987: 61), also writing from the British perspective, see professions as 'broadly circumscribed by the state because they owe their existence to a framework of law which provides the protection for their cartel'. According to them, models for regulating the profession must recognize that the only effectual discipline against a profession is the withdrawal of its privileges of self-regulation (1987: 62). They advocate reliance on the potential of that discipline and the (Durkheimian) group socialization processes of the profession to make lawyers public-regarding most of the time.

Halliday (1987) offers a more sophisticated rehabilitation of the social bargain approach for the legal profession from a US viewpoint. He argues that legal professional associations are now strong in collegial organization and resources so that they are free to move 'beyond a preoccupation with monopoly, occupational closure, and the defence of work domains' and to take on more public-regarding concerns, especially responsibility in liberal democratic government (1987: 347). The particular capacity which they can offer is the ability to advocate and help shape a legal system that emphasizes the integrity of the legal process and the primacy of the rule of law (1987: 360). Having moved 'beyond monopoly', the profession can now bargain meaningfully with the state to preserve its monopoly in return for working to make the law more effective and efficient:

> [I]n exchange for the state's implicit guarantee that the traditional monopoly of the profession will be largely preserved . . . the profession will commit its monopoly of competence and its organizational resources to state service . . . Should professions prove disinclined to contribute their technical expertise to a general public interest . . . and should they choose to honour a civic professionalism only in the breach, then moral claims must yield to economic constraint and regulatory adjustments. The state can alienate occupational territory from a profession if a constituency is too poorly—or too expensively—served by it. In short, given the moderate economic monopoly and autonomy granted professions by the state, a commitment to civic professionalism can be not only expected but enforced. (Halliday 1987: 370–1).

Certainly, as we have seen, these commentators are accurate in describing the way the legal profession has sometimes been forced to move its position to a more public-regarding one in dialogue with governments and regulators. But the approaches of Dingwall and Fenn (1987), Paterson (1995), and even Halliday (1987) seem to 'trust' in an effective social bargain between profession and state on the basis of their empirical analyses of the nature of the profession and recent changes to it. Their lack of normative vision for how to improve on this record suggests that they do not take seriously enough the evidence that negative outcomes are likely to be pervasive.[1] The models offered are still too static and statist to serve as normative ideals for governing lawyers' role in the justice system for two main reasons.

First, giving governments a bargaining chip in the genesis and dissolution of regulatory regimes is not sufficient. The history of the profession shows that regulatory schemes are born in historically contingent circumstances of moral panic or professional politics, and then remain in place largely unchanged for decades (Pue 1987*a*, 1987*b*, 1990*a*).[2] Thus English solicitors were granted a monopoly over conveyancing in 1804 by Pitt to stop them protesting increased stamp duties on both their practising licences and written conveyances (Abel-Smith & Stevens 1967: 23). They retained it until Thatcher's reforms in the 1980s. The regulatory regimes that governed Canadian and Australian lawyers until the 1980s and 1990s were shaped by both Pitt's politics and events in the English legal profession of the late nineteenth century. In the traditional social bargain approach, because the state acts as surrogate for the community in the bargain, and because it is only able to apply sanctions in the most drastic circumstances, the profession is not required to take account of community access to justice concerns on a day-by-day basis.

Take Halliday's (1987) leading approach to rehabilitating legal professionalism. He puts forward 'civic professionalism' as an ideal which would guide the legal profession to do part of the work of government as a good citizen. In his social bargain between the state and the profession, the state calls the profession to fulfil its moral responsibilities as a citizen by contributing some resources to state service; it exercises economic leverage over them by retaining the power to alter their monopoly if they do not do so. Yet this at once gives the profession too much and too little responsibility. It is neither dynamic nor deliberative enough. The profession is given the onerous responsibility of self-regulation and state service, but without a framework of accountability and responsiveness to dialogue with the community. Halliday's civic professionalism is certainly a public-regarding professionalism, but one devoid of democratic foundations. It flows from a top-down view of the sovereignty of the legislature or the executive state. In Halliday's social

[1] Indeed Dingwall & Fenn (1987: 62) are explicitly pessimistic about the possibility for any more dynamic approach than their social bargain.

[2] Pue shows how the regulation of the British bar was shaped by a series of moral panics in the 19th century.

bargain the state decides, without public deliberation, to delegate state functions to an unaccountable profession. Consumers and the community need a more dynamic and responsive way of institutionalizing both trust and distrust, self-regulation and public accountability. The mechanisms for governing the profession must be more capable of contextual fine-tuning on an ongoing basis at the option of community as well as governments.

Secondly, continuing to conceptualize the regulation of the legal profession as determined by a social bargain between state and profession does not ensure that it is the community's legitimate interest in advancing justice that provides the normative goals for the governance of the profession. It should be the access to justice ideals of both community and profession that meet in any social bargain about the governance of the profession. The traditional social bargain makes no room for ongoing contextual input from the community about the justice system, how justice should operate and, by derivation, what parts lawyers should (or should not) play. It runs the risk of allowing government or professional interests to control the agenda.

The English Legal Aid Board's franchising scheme illustrates the potential for even an ostensibly access to justice based bargain between profession and state to go off track if the possibility of input from community groups with access to justice concerns is not guaranteed. As at April 1997 under the English scheme 1,740 law firm offices had franchising agreements with the Legal Aid Board (out of around 12,000 paid for legal work during the year) (Smith 1997: 29). These firms must show they meet certain quality criteria, in return for which certain legal aid decision-making is delegated to the firm through block contracts (see Paterson 1996: 155, Smith 1997: 27). In theory the Legal Aid Board as a powerful repeat buyer of legal services uses its market-place power to monitor the quality and amount of work the client receives thus improving the 'access to justice' of the client and overcoming clients' incapacity to monitor the work they receive from lawyers due to informational asymmetry (see Paterson 1996: 155–6). However, the government, as ultimate controller of the Legal Aid Board through the Lord Chancellor's Department, has an equally, if not more, significant interest in keeping down the costs of legal aid and thus working against the access to justice of the (potential) legal aid client. Thus Roger Smith, director of the Legal Action Group, a legal services public interest group, has criticized the progress of legal aid franchising in meeting access to justice goals as limited by its origins in reviews aimed at administrative efficiency and cutting down legal aid expenditure (Smith 1997: 29): 'The Board's political agenda is unavoidably administration-driven: it is not necessarily linked to policy considerations about, for example, the desirable scope of eligibility for services' (Smith 1997: 35). In particular, the Legal Action Group has criticized the criteria used to measure quality as being too focused on processes and management and not enough on the substantive quality of legal advice and outcomes for clients (Smith 1997: 28–9, Travers 1994: 173). The National Consumer Council is also concerned that it will not include measures of client satisfaction with lawyers' services (Harris 1994: 25). While there is no evidence at the moment that the franchising scheme has had counter-productive effects on clients' access to justice, it is clear that schemes such as these can easily be sidetracked into procedural efficiency or cost-cutting if there is no regular input from public interest groups on their justice outcomes.

A democratic theory that is more attractive than the social bargain approach renders professional and parliamentary sovereignty more subordinate to the justice concerns of the people. It will consist of three crucial elements: (1) a public-regarding professionalism, (2) constituted by public deliberation that is not monopolized by the lawyers in the state and the profession, and (3) is held accountable to the justice goals of the community through dialogue over particular decisions and public reporting of performance indicators that profession, state, and community agree to be fair. If we accept such a democratic theory of public-regarding professionalism, it follows that there is no correct blueprint of accountability and deliberative process for lawyers. They are matters for deliberation themselves, the outcome of which will be different in Australia from what it might be in the USA or Indonesia. It is more important to render the profession subject to the justice of deliberative democratic accountability, than to the demands of either competition or traditional professionalism.[3]

In this chapter and the next one I set out three principles for implementing this deliberative democratic theory for regulating the legal profession.

First, decisions about which regulatory strategies to use when should be based on judgments about how they will help lawyers fulfil the

[3] As Brazier et al.'s (1993) research on the British legal profession shows, increasing democratic involvement in professional regulation is the most important motivation for reforms even though it may be the ascendancy of economic rationalism that makes reform possible.

ethical ideals aimed at justice outlined in Chapter 5. Multiple regulatory strategies will be necessary to cover each other's weaknesses in combating the multiple, sometimes inconsistent forms of domination of clients, the community, the justice agenda, and each other of which lawyers are capable. The important thing is to ensure that, whichever regulatory mechanisms are chosen, they are chosen because they will best operationalize access to justice ethics in the particular circumstances. From the evidence of the previous chapter, four strategies emerge as currently existing techniques that ought to be utilized in any new regulatory balance for lawyers. These are (1) nurturing professional community, (2) encouraging elements of self-regulation, (3) embracing competition reform, and (4) developing institutions of state and community accountability. The following sections of this chapter identify the particular strengths and weaknesses of each strategy in implementing the justice ethics outlined in Chapter 5. Table 7.1 summarizes the access to justice strengths identified for each.

Secondly, each of the regulatory mechanisms used should be subject to continual deliberation, evaluation, and contestation in which community and consumer voices are as important as state and professional ones so that regulatory decisions are not hijacked by professional self-interest or government ideology. The penultimate section of this chapter gives detailed attention to how we might nurture procedures of deliberative accountability between profession, state, and community that are informed by a framework of substantive access to justice concerns.

Thirdly, policy-makers need to focus on improving justice as an integrated strategy and then asking where lawyers or legal advisers will fit into that (if at all), and consequently how they must be reformed, organized, or governed, rather than assuming access to justice means access to lawyers and allowing existing conceptions of legal service delivery and access to justice to limit reforms. To this end, in Chapter 9, I propose one example of a way that we might start with an access to justice problem—everyday injustices within organizations—and work forward towards an integrated justice solution (using the principles outlined in Chapter 4) that has consequences for legal professionals, rather than working backwards from traditional legal service delivery towards reforms.

The theory presented here does not seek to rehabilitate the functionalism of the social bargain approach as an accurate description of the profession and its optimal regulation. It seeks to institutionalize trust

Table 7.1 *Strengths of different regulatory strategies for the legal profession*

Multiple regulatory strategies	Strengths in orienting profession towards access to justice ideals
1. Nurturing professional community	Source of professional identity and socialization into all four ethical ideals: • advocacy ideal (but only if external pressure from market forces or competition reform), • gatekeeper ideal (through identification with whole profession), • public interest ideal (through identification with professional subcultures), • ideal of collegiality (but needs to be turned inside out).
2. Encouraging responsibility for self-governance	• Nurtures professional community, and professional responsibility for access to justice. • Shares strengths and weaknesses of professional community.
3. Embracing competition reform	Strengthens advocacy ideal through: • Deregulation to make traditional legal services more consumer-oriented, and • Reregulation to ensure competitive market by increasing market power of consumers. Helps prevent lawyer domination of justice market through: • Deregulation to allow proliferation of new forms of legal service delivery, and alternatives to law.
4. Developing deliberative accountability	• Ensures regulatory strategies of professional community, self-regulation and competition are actually implemented and are oriented toward access to justice. • Provides forums for deliberative processes of regulatory reform in which access to justice is the overarching goal.

and distrust of lawyers by placing discussions about policies for regulating the legal profession within a more flexible framework. Competition, self-regulation, and accountability become options on a continuum of regulatory strategies, highly contextual choices about which strategies to use at different times and in different sub-areas of professional regulation that can be relatively quickly adjusted when they fail or circumstances change. Like the social bargain model, this approach recognizes that self-regulation is desirable where it works and that the threat of withdrawal of professional privileges can motivate lawyers to self-regulate in a trustworthy manner. But by seeking to insinuate the potential for deliberative justice into every aspect of legal professional regulation, organization, and service delivery, it affirms the everyday importance of public (as well as government and professional) voices in determining regulatory strategies and contesting regulatory decisions.

NURTURING PROFESSIONAL COMMUNITY

The informal social control of professional community is the indigenous ordering that forms the bottom layer of a pyramid of methods (see Fig. 7.1) for ensuring lawyers act out the access to justice ideals advanced in Chapter 5. Traditionally legal professional self-regulation has been organized and justified around the notion of professional community because of the effectiveness of socialization in gaining compliance with communal norms (Durkheim 1992, Parsons 1954*b*); 'people are socialised to accept norms of appropriate behaviour as so much a part of their definition of self that any violation of the norms provokes shame and guilt' (Haug 1980: 64; see also Kavanaugh 1976: 966–7). Informal

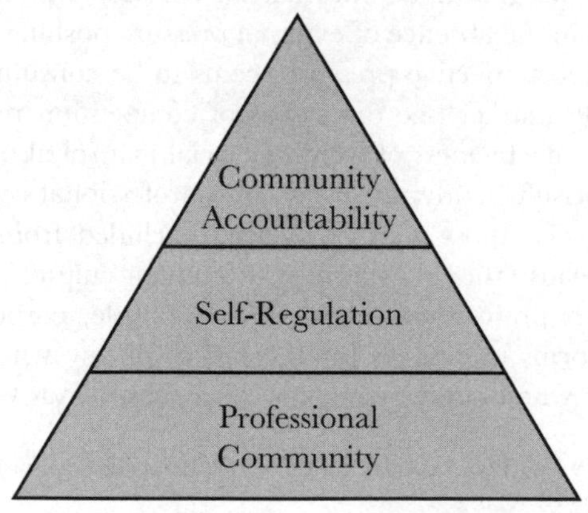

Fig. 7.1 A pyramid of lawyer regulation

controls of public criticism, gossip, embarrassment, and ostracism can equally ensure conformity.

As we have seen, critics argue that professional community is indeed good at informal social control, but that this control is aimed at ensuring that the whole profession is effectively oriented towards market control and status improvement, not access to justice or any other public good (Abel 1988*a*, 1988*b* 1989*a*, Larson 1977). In principle, however, there is no reason why informal social control cannot be aimed at nurturing a legal culture which upholds lawyers' special responsibilities to protect and facilitate access to the justice system. Communal control in this sense may take unexpected forms: large city law firms are often decried as symbolizing the breakdown of traditional professional community (Galanter & Palay 1995*b*), yet the management structures and socialisation processes of large firms may actually 'provide ethical obligations, expectations . . . information channels and social norms' (Arnold & Kay 1995: 339; see also Carlin 1966: 96–118) that broader professional associations no longer provide, if they ever did. Many firms have institutionalized the building up of social capital through increasingly widespread quality assurance programmes (Dal Pont 1996: 63–8, Lockley 1993),[4] and the development of ethics committees, mentoring schemes, and policies that decisions to take ethically uncertain actions should always be approved by a senior lawyer (Nelson 1996).[5]

The informal communal control of large law firms has been particularly effective at ensuring individual lawyers practise the advocacy ideal of high-quality service to clients. Yet, as Abel (1981*b*) so forcefully argues, there is no guarantee informal socialization will implement the advocacy ideal in the absence of external pressure pushing in that direction, and the most effective pressure seems to be consumer force in a well-functioning market (see discussion of competition reform below). Failures in the effectiveness of informal social control also occur where lawyers are not sufficiently integrated into professional community. As Chapter 2 showed those that have been excluded from professional community because they do not fit its dominant culture are also more likely to breach professional norms. For example, corporate lawyers may breach norms of respect for the justice of law when communal bonds with the whole profession are weaker than bonds with corporate

[4] Law firms may now be accredited under ISO 9001 for the legal profession (Salter & Friend 1996, Will 1996).

[5] Nelson's research describes how US law firms seek to curb sharp practice among their own litigators.

employers or clients. This may help explain why a powerful faction of in-house corporate counsel within the American Bar Association stopped new whistle-blowing rules requiring lawyers to report the illegal activities of clients being included in the 1983 model code of conduct (Schneyer 1992). In his seminal work on social theory and professional ethics Larry May (1996: 13) sees personal identity 'as a web knit from the various identifications and commitments that one makes with various social groups'. Professional socialization works by creating affective bonds between professionals as well as passing on cognitive skills (May 1996: 63). Thus an engineer relying on both cognitive and affective factors institutionalized in his or her professional identity, and assuming the support of professional colleagues, might blow the whistle on the use of unsafe construction materials in his firm, despite short-term organizational interests in doing the job more cheaply. If professional community is not strong enough in terms of socialization and support, short-term organizational interests are more likely to win out.

It is in professional communities which span different workplaces that lawyers are more likely to learn public regarding pride in lawyers' justice. It is there that they develop the self-identity that motivates them to stand up to clients and to employers when necessary to preserve the justice of law (social responsibility ideal), to do voluntary work as a matter of public service from time to time (justice ideal), and to respect one another (ideal of collegiality). However, in an increasingly fragmented legal profession, this need not occur in professional communities that span all 'lawyers'. There could be many legal professional communities, some covering many different types of work and workplace, and some convening as a group of legal advisers in only one industry or even one large company. The crucial factor for informal social control is that each individual lawyer identifies with at least one group of other legal advisers who hold to the basic values described in Chapter 5.

Indeed, as May argues (1996: 178–9), it is often better to implement professional ideals through the institutions of professional community than through disciplinary enforcement and penalties because it is the professional community that can support individual professionals' discretionary and contextual decisions to act on conscience or integrity. This would mean that professional associations should focus on supporting those who, for example, run the risk of losing their jobs by standing up for professional values. In the context of a discussion on whistle blowing by professionals, he argues,

> The ideals expressed by most professions in their codes of professional conduct (such as serving interests of safety, justice, health) would be given real strength if the profession were willing to support those of its members who, in the name of these ideals, blow the whistle on professional misconduct by their colleagues. The often flagging public confidence in scientists, as well as in doctors, lawyers and engineers, could be greatly bolstered if the public were to come to believe that strong professional associations would support their whistle blowing members. This is especially apparent where the member blows the whistle because of a concern for public safety or welfare. (May 1996: 178)

It is precisely because of the danger of identification with employer outweighing identification with professional norms that other professionals with social responsibilities such as equal opportunity officers (V. Braithwaite 1992), consumer complaints workers, and ombudsmen (James 1997) have found it desirable to group together as professionals, independently of their employers, to support and learn from each other, and maintain their commitment to certain ideals. When they do so, they are frequently more effective (V. Braithwaite 1992). Following May's prescription might mean that legal professional groups should be taking on campaigns to give in-house legal counsel protection from at-will employment and an entrenched independent position in corporate constitutions so that their advice can obey the dictates of justice without their personal job security being threatened. It might mean publicly honouring those lawyers and law firms who have stood up for justice or contributed to the pro bono work of the profession through awards and more routinely through coordinating and promoting pro bono schemes so that lawyers who gave up some of their time and energy to pro bono work would be recognized for it.

Subcultures of women, gay, black, or young lawyers may not be what traditionalists have in mind when they extol the virtues of professional community, yet professional subcultures also serve a crucial function in building up public-regarding professional communities. Indeed members of such subgroups are frequently more idealistic about the justice of law and being a lawyer than mainstream lawyers. 'Public interest subcultures', such as the groups of lawyers that run and volunteer at community legal centres, nurture commitment to the ethics of public service among diversities of lawyers (the justice ideal). Fostering such groups within the broader profession actively includes traditionally marginalized voices at the same time that it foments the reconstruction of legal professionalism (ideal of collegiality). The particular concerns and ideals of each subgroup are often a goad to the kind of discussion about the ideals of law and lawyering that is necessary for the professional community to continue to do its job of debating and passing on pride in the access to justice ideals of lawyering. This is not a matter for rules and regulations but for the strategies of social movement politics.

Special interest groups also strengthen community within the broader profession by building associations between lawyers from different workplaces. A feminist lawyer group is a community in which members share a common identity as lawyers and women despite their employment in different, competing firms, and in which they engage in thinking, discussion and action aimed at improving the law (Thornton 1996: 213–15). Where lawyers accomplish strong identity both with the whole profession and with a subset of it (either a firm in which social capital is strong or a special interest group that spans many firms), then there is greater scope for face-to-face informal control to work in harness with profession-wide ethics and values.

ENCOURAGING RESPONSIBILITY FOR SELF-GOVERNANCE

When lawyers are not adequately constrained by the bonds of community to advance access to justice norms, more formal controls must be brought to bear. Traditionally legal professional associations have seen it as consistent with the ideals of professional community that they take responsibility for disciplining their own members. They have also been responsible for formulating the rules and standards that will be applied in professional discipline. These formal aspects of communal control (discipline and rule-making) occur on a continuum with more informal methods of control such as socialization, gossip, and collegial criticism.

Giving professional associations formal self-regulatory powers has some efficiency advantages; the association internalizes regulatory costs, and mutual trust and greater expertise can make it easier for them to formulate, monitor and enforce standards (Ogus 1994: 107). But the strongest argument for legal professional self-regulation is that it supports the growth of professional community. As Wilkins (1992: 863) writes,

> [I]t would be a mistake to assume that there is nothing to the traditional argument that links independence and the opportunity for self-governance. By collectively engaging in the process of enacting and enforcing rules of professional

conduct, lawyers develop and reinforce the disposition for moral decision making.

A reformed legal profession in which no self-regulatory institutions remained would give lawyers little sense of the importance of their role as bearers of the culture of legal justice. As Chapter 6 argued, abandoning all elements of professional self-regulation means abandoning hope that lawyers will implement public-regarding professionalism. Allowing, even enforcing, elements of self-regulation encourages lawyers to take their public responsibilities seriously. It requires lawyers to create the institutions and associations in which professional community can grow and in which debate over ethical issues takes place.

The layering of self-regulatory institutions over informal communal control is the beginning of the constitution of a pyramid of lawyer regulation (see Fig. 7.1). Oversight mechanisms by which lawyers are made accountable to community concerns complete the pyramid, as I will argue below. The self-regulation advocated here is not licence for lawyers to pursue their self-interest; it is responsibility to implement public interest under the supervision of and in partnership with state and community. Thus the profession might be required to develop informal options for resolving disputes with clients and sanctioning lawyers that include lay involvement and an appeal to an independent tribunal. Encouraging self-regulation might even mean recognizing the existing complaints handling schemes of large firms (provided they meet appropriate standards). Professional association 'client care' rules in Britain and Australia are already requiring law firms to develop complaints handling policies and inform clients of them at the first meeting (Dal Pont 1996: 66–8, Harris 1994, James & Seneviratne 1995: 199).[6]

Not all self-regulation has to be by means of disciplinary mechanisms. 'Self-governance' may more accurately reflect what is required here than 'self-regulation'. In fact professional self-governance should continue to move away from its traditional sole reliance on discipline, which both failed to address consumers' concerns and also alienated non-elite practitioners who were worried that they would be the target

[6] Rule 15 of the (English) *Solicitors Practice Rules* requires solicitors' firms to have a complaint handling policy and to inform clients of it. Breach of the rule may amount to 'inadequate legal services' and serious or persistent breaches could amount to professional misconduct. See also the Law Society of Scotland's *Guidance Manual on Client Care and Practice Management.* In Australia the Queensland Law Society has made a similar rule, the New South Wales Law Society has issued a guideline to similar effect (NSW Solicitors Manual para. 13575) and the Victorian legislation governing the profession contains client care provisions (Dal Pont 1996: 66–8).

of unfair disciplinary attention. Professional associations and regulators might also focus attention on providing similar mechanisms for resolving problems between lawyers, particularly between employers and employees, including complaints related to sexual harassment, parental leave entitlements, and part-time work. Such a scheme is operating reasonably successfully in the Canadian province of British Colombia (Brockman 1997: 241).[7]

One of the problems of traditional self-regulation has been that consumer complaints have bottlenecked at the level of the professional self-regulatory association while the lawyers or firms that cause complaints have not developed the levels of consumer awareness necessary to solve their own problems. The best long-term strategy for better self-regulation in legal services is effective management within the firm where problems arise. An important priority for professional associations and regulators is to break the bottleneck by ensuring that firms take self-regulatory responsibility for problems upon themselves. This would leave (self-)regulators free to concentrate on (1) disputes that are particularly intractable, (2) serious misconduct, (3) monitoring and encouraging law firms' consumer/employee complaints schemes and (4) looking for patterns in complaints and changing professional rules and practices as necessary to address them. Yet despite the promulgation of 'client care' rules or guidelines by a number of professional associations including the New South Wales, English, and Scottish Law Societies,[8] many firms have not implemented a complaint handling system aimed at improving client satisfaction. In England, where it is compulsory, approximately 25 per cent of the whole profession and 60 per cent of sole practitioners (Harris 1994: 9, Jenkins 1994: 233) have not implemented a complaints handling system. Up to 50 per cent of firms in Scotland (MacMillan 1995: 14) and possibly more in New South Wales (North 1997), both jurisdictions where it is voluntary, have not done so. Professional associations might seek to ensure self-governance at the law firm level by providing resources and incentives for law firms to introduce not only consumer complaint mechanisms (as has been attempted through client care rules) but also anti-discrimination and equal employment opportunity policies and pro bono schemes. For example, one way of addressing lack of compliance with client care

[7] The Law Institute of Victoria (Australia) also proposed such a conciliation scheme for dealing with discrimination and harassment complaints in 1996 (Attorney General's Department and Department for Women 1996: 67–8).

[8] See n. 6 above.

rules might be for the Office for the Supervision of Solicitors (or equivalent) to award its costs of investigation of any complaint that has been inadequately handled by the firm concerned against the firm, whether the original complaint is substantiated or not (Smith 1994: 1741).

There is no reason why lawyers should have to continue to belong to the traditional professional associations geographically defined to cover all lawyers in that area, or even to a legal profession defined according to its current jurisdiction (Abbott 1988). Lawyers or firms could choose to which association they wished to belong. As long as each maintains appropriate ethics for whatever part they play in justice, there is no reason why all legal advisers need be part of one profession. The self-regulatory associations could each be required to report on their self-regulatory performance each year along certain performance indicators such as length of time in dealing with complaints, complainant satisfaction, procedural fairness for practitioners, and success at encouraging implementation of client care arrangements in private practices. Those associations not doing a good enough job would be deregistered, and the members would have to find another association to join.[9]

Self-regulation, however, shares the weaknesses of professional community as a means of implementing access to justice ideals. We have seen in previous chapters that historically it has been weak at enforcing the advocacy ideal in the absence of external pressures such as deregulatory and reregulatory competition reform. Relying on self-regulatory discipline alone also risks 'in-group solidarity of occupational incumbents, who frown on revealing to the public any unsavoury activities of an individual worker unless they become so blatant as to harm the whole group' (Haug 1980: 66). Self-regulation also has a bad record on the ideal of collegiality, tending to enforce a narrow vision of professional community.

EMBRACING COMPETITION REFORM

Historically, communal control and self-regulation have built up thick layers of unnecessary rules and restrictions that shore up legal professional domination of the justice market and are impermeable to client and community concerns. Competition reform as a deregulatory strat-

[9] See below for a discussion of holding self-regulatory schemes accountable. A scheme like this has been introduced in the Australian state of Victoria (Ross 1995: 91).

egy is necessary to break them down, and as a reregulatory movement to ensure a competitive and consumer-oriented market. Both aspects of competition reform can create external pressure pushing lawyers in the direction of regard for clients. Competition policy is not a regulatory strategy that adds a layer to the pyramid represented in Fig. 7.1. Rather it conditions communal practices and self-regulatory rules (abrogating lawyers' tendency to be unresponsive to consumer needs). Competition reform of the lower levels of the pyramid is a goal of institutions of accountability at the top of the pyramid.

As Chapter 5 showed, there ought to be a particular affinity between regulation by the market and the strengthening of the advocacy ideal. Competition reform can also help prevent legal professional domination of the justice market. Chapter 3 showed that making the legal services market more efficient by allowing advertising and price competition and abolishing anti-competitive legal professional rules can make traditional services more affordable, and that market reforms may also set the conditions for the proliferation of new means of providing legal services which might benefit consumers, including non-lawyer legal service provision, franchising, group legal service plans, legal insurance, and contingency fees. Since many competition reforms have already occurred in common law countries like Australia, Britain, Canada, and the USA, an important feature of a competition regime of regulation should now be to preserve the gains that have been made, preventing self-regulation from compromising them by cartelization. It will also be important to educate lawyers further in consumer-awareness so that they overcome their inherent conservatism and learn to take advantage of opportunities for competition that might benefit their clients.[10]

Embracing market reform should also mean introducing new regulation to increase the market power of consumers who would otherwise have little bargaining power with their lawyers. Powerful corporate clients have used in-house counsel to increase control over lawyers from whom they hire services (Chayes & Chayes 1985: 289–93). But the problems of information asymmetry and status differences still mean that lawyers have much greater market power than individual, especially poor, clients. Regulation which requires lawyers to give clients information about prices and services is crucial to overcoming the

[10] As mentioned above, Seron's (1996) research suggested that most US small firm lawyers have not taken advantage of relaxed rules that allow competition so that the benefits of competition are not accruing to their clients.

information asymmetry and therefore enabling clients actually to compare services so that competition between service providers occurs in fact and not just in theory. For example, 1993 reforms to the legislation governing New South Wales (Australia) lawyers requires them to inform clients in writing of how their bill will be calculated, an estimate of the likely costs, and their rights to have the bill reviewed. If the lawyer fails to do so, then the client has to pay only what an independent assessor decides the bill should be, and need not pay anything until that assessment has occurred.[11] Compliance with this type of rule is still weak in New South Wales (Brookman 1997, Lagan 1998, up to 75 per cent compliance for conveyancing matters), England (Harris 1994: 6, showing only up to 15 per cent regular compliance, Jenkins 1994: 234), and Scotland (MacMillan 1995: 19, between 30 per cent and 60 per cent regular compliance depending on the type of matter). Overall, the studies suggest that compliance is higher in New South Wales, where it is legislatively required, and solicitors' rights to remuneration depend on it, than in the other jurisdictions, where it is a voluntary or self-regulatory requirement. Improving consumer market power may also mean lifting restrictions on group legal service plans and profit-sharing between public interest groups and lawyers so that diffuse consumers can be subsumed under the umbrella of a larger more savvy, legal actor.

Liberalizing the market for legal services and for dispute resolution can also help decentre the legal profession from access to justice discourse. It may allow the development of informal community-based dispute resolution and the political use of law which were restricted while lawyers' justice monopolized access to justice. Licensing lawyers (exclusively or jointly with other occupational groups) to perform certain services can even help achieve the proliferation of other justice service providers if the grant of the monopoly or licence is limiting as well as capacitive. Lawyers may be licensed to provide certain services at which they excel (such as advocacy in the superior courts) but at the same time be prohibited from providing other services in tribunals and alternative dispute resolution fora. This might involve very specific regulation of lawyers in a variety of fora of formal and informal justice so that they do not hinder the development of non-legalistic means of justice. It may even mean licensing new occupations to perform new functions. For example reforms proposed in Manitoba would make

[11] ss. 175–83 Legal Profession Act 1987 NSW.

traditional occupational monopolies subject to contestation by 'para-professional' groups seeking a licence to perform work which they have previously been able to perform only under the supervision of the traditional professions (Brockman 1996). Clearly occupations that have already shown they are capable of competing with lawyers and providing quality, cost-effective legal advice services to consumers, such as accountants in the tax area, should immediately be recognized as entitled to give advice without technically breaching the legal profession's legislative monopolies by appropriate amendments to legislation.

More significant for improving access to justice at the lower end of the market might be the targeting of the development of new occupations to compete with lawyers in giving inexpensive legal advice and representation. One way of nurturing new groups to compete with lawyers is by using public money, especially legal aid money, to underwrite the development of competitors for lawyers by hiring non-lawyers to do legal work. The English Legal Aid Board's experiment with block contracting Civil Advice Bureaux to provide non-lawyer legal advice and possibly representation shows much promise in this regard (Steele & Bull 1996). Governments could also act more broadly to nurture non-lawyer legal advice professionals by hiring non-lawyers to perform certain legal advice functions, in much the same way that companies have hired accountants, human resource managers, health and safety officers, and others to perform certain legal advice tasks for them. Similarly legal expenses insurers might also be allowed by legislation to hire non-lawyers to provide legal services, provided they supervise their quality.

The main difficulty with embracing competition reform is that competition and communal professionalism often seem inconsistent. Increased competition is blamed for low standards of service and 'hired gun' mentality lawyering, while communal professionalism is seen as the genesis of cartels and anti-competitive practices. Competition among lawyers, however, can provide the external pressure which ensures that the internal pressures of informal social control are oriented towards giving the client the best product possible. Whenever companies compete with each other on the quality of the goods or services they provide, they must be competing with each other on the basis of the effectiveness of internal self-regulatory mechanisms which seek to ensure high-quality goods or services are produced (Ogus 1994: 110). Thus English legal firms now see the pursuit of quality accreditation as 'a [competitive] necessity, not a luxury' (Paterson 1996: 156; see also

Salter & Friend 1996). The British Legal Aid Board uses its power in a buyers' market to force up standards by offering franchises only to law firms that meet certain quality assurance standards (Lockley 1993). Deregulating to improve competition can therefore give consumers or mediators (such as the Legal Aid Board) more power to demand assurances of good service.

In the right conditions, then, competition can build up the advocacy ideal both by ensuring that lawyers give a cheaper more efficient service which increases access, and by stimulating lawyers to improve the quality of service offered. A further advantage is that by breaking down unnecessarily restrictive rules, competition reform can also have the effect of opening professional community beyond its traditionally exclusive bounds, thus helping repair the collegiality ideal. However, market reform is dangerous when it comes at the expense of professional community and effective regulation to implement all four access to justice ideals. In a vigorous market, lawyers may seek to please clients at the expense of other ethical commitments. For this reason the development of institutions of accountability to state and community is necessary to ensure that strategies of competition reform remain conducive to access to justice ideals.

DELIBERATIVE ACCOUNTABILITY

Communal control and self-regulation are not sufficiently responsive to the needs of clients and the wider community satisfactorily to implement access to justice ideals on their own. Competition reform may assist lawyers in responding to client demands and in opening up professional community to a wider group, but it does not sufficiently assist clients who lack market power to gain access to quality legal services. It provides no check on lawyers who are willing to do anything for unscrupulous clients, and it is not self-implementing; left to themselves lawyers may not introduce or sustain competition in the legal services market anyway. The failures of communal control and self-regulation must be remedied, and the pressure of market forces made effective, through institutions in which lawyers are made accountable to community access to justice concerns.

As I have argued, legal professional regulation requires more than a static social bargain, the terms of which are changed in emergencies, more than tinkering with individual regulatory institutions. It is an indication of the completeness of legal professional domination of their own regulation and organization that institutions in which lawyers discuss their practices with government and community are still rare. Deliberation about the practices and institutions of legal professionalism will automatically raise the substantive ideal of access to justice as an idea to which lawyers' regulation ought to aspire. Governments, clients, and community groups will certainly use the opportunity to articulate their access to justice concerns (discussed in Chapter 2). The deliberative process would also require the profession to justify its practices within the terms of the public good, a process that would encourage lawyers to rediscover traditional shared ethical ideals which have access to justice appeal (such as the ideals set out in Chapter 5). We need to build the capacity for the culture of the profession to become subject to the texture of deliberative democracy on a daily basis, not just in the unusual conditions of a law reform commission report. This should be tackled from two different angles; *from the outside in*, by establishing groups external to the profession which can draw it into dialogue and by developing institutions where the dialogue will occur, and *from the inside out*, by nurturing deliberation about access to justice values within the profession itself so that lawyers are better equipped to engage in, respond to, perhaps even influence, community concerns.

From the outside in

The success of deliberation as a strategy for improving the legal profession's responsibility for access to justice depends on finding opportunities to engage the profession in public dialogue about its goals and practices. Governments and quasi-governmental organizations have had some success in this endeavour in recent times. Broad-based community groups have had an influence on the legal profession through public consultation by law reform commissions, but their capacity to participate in an ongoing debate has been limited. From the outside of the profession, we must create institutions for wide-ranging and ongoing deliberation about legal professional institutions and we must also find or create groups that will represent public and client concerns in this debate. There are three main ways of building such institutions. First, the general law governing lawyers could be made strong enough for lawyers and third parties to be able to bring lawyers to account when necessary and for lawyers' insurers and risk managers to demand changes in lawyers' practices. Secondly, judges and regulators could hold lawyers accountable for things they do over-zealously for clients. Thirdly, there should be pyramids of regulatory control governing lawyer regulation powerful enough to deal with particular complaints and decisions and also to make recommendation on institutions, practices, and patterns of dealing with things. To date ombudsmen and advisory councils have not generally been given enough powers to sit at the tip of these pyramids and hold lawyers sufficiently accountable.

Liability in general law

The general law often provides adequate means of external accountability for lawyers' breaches of the advocacy or gatekeeper ideals if only victims of lawyers' conduct were suitably empowered to use it. Lawyers and law firms can be sued in tort, contract, or equity for harms caused to clients and to opposing or third parties (Evans 1996, Ross 1995: 193–222, Weisbrot 1990: 210). They can also be sued under consumer protection legislation including legislation specifically governing lawyers (Weisbrot 1990: 215–16), and, in egregious circumstances, they might be prosecuted for criminal behaviour. Insurance schemes and fidelity funds ensure that there are funds available to settle claims in many circumstances, so that such a course is sensible when what is required is financial compensation or reparation.[12]

Such actions may also be suitable where a third party (not the client) has been harmed (Wilkins 1992: 833). For example in Australia and Britain lawyers have been held liable to beneficiaries under wills when they have been negligent in the way they have carried out their duties as drafters and holders of the will.[13] In the USA, Wilkins (1992: 834) cites the case of *In re Flight Transportation Securities Litigation*[14] in which a class of investors sued a leading New York law firm alleging that it had engaged in a number of false or deceptive practices on behalf of its corporate client (a failure of the social responsibility ideal). In each case successful court actions against lawyers also led to significant discussion and awareness within the profession and thus the potential for a change in lawyers' conduct. If lawyers' own fear of liability is not enough to change harmful practices, their insurers may have the capacity to

[12] But while professional negligence liability has been generally expanding, barristers in Australia and Britain continue to have immunity from negligence liability for their appearances in court. See *Giannarelli* v. *Wraith* (1988) 165 CLR 543, and *Saif Ali* v. *Sydney Mitchell & Co.* [1980] AC 198. There no immunity doctrine for work performed in court in the USA and Canada (Ross 1995: 218).

[13] *Ross* v. *Caunters* [1980] Ch. 297; *Hawkins* v. *Clayton* (1988) 164 CLR 539.

[14] 593 F. Supp. 612 (D. Minn. 1984).

require certain standards of them as a condition of retaining their (compulsory) insurance.

More effective utilization of remedies under the general law means less time and resources need to be devoted to specific regulation of lawyers. More support should be given to legal consumer movements that will educate people about their ability to use these legal remedies to negotiate settlements with lawyers. Indeed one conclusion of this chapter will be that the nurture and funding of legal consumer groups should be a priority for state spending on lawyer regulation. These groups could also use the general law to challenge rules and practices of professional associations where necessary, perhaps on the grounds of discrimination or anti-competitiveness.[15]

Third party enforcement of lawyers' ethics

Pyramids of disciplinary controls and the utilization of general law discussed above rely on the victim of a lawyer's conduct pursuing a complaint or suit. Yet the victims of lawyers' conduct are often not suitably empowered to do so. Sometimes there is no victim. For example, breach of the social responsibility ideal may often benefit the client and harm only some broadly conceived public interest, or a group of third parties who have no idea they have been harmed.

However, other powerful actors often become aware of such breaches and have the capacity to remedy them. Judges and courts already have responsibilities to ensure that litigation lawyers do not overstep the mark of justice in representing their clients, although they do not tend to exercise them very proactively. Corporate regulators and administrative officials might also have the capacity and incentives to observe and regulate lawyer conduct which harms either the client or a third party:

> In the ordinary course of business, SEC officials review formal submissions and public documents prepared by lawyers. These efforts undoubtedly provide some tentative information about lawyer conduct . . . Moreover, as part of their normal duties, SEC officials investigate specific market transactions to determine whether the relevant parties have complied with applicable provisions of the securities laws. These investigations also produce a significant amount of information about lawyer conduct. Simply as a result of their participation in an ongoing process, therefore, trial judges and administrative officials are likely to uncover information about lawyer misconduct that would escape the attention of disciplinary officials. (Wilkins 1992: 835–6).

[15] It was anti-trust actions brought against US bar associations that led to much of the reform in the American legal profession over the last twenty years (Powell 1985).

Giving these actors greater responsibility and greater power to hold lawyers accountable deflects some of the regulatory burden from an overburdened lawyer disciplinary system, and complements the efforts of consumer and community groups to improve education about lawyer conduct. In the USA from 1989 to 1993 regulators brought over ninety cases against law firms which had been uncritically cooperative with the financial schemes of savings and loan association clients which later collapsed (Galanter & Palay 1995*b*: 196). Two large firms, Kaye Scholer and Jones Day Reavis and Pogue, have settled claims at $41 million and $51 million respectively and, in each instance, 'the case was resolved by a consent decree that set out stiff new rules for the respective firm's banking practice' (Galanter & Palay 1995*b*: 196–7; see also Weinstein 1993). Corporate regulators charged with administering a particular legal regime will have a much stronger incentive to prevent lawyer misconduct that damages the legal framework than will lawyers' clients (Wilkins 1992: 836). As this example shows, they might even have the capacity to force lawyers to overhaul their ethics and practice for the future through their ability to refuse to allow lawyers who do not comply with certain standards to practise before them.

Pyramids of regulatory controls

Most obvious is the need to have methods by which (1) individual lawyers and law firms can be brought to account for day-to-day conduct which harms clients, third parties, the framework of law, or other lawyers when communal control and self-regulation fail, and (2) the ongoing exercise of regulatory strategies is made contestable at the option of consumers, the community, government regulators, or even the profession. For example, the profession might be allowed to make rules and arrangements for its own regulation and organization, but governments and community members might also be given the standing to challenge any of those rules or arrangements on the grounds that they are not in the public interest before an independent regulator or commission. In the same way, the profession might agree to be responsible for certain disciplinary matters, but to allow any party who is unhappy with the outcome to appeal to a body consisting of government, community, and professional representatives. That body might also receive reports on the outcome of all cases from which it could judge whether there were any problem areas that should be brought to the profession's attention or regulated in some other way. A consumer or community group through its representative on the body might have access to information about patterns of structural inequality or domination that would found campaigns to change lawyers' practices or educate the public. Chapter 6 showed that a scheme with some of these elements was adopted in the state of New South Wales after a process of negotiation between the profession, the government, and reform agencies.

A condition of any regulatory regime which gives the profession self-regulatory privileges and responsibilities should be that it also provide a way to make self-regulatory decisions contestable by consumers, the community, or a government regulator. Thus, complainants would have a pyramid of options in pursuing their grievances against lawyers and law firms, perhaps starting with a complaint to the firm involved, moving on to an informal conciliatory process sponsored by the professional association, and then to a more formal self-regulatory disciplinary process which is supervised by a commissioner or board completely independent of the profession. Many of the independent officers or institutions that have been introduced to make professional self-regulatory powers more accountable have not been powerful enough to be effective at the tip of a pyramid of lawyer discipline. For example the 'lay observer' who was introduced into many Commonwealth jurisdictions had few formal powers and no ability to remedy problems. The British Legal Services Ombudsman improves upon the lay observer model but still lacks the power adequately to supervise professional self-regulatory bodies. The Ombudsman only has jurisdiction in relation to complaints that have already been dealt with by the professional bodies and where the complainant makes a formal complaint to the Ombudsman's office, and the Ombudsman has no power to compel the professional complaints bodies to reconsider action they have taken or to change their practices (Hansen 1994: 93–100, James & Seneviratne 1995). A better model is the Office of the Legal Services Commissioner introduced by the 1994 New South Wales reforms. That office receives all complaints about lawyers, and refers these complaints to consumer-oriented mediation or to self-regulatory institutions for barristers and solicitors. If a complainant is not happy, the decision is returned to the Legal Services Commissioner for review and the Commissioner has power to substitute a new decision. The Commissioner also oversees all self-regulatory complaints handling as it occurs, and is empowered to take over an investigation if it is unhappy with the way the profession is dealing with it. Ultimately, serious matters go to an independent tribunal for decision, the Legal Services Tribunal.[16]

[16] Part 9, Legal Profession Act NSW 1987 (as amended).

An effective independent regulator at the tip of the pyramid would not only have sufficient powers to hold the profession accountable, but would itself be subject to the contestations of groups which represent the lay public or consumers so that the office is not 'captured' by the profession. As Ayres and Braithwaite (1992) argue, participation of empowered public interest groups in decisions about the implementation and enforcement of regulation prevents professional interests capturing the regulators, or using their power to get away with a lower standard than that required by the law. This kind of participation in regulatory decision-making achieves a much more dynamic and effective democracy than either self-regulation or simply leaving the implementation of regulation to legislators and government agencies. I will argue below that one of the most significant things governments can do to reform the profession is to create opportunities for community and consumer groups to take part in legal professional regulation. Perhaps representatives of such a group should actually be paid to spend a day a fortnight discussing the Legal Services Commissioner's most difficult decisions with him or her and checking through the pattern of decision-making in other cases.

Finding people to speak for the community in deliberation about the regulation of the legal profession may seem difficult. Consumers of legal services have been too diffuse in the past to organize themselves to hold the state and the profession accountable for lawyers' regulation. Few consumer groups have consistently focused attention on the legal profession, and the lay representatives involved in professional regulation have done so as individuals or government nominees (e.g. Weisbrot 1990: 209). In recent years the consumer movement has begun to take a more concerted interest in lawyers.[17] A range of broad-based community groups exist who ought to be able to provide and support members who will take part in negotiations with the legal profession about its regulation.[18] The British consumer movement, especially through

[17] For example in Australia a Consumer Justice Charter was developed by a coalition of consumer and community groups initiated by the Australian Federation of Consumer Organisations (Consumer Action 1995).

[18] If a representative from one group consistently puts positions that are unacceptable to the broader public, there are enough consumer groups with an interest in the issue to move to destabilize and delegitimize their place at the negotiating table (Ayres & Braithwaite 1992: 83–4). Ayres & Braithwaite argue that the key to effective involvement by public interest groups in regulation is making sure that public interest representatives are democratically chosen from groups with broad-based support, and that any one group's place in regulatory negotiations is contestable by another group that can show it enjoys more widespread public support.

the work of the National Consumer Council, for example, has contributed much to the reform debate in that country (e.g. Hansen 1994, Harris 1994).

Two of the most crucial things governments can do to change the regulation of the legal profession might be to increase the number of fora for supervising the regulation of the profession at the tip of the pyramid in which representatives of community and consumer groups must be involved, and to spend money nurturing groups that will provide representatives. This means introducing boards and tribunals made up of lawyers and consumer/community representatives not only to hear appeals on particular disciplinary decisions but to monitor the entire regulation of the profession and provide fora in which concerned groups can air their worries. Providing such opportunities encourages broad-based consumer groups to expand their interest in lawyers. To date new independent bodies such as the New South Wales Office of the Legal Services Commissioner have hired mainly lawyers and individual non-lawyers but have not required the institutional input of consumer and community groups. To remedy this, independent regulators should be required, for example, to hear consumer group representations on patterns of problems and particular instances of injustice. Community or consumer group representatives should have some capacity to check over regulatory decisions to ensure the regulator is not being captured, as I argued above; and legal professional representatives should have a similar capacity to have input into the process.

It may be necessary for governments to invest resources in more proactively encouraging the creation of community groups with an interest in lawyer regulation. One useful model of a way to solve the problem of the lack of specific public interest groups with an interest in lawyers is the idea of creating a peak public interest group relating to lawyers and legal services (New South Wales Law Reform Commission 1982). Such a group should consist principally of non-lawyers and have the functions of investigation, consultation, the expression of views, and the selection of non-lawyer members for the main self-regulatory institutions of the profession. It would take the initiative in considering issues and making public and private reports and statements on the profession, and would be suitably resourced to play a watchdog role over the whole profession (see also Disney et al. 1986: 206–35). In order to be effective such a group should have the power to ask the government to review regulatory mechanisms that are not working properly. It should have the power to access material relating to the independent regulation of the profession and the standing to contest decisions of any independent regulator of the profession to ensure that it is not captured by the profession. In England such a body has been created in the form of the Lord Chancellor's Advisory Committee on Legal Education and Conduct, and in New South Wales in the form of the Legal Profession Advisory Council. In both cases the body has the function of advising the Attorney General/Lord Chancellor in the use of his or her powers to disallow a rule made by the professional associations or to make his or her own regulation for the profession. This means that its influence and effectiveness are very much dependent on the will and engagement of the Attorney General/Lord Chancellor in the regulation of the profession. A more democratic regulatory structure for the profession might give the council its own power to veto rules, and might also give it a role in advising and overseeing the complaints handling body in the way it decides to handle cases and address recurrent problems in the profession. Consumer and community groups need a forum where their voice will count in deciding how the profession operates on a day-by-day basis. A more powerful council could be very important in giving consumer groups a say in ensuring the profession does not capture the complaints handler and also in giving the complaints handler a forum for raising problematic patterns of behaviour that it notices. The council should also be funded at a level that allows it to sustain a secretariat that could regularly publicize its opinions on decisions and actions by professional bodies, so that the profession feels the accountability of publicity.

Where ordinary consumer groups are not powerful enough to make a difference, big business and business peak councils can be strong consumer advocates in the legal services market. The business community (as well as government departments and legal aid boards as consumers of legal services) has already shown that it has the power and the will to force lawyers to be less expensive and more efficient. Harnessing this energy by including business consumers in regulatory negotiation with the state and the legal profession would ensure that at least some aspects of community interest in competitive and effective legal services are adequately represented.

However, these reforms will not make much difference to the profession if there is no overall climate change in the wider community about the extent to which lawyers are expected to account for and justify their practices and regulation. The lack of community groups with an interest in lawyers is partly an artefact of the paucity of general community knowledge about the legal system. Democratic decision-making about professional practices should ultimately be a matter of deliberation between individual clients and their lawyers, and between law firms and their stakeholders, as well as dialogue at the level of professional associations, consumer groups, and government agencies. Basic things like improving citizenship education about law, legal procedures, and legal rights and duties in schools, workplaces, and government institutions will help equip people to demand more of the legal profession.

In a society where the access to justice pyramids of Chapter 4 were reality, where civic education included justice education, and where access to justice policies were an ordinary part of the cultures of most institutions and organizations, the possibility of holding lawyers deliberatively to account on a regular basis might not be such a naive hope. Reforming the profession 'from the outside in' ultimately means spending less time on specific regulatory regimes for lawyers and more time improving justice without lawyers. The structural transformation of justice advocated in Chapters 3 and 4 is the best guarantee that the legal profession can be brought to account before the justice of deliberative democracy. It is in a society where access to justice has become more than lawyers' justice, where alternatives proliferate, and many voices in many rooms contribute to the practice of justice, that citizens are best equipped to articulate the access to justice ideals to which they want lawyers to conform. A society in which lawyers' justice dominates justice discourse is a society in which lawyers will also dominate their own regulation.

From the inside out

A climate of willingness and ability to deliberate about the legal profession, its practices, and institutions must not only exist outside the profession, but must permeate it from the inside and work its way out into public deliberation. The socialization of law students and young lawyers, and especially their growing awareness of the significance and content of ethical norms, will be crucial in this process, as will debate and discussion about the ethics and justifications for lawyering among practising lawyers. In this process of debate, subcultures of lawyers and their visions of law and lawyering will be key provocateurs, as already prefigured above.

Powell (1985) shows that many of the reforms in the US legal profession over the last thirty years had their genesis in the internal dynamics of the profession, rather than the direct application of external social forces. For example, it was not consumers of legal services who used litigation to challenge restrictive rules such as the bar's prohibitions on advertising, but two lawyer-entrepreneurs of legal services clinics, Bates and O'Steen (Powell 1985: 286): '[T]he rise of consumerism was important not so much for aggregate changes in individual client behaviours as of the appearance of consumer advocates within the bar itself' (Powell 1985: 284). In these groups community interests and concerns permeate the profession from the inside, through the dual identification of lawyers with legal professionalism and wider community concerns. Chesterman (1996) shows how in Australia the new left culture of protest outside the legal profession gave birth to the 'new left lawyers' who started Fitzroy Legal Service, Australia's first non-Aboriginal community legal centre, and worked to remove the mystique of law and the power of lawyers.

Chapter 6 showed that legal professional reforms in other countries have also been frequently initiated or facilitated by segments within the profession. In Britain the activities of the Legal Action Group, an alliance of lawyers and consumer activists, has been a good example of the way that lawyers can help keep up the pressure to reform their own profession (Downes et al. 1981: 127). In the USA, Canada, Australia, and Britain movements of lawyers concerned with offering legal services to the poor have also acted as a catalyst for change and reform. Abel (1985: 6) argues that these 'fringe' lawyers are

> a vital source of new ideas and experimentation in the delivery of legal services. The neighbourhood law office, for instance, which became the centrepiece of the Legal Service Corporation and, in different guises, the principal form of the American legal collective, the English law centre, the Canadian community legal clinic and the Australian legal centre, originated in a private initiative in Philadelphia in the 1930s. Progressive practitioners also are a constant gadfly within the legal profession and an important goad to change: advertising by politically motivated private practitioners and by English and Australian law centres has been a major stimulus to the general relaxation of professional prohibitions.

Such groups frequently have a keener sense of traditional professional ideals and their importance in contemporary circumstances than many lawyers in ordinary business. It has already been argued above that subgroups of feminist, indigenous, or politically motivated lawyers can have a similar culture and impact; segmented professions can be more robust self-regulators than unified ones.

Lawyers' engagement with external social movements need not be completely benign: corporate counsel in the USA as 'a newly organised segment of the bar provide, wittingly or unwittingly, an avenue for the representation of the interests of a powerful group of clients within the bar itself' (Powell 1985: 291; see also Schneyer 1992). Yet on the whole the existence of social movements within the profession provokes internal debate and deliberation about the quality of and access to lawyers' justice. An important support for this process is opening up the legal profession to people from many different groups who will bring their interests and perspectives and pre-existing social commitments to the legal profession, the 'turning inside out' of the ideal of collegiality.

As community concerns permeate the profession through the medium of legal professionals themselves, lawyers are also more likely to reach out to non-lawyer citizens, and help them achieve a deeper access to legal justice than they would otherwise enjoy. Indeed this action on the part of the profession is necessary if certain groups are ever to enjoy access to the justice of law:

> The development of a more competent citizenry and of the opportunities to exercise both the skills and rights of citizenship depend, in part, on a different kind of professionalism, one that stresses 'outreach' tactics and a more participatory role for the client. This kind can be found in proactive law centres, which seek to provide clients with the knowledge and resources they require to participate in local policy issues, to criticise existing policies, and to propose alternatives. (Stephens 1985: 80)

Groups such as Civil Liberties Councils and human rights groups are often lawyer-dominated but outreach-oriented. They arise as movements within the profession but they take lawyerly concerns and values about human rights, due process, and even political and cultural empowerment to the wider society and to the state. Thus a broad access to justice agenda and vision of what law should achieve is propagated from inside the profession outwards.

A key component of any strategy for increasing access to justice deliberation within the legal profession ought to be legal education (see Webb 1998). Yet most empirical studies suggest that while there is considerable idealism among students entering law schools, the process of legal education and socialization undermines it (Erlanger et al. 1996, Goldsmith 1995, Granfield 1992, Stover 1989). About a quarter of Granfield's sample of Harvard students said they entered law school to help people, seek social justice, or achieve social change (1992: 38). Yet during their education most students replaced a justice-oriented consciousness with a cynical, game-oriented consciousness (Granfield 1992: 52).[19] Stover (1989: 12) found that the number of students expressing a preference for doing public interest law work after law school was halved between the first and final years (originally approximately a third of his sample expressed such a preference).

Both Stover and Granfield concluded that those students who were best able to preserve more idealistic conceptions of legal practice were either those who joined subcultures with a public interest vision of legal justice while at law school, such as the National Lawyers' Guild or legal services offices (Stover 1989: 103–15), or those who came to law school later in life with pre-existing commitments and kept up their relations with groups outside the law school with the same concerns. Perhaps law schools should be doing more to encourage what Stover calls 'public interest subcultures':

> In sum, contact with a public interest subculture appears to have insulated students from the influence of the dominant culture in several ways. First, the alternative professional communities communicated support for the norm of professional altruism. Second, they conveyed an image of public interest practice sharply at odds with the prevailing image of public interest ineptitude and marginality. Third, they provided altruistically oriented students with the assurance that they were not alone in their beliefs but belonged to a broader community of like-minded persons. Fourth, they provided students with role models. And fifth, in the case of the Lawyers Guild, contact with a political point of view that heightened their commitment to public interest goals. (Stover 1989: 109)

Erlanger et al.'s (1996) study of lawyers' first jobs after graduation compared with pre-law school interest in public interest work also showed that political commitment and involvement with a supportive subculture during law school were significant factors in determining whether students who had been interested in non-traditional practice actually took a job in public interest law. The proliferation of feminist law student groups and clinical legal education units in local community legal centres are examples of how contact with public subcultures can be increased for students. Much is being written on other ways to encourage students to take ethical development and critical reflection upon the role of lawyers in society seriously through educational techniques such as the 'pervasive method' (Rhode 1994), which advocates

[19] Turow's (1977) novelistic account of his first year at Harvard Law School tells the same story.

the discussion of ethical issues in all substantive law classes and teaching law in its social and political context (e.g. Goldsmith 1996). The recent psychological evidence on university-level education is encouraging: Deborah Rhode (1995: 149) cites 'over 100 studies evaluating ethics courses [that] find that well designed curricula can significantly improve capacities for moral reasoning', and recent psychological evidence showing that 'significant changes [do] occur during early adulthood in people's basic strategies for dealing with moral issues'. Whatever the method, law teachers should aim not only to teach the law, but to encourage students 'to critically evaluate the law and professional institutions as they learn about them . . . to develop and apply their own values and decide for themselves what justifications [for legal professional institutions and practices] are relevant' (Sampford & Parker 1995: 20; see also Parker & Goldsmith 1998).

An aspirational tradition

The goal is to create lawyers who are equipped to become part of what Croft (1992) calls 'deliberative moral community' in the legal profession. Croft sees a moral community as a group of persons who identify themselves as the present participants in an aspirational tradition the precise normative content of which is constantly open to modification at the option of its current bearers. Creating deliberative moral community in the legal profession involves discovering and recognizing the normative and ideological traditions lawyers already carry, and discussing how and to what extent they should be applied and reconceptualized on a day-by-day basis. Croft argues that while this dependence on deliberative change to ethics seems to raise 'the spectre of standardless relativism',

> Adoption of the deliberative moral community model should not be understood as tantamount to abandoning the quest for certain baseline, aspirational norms, but rather is viewed best as directing professional discourse to articulate such norms in recognition of the variability of modern practice, and as fostering an attitude that such an endeavour is worthy of professional interest. To this end, deliberative moral community envisages a foundation of aspirational professional norms, supplemented by more context-specific codes of conduct where necessary. (Croft 1992: 1325)

The most basic aspirational norm of the legal profession emergent from the process of iterative adjustment between facts and norms in this book is access to justice. The aspiration is brought to life in four traditional ethical principles that most lawyers broadly accept. (Croft sets forth his own four candidates which are not dissimilar to those set out in Chapter 5.) While aspirational norms like this may be criticized as too indeterminate, it is precisely this openness that should make them attractive to large heterogeneous moral communities (Croft 1992: 1326; see also Sunstein 1996). 'Deliberative moral community' consists in sharing debate, discussion and reflection from different perspectives and experiences in order to 'distil the contours' of a few broadly accepted principles. It does not imply pre-existent agreement on normative details. Organized professional associations should be places where a variety of voices in the profession can spark debate about the contemporary meaning of traditional ideals.

The evidence suggests that, despite lawyers' many failures to live up to their ideology, from time to time idealism about legal and professional values becomes more than rhetoric and reasserts itself in action that is at least partially public-regarding. Gordon's (1984) classic paper on New York City lawyers between 1870 and 1910 demonstrates that between 1870 and 1890 their ideal was one of perfecting a 'legal science' which would define the rights and duties of their clients in a socially harmonious way. While such a role was in their material interests, Gordon shows that to them it was also an ideal of (republican) public virtue contributing to the making just of American society. He also demonstrates how the ideal disintegrated with the realities of emerging corporate practice, revealing how the market will corrupt the lifeworld of communal lawyering in the absence of institutionalized deliberative processes that will bring the profession back to its access to justice aspirations.[20]

We have seen that in contemporary legal culture, it is often the subcultures of legal services lawyers, of feminist lawyers, or of civil liberties lawyers who continue to bear the burden of sparking discussion about the traditions of ethical ideals that can further lawyers' part in access to justice. As Gordon (1985: Lecture 2, 18–19) notes, those historical lawyers' movements that made the most impact on the practice of law as a contribution to the practice of justice in the USA—the Federalist lawyers of the early republic, the Progressive lawyers of the late nineteenth century and the New Deal, and black civil rights movements of the 1970s and 1980s—were themselves intensely political and controversial movements. Gordon's (1985: Lecture 2, 20) prescription for

[20] Roeber's (1981) study of lawyers in Virginia from 1680 to 1810 tells a similar story of commitment to the rule of law and the republican principles of the American Revolution.

improving lawyers' justice in the future is similar to that advocated in this section; that groups of lawyers should take collective action to form 'political conspiracies aimed at recapturing their profession's sense of virtue'.

ASPIRING TO ACCESS TO JUSTICE IN LAWYER REGULATION

The key to reforming the regulation of the legal profession for access to justice is for the justice aspirations of the community to meet the justice aspirations of the legal profession in public deliberation about how the profession should be reformed and regulated, and what the public can reasonably expect the legal profession to achieve. In building a profession which is better at helping to deliver access to justice, four regulatory strategies are available. Professional community is the context in which ideals and norms must be learnt, discussed, and passed on. Self-regulation institutionalizes the necessity for the profession to take responsibility itself for considering how it does justice to clients, the public, and within its own community. Competition reform helps encourage lawyers to deliver services in an effective, efficient manner to consumers, and creates the conditions in which alternatives to legal justice can exist. Institutions of accountability help ensure that public-regarding interests are institutionalized in lawyer practices and self-regulation, rather than irrelevant, irrational, or purely selfish ones. These four regulatory strategies need to be interlocked in particular circumstances and contexts in order to nurture the four ethical ideals which can motivate lawyers towards access to justice.

In a well-functioning democracy citizens will be able to find fora in which they can voice their concerns and aspirations about lawyers' part in access to justice in ways which will have an effect on the ongoing reform of the legal profession. The legal profession would also have its own internal dialogue and debate about its aspirational tradition perhaps provoked by groups of lawyers who are themselves engaged with external social movements. The existence of (1) groups with something to say about what the profession should achieve in terms of justice, (2) a profession which considers its own ideals and responsibilities seriously, and (3) regulatory and reform processes where they can deliberate, creates the conditions in which access to justice aspirations can begin to be institutionalized in not only the regulatory practices of the profession, but its communal consciousness.

8 Speaking Justice to Power: A Fifth Wave of Access to Justice Reform?

INTRODUCTION

The access to justice strategy set out in Chapter 4 asks us to reimagine access to justice as something other than a professional system controlled and rationed by lawyers and judges (with a few alternatives tacked on). If access to justice is to be significantly improved, a priority is to ensure that justice is being done in everyday transactions and interactions and that legal and alternative individual dispute resolution options are placed within a context of community and political action. Chapter 7 concluded that access to justice strategizing should start by addressing concrete problems of justice and only then move to considering what role legal professionals should play. The focus of a 'fifth' wave of access to justice reform would therefore lie in creating and improving everyday justice practices, rather than relying solely on elaborating professional systems of justice that are only ever utilized by the rich and the desperate.

People experience domination in the places where they spend their daily lives in the presence of more powerful others—families, schools, workplaces, shops, government departments, and community organizations. Because commonplace dominations make up most injustice, it is in these institutional loci that citizens will frequently experience injustice (or be enriched by justice). As Galanter (1981: 161–2) writes,

> Just as health is not found primarily in hospitals or knowledge in schools, so justice is not primarily to be found in official justice-dispensing institutions. Ultimately, access to justice is not just a matter of bringing cases to a font of official justice, but of enhancing the justice quality of the relations and transactions in which people are engaged.

Many of the places where injustice occurs will be powerful organizations with the capacity and money to ensure that customers, employees, shareholders, and other citizens within their domains have access to the necessary justice options. This chapter suggests that it is strategic to conceive the next wave of access to justice reform (the fifth wave) as requiring these organizations to create, implement, and finance for themselves responsive access to justice policies for those affected by their power; local access to justice plans for dominations that are predominantly local, or 'glocal' in the case of a global corporation that dominates a galaxy of local sites. Indeed, in a globalized world in which geographically bounded states are of decreasing relevance, democratic justice can only be secure when it is 'based on the multiple lodging of the rights and obligations of democratic law in the organizational charters of the agencies and associations which make up the spheres of politics, economics and civil society.' (Held 1995: 277).

Because wave five would require organizations above a certain size to create and pay for a significant proportion of citizens' access to justice, governments should then focus their financial resources on improving (waves one to four) access to justice in relation to less centralized, smaller (but very powerful) institutions such as families, small business, private housing markets, and community groups. This chapter advocates enforced self-regulated access to justice for large organizations, by requiring them to develop access to justice plans for those under their influence, combined with education for voluntary improvement of justice within small organizations including families.[1] Because voluntary self-regulation provides less robust guarantees of access to justice than enforced self-regulation, public resources dedicated to waves one to four access to justice (legal aid, public interest law, ADR, and competition policy) should be concentrated on access to justice in small organizations like families.

Such a policy does not ride the tiger of legal professional fees and culture. Rather it requires organizations and the citizens affected by them to decide for themselves how to build pyramids of access to justice options using alternative grievance mechanisms where appropriate, and law and lawyers only where necessary. The first section of this chapter shows why a strategy that escapes the problem of legalistic domination of access to justice is necessary. The second outlines incipient manifestations of the access to justice policy idea for large organizations and argues that organizations should be required to develop

[1] When injustice from small organizations like families properly becomes a matter of public concern, enforced self-regulatory strategies may become relevant here too. For example when a minor commits an offence the state might require family conferencing, an enforced self-regulatory strategy. See Braithwaite & Daly (1994), and Braithwaite & Pettit (1990) for a discussion of when an action properly becomes a matter for the intervention of the state by criminal law.

comprehensive and systematic access to justice policies. The third section sets out how organizations might be required and persuaded to comply with such a regime as a matter of enforcement and self-interest. The fourth shows how legal culture and communal ordering would each be important in constituting organizational practices that do justice rather than injustice, and how this might affect the organization and regulation of legal professionals.

BREAKING THE LEGAL STRANGLEHOLD ON ACCESS TO JUSTICE POLICY

Chapters 3 and 4 have shown that access to justice encompasses much more than law and that indeed law usually is and ought to be a last resort for citizens who wish to secure just social relations. Yet legalism has frequently dominated the access to justice reform agenda: Macdonald's (1990: 290) critique of access to justice scholarship argues that society's concerns have moved 'from justice to law (or more precisely, from complex justice to legal justice); and . . . from substance to access (again, more precisely, from the outcomes of institutional processes to the potential for their invocation)'. Geerts (1980: 219) shows that lawyers are guilty of perpetrating two exaggerations of the significance of law which affect both policy-making and citizens' desires: On the one hand they overestimate the 'social engineering' function of law, its ability to achieve beneficial social change, while on the other, they over-accentuate the importance of access to law as an end in itself.

Concerns at the ascendancy of legalism in practical justice discourse and policy-making echo the Weberian apprehension at the rise of technical rationality at the expense of other forms of social action (Shils & Rheinstein 1954), the warning of Habermas (1987: 361–73) that communicative action may be easily supplanted by legal norms ('juridification'), Luhmann's (1985) concern that the rationality of the legal system may destroy other patterns of social ordering (see also Teubner 1987), and popular misgivings about increasing 'legalisation' (Galanter 1992), and over-lawyering (especially in the USA, see Galanter 1994).

The history of access to justice reform can be seen as an attempt to break away from legalism in institutions of justice delivery. But in practice it was generally an unsuccessful manœuvre. At each stage legalism and lawyering have dominated. The legal aid model relied on organizing and regulating lawyers as a public utility employed by the state to provide services to citizens (Leubsdorf 1982: 1035). As a result it has been so expensive as to provide only a tiny minority of citizens with a narrow range of legal services. The public interest law movement was an attempt to use innovative legal techniques and politics to achieve more substantive justice for under-represented groups and individuals. Because it depended on lawyers acting conscientiously to help reform the legal system, give free services, and become involved in community action (Leubsdorf 1982: 1048), it remained entrenched in legalism (Trubek 1990). While there was progress in (unsystematically) taking on more structural injustices, only injustices of such structurally aggregated character as could be accommodated within the formal legal paradigm of the class action could ride wave two. It did not necessarily provide remedies for the fragmented, diffuse injustices arising from local dominations. The free market model too concentrated on reform of the legal profession, dismantling lawyers' monopolies and restrictive practices (Leubsdorf 1982: 1026). But this is a limited strategy even for the smaller task of orienting lawyers more towards access to justice. It can make legal justice cheaper for those who can afford to pay. But those who cannot afford to pay at all had already learned to 'lump' injustice before wave three arrived and continue to do so.

The ADR movement was the most promising attempt to break the legalistic stranglehold on access to justice policy. Lawyers often colonized the alternatives that reformers developed, however, dragging them back into legal culture and professionalism. Empirical work in the law and society and law and anthropology traditions repeatedly shows how vulnerable the institutions of informal justice are to the colonization of law and legal professionalism (see Abel 1982*b*, Auerbach 1983, Galanter 1981, Merry 1993, Naffine & Wundersitz 1991). Reforms that initially sought to eliminate lawyers by creating informal alternatives to law such as commercial arbitration, workers' compensation boards, small claims tribunals, and juvenile courts have frequently been taken over by judges and lawyers and absorbed into dominant legal categories.

Lawyers and judges easily assume the administration of institutions of informal justice, bringing with them the discourse of formal law and their codes of professionalism (Merry 1993: 60). Such is the potency of the imperialism of legal discourse that even occasional appearances by lawyers 'may lead an informal tribunal to restructure its proceedings, perhaps bringing them more in line with lawyer expectations' (Lempert & Monsma 1988: 137). Lempert and Monsma concluded from their study of a public housing eviction board in Hawaii that lawyers appearing sporadically before the board often proceeded in a legalistic way, attempting to transform hearings into more court-like encounters.[2] The existence of a credible threat of appeal to institutions of formal justice also increased legalism: 'Without making great changes in the way eviction hearings were held, the Authority acted to bring its eviction process more closely in accord with the requirements of formal law' (1988: 178). Thus ADR and informal justice practitioners learn to gain acceptance and secure immunity from formal legal appeal by mimicking the processes of the formal system (Merry & Milner 1993: 5).[3]

Options that appear to be alternatives to the formal legal system turn out not to be alternatives at all but part of the whole process of 'litigotiation' controlled by lawyers and judges. Thus Roberts (1995; see also Genn 1987) shows how lawyers have had a traditional monopoly on the settlement (not just the adjudication) of disputes using a long-drawn-out process in which negotiations are pursued simultaneously with preparation for trial. As ADR and mediation have become popular, lawyers and judges have successfully co-opted them into this process of 'litigotiation'.

The co-option of popular justice by lawyers' justice might also help to explain the research summarized by Cranston (1995*a*: 48–9) that shows that settlement conferences, case management, and other mechanisms designed to give potential litigants ADR type alternatives often fail to produce any savings in costs or time, and may not even lead to a higher number of cases settling. Similarly Cranston (1995*a*: 50) reports that the British small claims courts that were supposed to provide a quick, cheap, and accessible way for people to solve small disputes are rated poorly by their users on image and approachability and that most people still require legal advice before using them. Cranston

[2] Lempert & Monsma (1988: 158–9) imply that lawyers who did appear before the board seemed to have unreasonably high expectations about procedural safeguards.

[3] See also Merry & Milner's (1993) edited collection on the operation and history of the San Francisco Community Boards which shows how popular justice is both co-opted by state law and resists co-option. As Merry (1993: 61–2) writes in her piece in the collection, 'The fact that SFCB did not create new forms of neighbourhood ordering in San Francisco is not surprising. This reproduction of power relation occurs, I think, because popular justice rarely grows out of a base of power outside the state or the dominant classes. It is usually more closely tied to state law than to indigenous ordering. Anarchic popular justice is the most direct political challenge to existing power relations and is usually quickly quashed. Popular justice that grows out of indigenous ordering, the communitarian and anarchic traditions, has a greater possibility of challenging the hegemony of language and form exerted by state law.'

does however report evidence that such mechanisms are likely to improve the quality of the ultimate trial if the matter does not settle, and that the introduction of court settlement programmes which include options like arbitration actually gave more parties what they wanted, a forum in which their disputes were adjudicated. While the co-option of ADR type mechanisms by lawyers and judges might improve the quality of formal legal justice (as elements of indigenous ordering filter up the pyramid), we should be vigilant not to mistake the adoption of some elements of ADR in the formal system for the proliferation of accessible, informal justice.

Chapter 2 showed that the main criticism community and clients make of lawyers is that they do not do enough justice. The history of access to justice reform suggests that lawyers simultaneously over-promote law. Reforms that begin and end with legal services, judicial case management, and legal arbitration perpetuate the problem of too much law and not enough justice. Tinkering with the apex of the pyramid without a focus on developing a variety of justice options in the places where people need them most is not enough.

SPEAKING JUSTICE TO INSTITUTIONALIZED POWER

An important criticism of communitarian ADR as a movement is that it has relied too much on encouraging *neighbourhood* informal justice. In pre-industrial societies where politics, work, education, religion, and child-rearing were all geographically localized, neighbourhood-based informal justice was of great significance. In the contemporary world the main arena of justice is in non-neighbourly networks of institutions that enmesh us wherever we go. It is here that improving 'grass-roots' justice options can make a significant difference. Governments and companies are already recognizing this as an important issue in a variety of discrete areas such as discrimination in employment and environmental justice. Specific initiatives in these areas ought to be broadened and systematized into a more comprehensive strategy in which organizations are required to have their own access to justice policies or plans. The aim is to speak justice to the power that these organizations already exercise in dealing with (or failing to deal with) many local dominations.

Incipient access to justice within organizations

There are many informal and semi-formal ways in which institutions routinely do justice and injustice to citizens. Even an organization that has never developed an explicit policy about the justice of its processes still has policies that deal justly or unjustly with citizens' justice claims. Examples of ADR and informal justice processes already formed as a result of indigenous orderings and market pressures include shareholder grievance mechanisms, consumer complaints procedures (TARP 1995*b*),[4] management strategies for dealing with employee complaints of exploitation, discrimination, or harassment (Edelman et al. 1993),[5] policies for dealing with debtors and creditors, practices for firing staff, and methods of consulting with and taking account of community interests in institutional decisions such as where to locate a new factory or office.

The introduction of self-regulatory complaint and dispute resolution schemes at either an institutional or industry level is sometimes a spontaneous reaction to market forces and customer and employee complaints. It may also occur as a result of state action. Much justice reform in recent years has been oriented towards encouraging and improving the quality of informal and semi-formal complaints and dispute resolution schemes within government departments and industry. The deregulation of state utilities in many countries has occurred only under the legislative condition that adequate schemes for consumer complaints and feedback be developed or maintained (Hood & Scott 1996). Thus in Australia when the telecommunications industry was liberalized, the telecommunications carriers were required as a condition of their licence to participate in the Telecommunications Industry Ombudsman scheme and to fund the scheme proportionately to the number of complaints made against them (Trade Practices Commission 1995*b*: 22). 'Regulatory crime' laws, such as trading standard and consumer protection statutes, frequently encourage self-regulation by providing businesses with a defence to offences if they can show they exercised 'due diligence' by having in place management and quality assurance systems aimed at ensuring compliance with the standards (Scott 1995).

[4] Sixty-five per cent of TARP's (1995*b*: 4) sample of Australian companies had a department or an individual responsible for handling consumer enquiries and complaints.

[5] In the USA Edelman et al. (1993: 512) found that institutional employers were motivated to have internal dispute resolution mechanisms to deal with equal employment opportunity and affirmative action issues in order to keep them out of external state agencies and the formal legal system.

The 'big bang' in the delivery of British financial services revolved around the reforms of the Financial Services Act 1986 that required the establishment of a complicated network of self-regulatory organizations all supervised by the Securities and Investment Board (Page 1987). NGOs are also using this strategy in attempts to improve corporate conduct. For example, Consumers International have developed the Consumer Charter for Global Business which transnational corporations are being asked to sign if they can demonstrate that their operations comply with its standards of ethics, competition, marketing practices, product standards, and consumer information. Signing the charter also means compiling a bi-annual report on the corporation's activities and compliance with the standards which can be made available to members of Consumers International (ACT Consumer Affairs Bureau 1996).

As internal complaints and grievance processes become common, governments and industry have become concerned to assure or regulate their quality. Under the British government's 1991 Citizens' Charter, a complaints task force has been established to advise public bodies on the best methods for dealing with grievances (Birkinshaw 1994: 40). Standards Australia have produced a standard by which internal consumer complaints schemes can be accredited.[6] In the USA and Australia standards which might provide a model for internal justice policies are also proliferating for effective compliance programmes in areas such as trade practices, consumer protection, and securities regulation (Brown & Kandel 1995: 7–29, Harvard Law Review 1996: 1789, Trade Practices Commission 1995*a*: 27–30).[7] The Australian

[6] Standards Australia, Australian Standard Complaints Handling, AS 4269—1995. The Australian Competition and Consumer Commission (ACCC, formerly the Trade Practices Commission) have also concerned themselves with helping companies understand the standards which should be applied to internal complaints handling schemes. See Trade Practices Commission (1995*b*: 18) for one list of elements for an effective internal complaints handling process; committed management, fairness, accessibility, adequate, properly resourced staff, appropriate remedies, feedback, review.

[7] For example the US Sentencing Commission's Sentencing Guidelines for organizations look to at least the following factors in determining whether a compliance programme is effective; high-level management responsibility for compliance, written polices and procedures promoting compliance, programmes and publications to educate employees about these policies and procedures, an auditing system to detect illegal conduct and allow employees to report violations, reasonable steps taken by management to prevent further violations if illegal conduct is discovered, consistent enforcement and disciplinary sanctions against wrongdoers, avoiding delegating authority to persons with a propensity to engage in illegal conduct (Brown & Kandel 1995: 7–29, Harvard Law Review 1996: 1789).

The Trade Practices Commission (1995a: 27–30) suggests that effective compliance

Competition and Consumer Commission and Association for Compliance Professionals with Standards Australia have even developed a generic standard for all compliance programmes (AS 3806) which was launched in early 1997.

Majone (1994, 1996: 47–60; see also Braithwaite forthcoming, Parker 1999, Power 1997: 41–67) has characterized the rise of such developments in Europe as the rise of a 'new' regulatory state following on, but conceptually distinct, from the earlier regulatory state inaugurated in the US New Deal. Instead of a state providing telecommunications or job placement for the unemployed, it specifies the outcomes it wants from either private or public providers of those services and then regulates to secure those outcomes. Increasingly, as the Telecommunications Ombudsman instantiates, one of the outcomes specified by the new regulatory state is access to justice. The fifth wave of access to justice proposed in this chapter therefore has its incipient manifestations in the new regulatory state. Indeed the fifth wave is very much attuned to the ethos of reinventing government so that the state gives priority to steering rather than rowing (Osborne & Gaebler 1992). It is, therefore, a practical not a romantic strategy for a world that refuses to accept totally unregulated market or Weberian bureaucratic control of its problems. Indeed it is so practical that there are already many incipient manifestations of it.

Models of enforced self-regulation in organizations

Strategies of 'enforced self-regulation' (Ayres & Braithwaite 1992: 101), such as the access to justice policy regime proposed in this chapter, are increasingly used to ensure that institutions take responsibility for the ways their activities can affect others both inside and outside their own organizations. In a variety of areas the state requires corporations and other powerful organizations to audit their own activities, to consider what effects their power might have on others, and to develop policies

programmes might involve; training and advice, commitment at all levels of the organization, adequate resources for compliance, a senior manager with responsibility and direct access to the CEO or audit committee of the board, compliance policies clearly stated and targeted, being well publicized, formal reporting relationships, action plans for when problems reported, record keeping, complaints handling system established, inclusion of agents and subcontractors as well as employees, monitoring against performance standards, regular review for effective outcomes, liaison with enforcement authorities and compliance organizations, continuous improvement philosophy, systematic identification and management of risks.

to remedy those effects (see Baldwin 1997, Grabosky 1995, Manning 1987). They are usually made accountable by being required to report the results of their deliberations to the government and to the community at large.

Corporations are now finding it desirable to initiate their own compliance audits before outside regulators do it for them. Sigler and Murphy (1988) describe compliance programmes that American corporations use to help them negotiate antitrust, environmental law, equal employment opportunity, and occupational health and safety.[8] They report that,

> For America's larger corporations, it is commonplace to find substantial legal departments among whose purposes are to assure that the business can continue its activities without running afoul of the law. Beyond merely consulting with lawyers, most of these companies have more active efforts to ensure that their personnel understand the legal risks and the rules that apply. (Sigler & Murphy 1988: 55)

Environmental regulation already requires corporations to take responsibility for the effects of their activities on the environment by preparing environmental impact statements about the consequences of proposed developments. There is a trend towards expecting corporations to environmentally 'audit' all their activities, not just new developments (e.g. International Auditing Practices Committee 1995). The new international environmental management standard, the ISO14000 series, requires companies to set objectives for continuous improvement in environmental stewardship and then to audit independently to ensure that each year's performance is better than the previous year's (Cascio 1994, Gunningham & Sinclair 1999).[9] Fischer and Schot's (1993: 5; see also Hoffman 1997) international research on industrial firms suggests that 'somewhere in the mid-1980s firms changed from fighting or resistantly adapting to external pressures to embracing them and incorporating environmental considerations into their policies in a more rigorous way'.[10]

[8] Sigler & Murphy (1988: 57) argue that compliance strategies are most advanced in relation to antitrust which they say is directly related to the severity of antitrust laws and the government's practice in enforcing them.

[9] Unlike the situation with European environmental management standards, under the ISO 14000 series, continuous improvement will not be on environmental outcomes, but on environmental management systems (Gunningham & Sinclair 1999).

[10] Gray et al. (1996: 143, 148, 172–3) have also found that internationally environmental reporting is the most common type of social reporting in which corporations engage.

Equal employment opportunity (EEO) and affirmative action (AA) regimes require companies, government departments, and universities to consider whether women (and sometimes other minorities) are discriminated against within their organizations and in their employment practices, and to develop corporate plans for improving their position (V. Braithwaite 1993). In the USA Edelman et al. (1993: 512) found that institutional employers were motivated to have internal dispute resolution mechanisms to deal with equal employment opportunity and affirmative action issues in order to keep them out of external state agencies and the formal legal system. A regime of enforced self-regulation is becoming common for occupational health and safety (Rees 1988, Smith et al. 1993) and Rees (1988) found some evidence that self-regulation based on labour-management cooperation facilitated by the regulatory agency was more effective than command and control regulation judged by accident rates and the evaluations of the leading participants.

Sheikh (1996; see also Dierkes 1985, Gray et al. 1996) discusses the concept of requiring companies to conduct 'social audits' in the growing number of fields in which the law and the community recognize corporate social responsibilities. Social audits evaluate the corporation's performance in its social environment in areas such as employee welfare, occupational health and safety, responsibilities to shareholders and creditors, consumers and clients, and also 'a company's social performance on matters such as environmental pollution, waste, misleading advertisements, unsafe consumer products and product quality' (Sheikh 1996: 193). Sheikh's own survey of British companies showed that well over half had already begun regularly to audit more than one area of social activity (Sheikh 1996: 194).

Improving indigenous access to justice within organizations

Instead of introducing complaints and dispute resolution schemes piecemeal, a fifth wave of reform might focus on ensuring that informal justice options and indigenous orderings exist in large organizations, and that those already in place are of sufficient quality and are sufficiently integrated with more formal justice options to do justice rather than injustice. They should adopt 'within their very modus operandi, a structure of rules, principles and practices compatible with [deliberative] democracy' (Held 1995: 251). Enforced self-regulatory activities in the domains of the environment, occupational health and safety, and affirmative action provide partial models for public and private organizations to audit comprehensively the ways they provide access to justice for customers, employees, shareholders, creditors, and others, and then to improve them. The access to justice policy regime would require them to examine critically these private orderings, discuss them with stakeholders, and consider whether they do justice or injustice and where they have gaps. It would incorporate schemes of the types described above into explicit and comprehensive access to justice pyramids. It would give institutions responsibility for the effects of their own power by insisting that they audit their own justice practices and develop policies with their stakeholders about how they will ensure access to justice for all (whether customers, creditors, employees, students, or anyone else) who may suffer domination within their institutional network.

Thus a corporation or government department might introduce consumer complaints schemes, natural justice for employees in danger of losing their jobs, grievance processes for employees who experience discrimination or harassment and for debtors who feel they are being aggressively hounded for their debts. It might join an independent industry ombudsman scheme to which a grievant could appeal if their grievance was not resolved internally in a satisfactory way. It might even decide to pay for legal advice or representation for citizens who were unhappy with the justice meted out in informal and semi-formal fora.

This proposal would solve the problems of relying on lawyers' charity or subsidizing lawyers' fees to enhance justice in crucial places. Rather it relies on effectively mobilizing the resources of the organizations in which domination occurs to deal with the problems they help to create. If one turns to lawyers for access to justice strategies, responses are frequently limited to after-the-fact remedies. If one turns to those who hold organizational power, one can prevent injustice. While the lawyer can get compensation for citizens who suffer from a polluted river, the manager can engineer the production process to minimize or eliminate waste.[11]

[11] Moreover he or she is likely to be able to do this at negative cost much of the time given that production processes that generate a lot of waste are probably inefficient (Porter & van der Linde 1995). See discussion below.

WHY EMBRACE THE ACCESS TO JUSTICE POLICY REGIME?

Perhaps this sounds romantic. Why should cost-conscious executives fund comprehensive enhancements to their private justice systems, and why should the public entrust a significant amount of the provision of access to justice for citizens to large and already (dangerously) powerful organizations? Three reasons will be considered below. First, it may be rational for executives of large organizations to adopt access to justice policies because flexible access to justice regimes that are private can deliver competitive advantage for just organizations over unjust ones. By virtue of their justice they can keep customers, hold and motivate quality employees, enjoy a capacity to restructure in response to changes in the competitive environment with minimum friction, and keep at bay greens, consumerists, unionists, EEO, privacy and disabled activists, and others who can threaten their legitimacy. Secondly, organizations might comply with an access to justice policy requirement imposed by the state in a process which allows them to do justice in their own way. Finally, an advantage for the public is that if large organizations provide a significant amount of access to justice then public resources can be focused on areas where they are really necessary, and models can be developed for improving the culture of justice in smaller organizations.

Advantages of access to justice policies for organizations

The development of corporate access to justice policies could improve business for competitive corporations. The efficiency of such schemes means that although they will require a significant devotion of resources and administrative expense to implement, and may be costly, they can be cost neutral overall, or even save money in the long term.

Harvard Business School professor Michael Porter (1990: 652) sees well-publicized consumer complaints systems as a stimulus to improvement in business practices leading to better productivity and profitability. Laura Nader argues that effective consumer complaints schemes can be the basis for an information loop that improves products and services (Nader 1979: 1018). A benchmark study of consumer complaint behaviour conducted for American Express and the Society of Consumer Affairs in Business (TARP 1995*a*, 1995*b*) shows that effective corporate complaint handling practices can produce significant marketing advantages. The study found that where consumers were satisfied or more than satisfied with the way their complaints were handled they were much more likely to repurchase than if they did not complain, or were dissatisfied or merely 'mollified' by the way their complaint was handled. Indeed where consumer complaint handling exceeded consumer expectations, the consumer was almost as likely to repurchase as if there had never been a problem (TARP 1995*a*: 18).

Similarly the implementation of anti-discrimination measures such as AA and EEO regimes may increase the efficient utilization of underused labour resources. An organization that refuses to promote its best women because they are women is investing its human capital foolishly. Occupational health and safety regimes can reduce costs by reducing problems and accidents that shut down production (Gunningham 1984: 320). This accomplishment is vividly illustrated in coal mines where productivity and safety are positively correlated (Braithwaite 1985: 169).[12] The evidence is compelling that 'pollution often reveals flaws in the product design or production process'; processes that produce wastes harmful to the environment are generally also inefficient so that improving environmental performance is often cost neutral (Porter & van der Linde 1995: 122). Porter and van der Linde (1995) see this as an instantiation of a general principle that business now accepts—that innovation can improve quality and lower cost simultaneously.

Institutional access to justice policies could also engender higher productivity from workers who appreciate being treated more justly, and higher satisfaction from customers/employees/students who prefer to get justice within an everyday setting rather than having to go to an external forum. This is consistent with Fisse and Braithwaite's (1993) argument that corporations ought to be made initially responsible for doing justice to corporate criminals within their own organizations. Their evidence suggests that in some cases employees feel that they receive a fairer deal from employers' corporate justice systems (which handle a massive volume of informal adjudication of criminal allegations such as employee theft) than from the state. They compare this with a literature (consistent with the evidence presented in Chapters 3 and 4) 'showing more generally that citizens who experience informal justice—court-annexed arbitration, plea bargaining and mediation—are more likely to come away with a perception that they have been treated fairly than are citizens who have been dealt with by a court'

[12] But compare Hopkins's (1995: 140–57) reading of the data on coal mine safety and productivity that suggests this is not always true.

(1993: 170; see also Lind & Tyler 1988). This in itself may improve competitiveness and efficiency since employees and others who feel they are treated fairly by their employer may also be more cooperative with company (or government) efforts to restructure.[13]

Finally, the institutions themselves will have something to gain by having their own policies that allow them to do justice before they are challenged more formally. They will spend less down-time fighting with customers, workers, and creditors and be more trusted by government who will therefore resort less often to direct regulation of the firm. They can decide for themselves how to structure their management and transactions to ensure justice rather than having someone else impose inconvenient schemes or requirements on them. Managers are also more likely to come up with creative ways of providing access to justice that are good for business and fit in with corporate culture than are governments (see Fisse & Braithwaite 1993: 197). This sort of responsiveness to core values of society positions business firms in an advantageous market position while also satisfying government by anticipating some of its demands (Sigler & Murphy 1988: 53). They can win by playing ball well with the new regulatory state (Hood & Scott 1996, Majone 1994).

A regime that promotes compliance

A regime which gives organizations the responsibility for doing justice to those under them and for doing it in their own way will more successfully engender compliance and changes in corporate cultures, policies, and processes to produce more justice than formal legal remedies imposed from above (for all the reasons that dialogic, persuasive mechanisms for justice are more likely to be successful as outlined in Chapter 3). Lawyers and political philosophers are disinclined to think of the challenge of justice as a challenge of management creativity. The idea of institutional access to justice plans is to nurture and harness management creativity to encourage the discovery of a plurality of approaches to increasing justice within institutions and industries. Just as Porter and van der Linde (1995: 120) argue that 'properly designed environmental standards can trigger innovations that lower the total

[13] As Leibfried & Rieger (1995) point out, contrary to expectations, large welfare states are generally more successful in the global market than other states because the safety net they provide means that businesses can more easily restructure in line with competitive pressures with more cooperation from workers who know they will be provided for.

cost of a product or improve its value', so the access to justice policy regime should be aimed at improving access to justice through liberating organizational innovations. The whole purpose could be easily defeated by having formal schemes introduced precipitately from on high.

The Australian affirmative action regime is a useful model in this respect. It was introduced by means of a pilot programme involving twenty-eight private sector companies and three higher education institutions which volunteered to implement affirmative action programmes. Extensive consultation occurred both before and after the pilot programme. The variety of companies participating in the pilot programme meant that a plurality of approaches and courses of action were developed. Later all private sector organizations with over 100 employees and all higher education institutions were required to report on their development and implementation of affirmative action programmes (V. Braithwaite 1993, Ronalds 1991). Valerie Braithwaite's (1992: p. i) study of the implementation of affirmative action regulation in Australia concluded that the way it was introduced and its enforced self-regulatory approach were keys to what success it had.

> In general, the business community saw compliance with the affirmative action legislation as part of being a good corporate citizen. They regarded the legislation as reasonable in that it was not particularly intrusive, it was effective in raising awareness and making employment practices fairer, it was not difficult to implement, and offered favourable outcomes for business.

In the first instance the objective might be simply to create the capacity for quality access to justice policies to be introduced in a wide range of organizations. As in the Australian affirmative action regime, some lead organizations could volunteer to develop models of access to justice.[14] The state could be a moral exemplar by volunteering one of its own departments, and some private companies which are attracted to showing leadership might also volunteer. For those organizations who are already leaders in areas such as consumer complaints schemes and employee natural justice, the development of models for comprehensive access to justice policies would be a matter of building on things that are already happening. Managers and consultants would later be able to draw on the expertise developed and documented by exemplary programme research.

[14] See Eveline (1994) for a study of one Western Australian mining company that volunteered to implement affirmative action ahead of time.

In the second stage, regulation would be introduced requiring all organizations above a certain size to develop and submit their own access to justice policies.[15] In the affirmative action case, the strict deadline for reports and the fact that companies would be named in Parliament if they did not submit a report was of some use (V. Braithwaite 1992: 89). In 1992 a further sanction was added; companies would be ineligible for government contracts if named in Parliament. This process of increasing the seriousness of the sanctions available for non-compliance over time is useful where it might take organizations years to adapt and become committed to a completely new type of regulatory regime. Although the results of the affirmative action regime have so far been limited (Burton 1991), by 1992 it had been successful in getting 95 per cent of organizations required to do so to submit a report (Affirmative Action Agency 1992: 1) and had achieved modest gains in actually getting companies to implement affirmative programmes (V. Braithwaite 1993). Other research has shown that women's managerial representation has increased at a significantly higher rate in firms covered by the legislation than in those that are not, and that affirmative action programmes in general have steadily improved since the regime was introduced (Affirmative Action Agency 1998: 22).

A particularly relevant sanction for failure to implement an effective access to justice policy might be the award of exemplary damages against organizations where an injustice occurs that should have been prevented by a suitable policy. Governments and courts are already willing to use awards of costs to discourage a party causing unnecessary cost and delay. Extra damages might be awarded in a court action arising out of a matter that the court thinks should have been dealt with internally by the losing organization. The extra damages might compensate the plaintiff for the fact that they have had to spend more time and money getting the matter resolved by going to court than if it had been dealt with internally in the first place, and will also be an incen-

[15] Size could be defined by number of employees, as in the affirmative action regime, or by size of budget. The affirmative action regulation requires companies to (1) issue an equal employment opportunity policy statement to all employees, (2) assign responsibility for affirmative action to a senior officer, (3) consult with trade unions, (4) consult with employees particularly women, (5) collect statistics to observe gender by job classification breakdown, (6) review personnel policies and practices, (7) set forward estimates and objectives, (8) monitor and evaluate the programme (see V. Braithwaite 1992: 1). Progress on these eight steps must be reported in a document sent to the Affirmative Action Agency each year.

tive for plaintiffs to make institutions accountable in court for the way they do justice. If it were felt that letting plaintiffs keep the excess would give them a windfall benefit, the excess could be assigned to legal aid or to some other access to justice funding.

The US Congress has already implemented a scheme recommended by the US Sentencing Commission for using decreased fines to encourage corporations voluntarily to put in place compliance programmes to help them avoid committing offences (Gruner 1994: 444, 817–94; see also Bloch 1992). A base fine is adjusted according to a corporation's 'culpability score' in relation to a particular violation:

> Each corporation starts with five points on its culpability score. Judges can add points for aggravating factors . . . Similarly, judges can subtract points for mitigating factors, such as if the organisation has in place an 'effective' compliance program; accepts responsibility for the crime; cooperates with the investigation; or voluntarily reports the offense. Depending on the final score, the actual fine may range from as little as one-twentieth to as much as four times the base fine. Additionally, if a convicted organization with fifty or more employees does not have an effective compliance program in place the Guidelines require that the organization be placed on probation until it implements such a program. (Harvard Law Review 1996: 1785–6)

By mid-1995 208 organizations had been sentenced under the guidelines. Only one was found by the court to have an effective compliance programme, and only three others bothered to claim that they had such a programme. Fourteen per cent were ordered to implement compliance programmes and sixty-one per cent were placed on probation (Harvard Law Review 1996: 1786–7). Yet there is evidence that the guidelines have had some of the effects desired; a survey of 300 US businesses found that almost 45 per cent added vigour to their compliance programmes because of the guidelines and another 20 per cent added compliance programmes (Harvard Law Review 1996: 1787). However, only about 40 per cent used audits to check their own compliance (Harvard Law Review 1996: 1788). Similarly in Britain the existence of a self-regulatory system for avoiding risk can be a defence to offences of strict liability in consumer protection and trading standard cases (Scott 1995),[16] and in Australian trade practices case law the existence of a compliance programme is a mitigating factor in the assessment of penalties.[17]

[16] *Tesco* v. *Nattrass* [1972] AC 153.

[17] TPC 1995*a*: 8–9, *Trade Practices Commission* v. *TNT Australia Pty Ltd.* (1995) ATPR ¶ 41-375, *Trade Practices Commission* v. *CSR Limited* (1991) ATPR ¶ 41-076.

The most draconian option is to make it an offence to fail to have an access to justice plan, ultimately punishable by corporate capital punishment – withdrawal of the firm's licence or charter. As draconian as this sounds, enforcement action up to licence revocation can already be taken in relation to a variety of types of business (including professionals such as lawyers). For example, some US states effectively do this with access to justice for nursing home residents. Unless nursing homes come up with effective plans for improving access of residents to rights such as freedom of movement and choice of treatment, enforcement action up to licence revocation can be taken (Fogg 1994: ¶ 200).

Improving access to justice in other domains

Part of the access to justice problem has been that access to justice resources have been under pressure from so many directions that it has been difficult for them to deliver everything. This is especially true of state legal aid resources. The proposed fifth wave expands access to justice by putting much of the onus for providing access to justice in relation to institutional power on the institutions involved. The state must continue to prioritize the areas which really need state access to justice resources. This includes the state responsibility to continue to support the infrastructure of formal justice, but it will be especially important to target the access to justice problems of those who suffer domination in non-institutional settings. The most important neglected problem is how to improve justice for women and children within the family, the smallest, yet most ubiquitously powerful unit in post-industrial societies.

While much can be accomplished through access to justice plans for greater equality for women who work for or are victimized by large organizations, these are not the only, or perhaps even the primary sites for unjust treatment of women (and children). The problems within families especially of women and children ought to be a priority for state access to justice spending. At the apex of the pyramid this would mean improving the availability of legal aid for formal justice for matters that concern women and children and continuing to improve the way the law and formal processes treat women and children. It might also mean improving funding for women's and children's legal services which take important test and other cases, and lobby for improvements in law and court procedures. At the base it should involve prioritizing funding for women's and youth refuges, crisis centres, and counselling services, and in the middle it would involve continuing to work for better-quality mediation schemes in family law matters.

'Fifth wave' access to justice reform might also have a beneficial effect on institutional domains other than large organizations through modelling, even if they are not under legislative obligations to develop access to justice policies. Schemes developed by larger organizations would inevitably become available to citizens in a variety of other arenas as well. For example industry-wide consumer complaint schemes developed by larger organizations as their legislative duty would also be available to the customers of smaller businesses. Smaller businesses often naturally follow the lead of larger businesses, suggesting that internal access to justice policies developed and found to be successful in large organizations might eventually be adopted as standard in smaller organizations as well. Indeed smaller businesses are often dependent on larger organizations as suppliers, distributors, or customers (some even model themselves on larger businesses in order to become more attractive takeover targets) so that an access to justice regime which required or encouraged large institutions to ensure that the businesses with which it dealt also had access to justice policies might help increase access to justice.[18]

Apart from the direct effects that the development of access to justice policies in large organizations might have on small organizations, the development of capacity and know-how in relation to grass-roots justice schemes would also have a positive effect. For example developing benchmarks and quality indicators for intra-organizational access to justice policies in large organizations could also be adapted for use in evaluating and accrediting ADR schemes developed by community groups. Social movements which developed and advocated ADR strategies within organizations could use the same know-how in developing neighbourhood and family alternative justice processes; the consumer movement and unions would be as relevant in finding solutions to problems with small businesses as with larger companies. The time might come when lawyers realize that in the era of the new regulatory state it is time to facilitate modelling explicitly by establishing an ISO committee to commence work towards an international access to justice voluntary standard grounded in the philosophy of continuous improvement and publicly reported audit of outcomes.

[18] This approach is taken in quality assurance schemes where to assure its own quality a company must ensure that its suppliers are also quality-certified. Hopkins (1995: 69–72) found that larger businesses often required smaller subcontractors to meet high occupational health and safety standards.

Mandated restorative justice programmes in schools could teach all students how to claim and to do justice in ways that might be translated into myriad families, community groups, workplaces, and commercial organizations, small and large, when the students leave school. Indeed education for doing justice informally, and education about legal norms, rights, and responsibilities for all, are linchpins of successfully improving the access to justice culture of a society. It is often said that there should be more civics education and more law in the curriculum; an implication of the research reported here is that there should be more law *and* more informal justice education in the curriculum for the masses while there should be less law and more justice in law students' curricula so that access to justice becomes the domain of the people, not just of the profession. One way to ensure that the justice lessons learnt in large organizations like companies, government departments, and schools begin to be translated into other smaller institutions like families, clubs, and small business might be to develop educational materials targeted at these groups, teaching and encouraging them to deal with their own justice problems internally.[19]

ENSURING THE QUALITY OF ORGANIZATIONAL CULTURES OF JUSTICE

Dangers of institutional access to justice strategies

There are dangers in allowing institutions to be solely responsible for access to justice arrangements for those over whom they exercise power. Those arrangements may not provide access to justice at all, or the 'justice' they provide may replicate patterns of domination and oppression already established in the culture of the organization. Indeed access to justice options offered by institutions may often magnify the problems of informal justice discussed in Chapter 4 because of the inbuilt and obvious inequality between the grievant and the institution within which they make their claim. Laura Nader (1979: 1006) summarizes a number of studies of complaints made to organizational complaints schemes and concludes,

> Instead of providing easy access to swift relief, many of the programs obstruct the complainants' path with complex procedures and repeated delays. Some fail

[19] See Nelsen (1996) for an example of the sorts of materials that might assist families to do justice.

to disclose to the complainant the steps necessary in order to process a grievance; some department stores even hide their customer-service offices from view. Intermediary organisations are often understaffed, underfinanced and overworked, and the resulting backlogs and inefficiencies can discourage consumers from pressing their complaints. There is evidence that some organisations deliberately dissuade individuals from pursuing relief. In sum, complaint-processing methods often make it so difficult for complainants to persist that they are likely to 'lump it,' and even likely to avoid raising claims in the future.

Edelman et al. (1993) show that internal complaint handlers reconstruct employees' civil rights complaints as depoliticized management concerns, that their complaints handling procedures lack fundamental due process protections and are unconcerned with issues of party inequality and with elaborating standards of discrimination. Finkle and Cohen (1993: 113) criticize American laws which induce manufacturers to provide ADR for consumers for favouring manufacturers and not being well supervised by governments. A policy of decentring legalism and encouraging institutions to develop their own access to justice strategies could be dangerous if it means that the indigenous ordering of management perpetuates domination and oppression up the pyramid. The aim of a fifth wave of access to justice reform must therefore be not just to create more private justice options, but to check domination in those that already exist.

As Finkle and Cohen (1993: 113) conclude from their research on Better Business Bureaux in Canada and the USA, 'It is possible to design a process which is paid for by sellers and that appears to be even-handed.' Yet it will take great vigilance. The development of standards and best practice for access to justice schemes from the bottom up by those who are actually implementing them can improve their quality, as can external supervision by independent complaints handlers, courts, lawyers, and representatives of social movements. The aim, as outlined in Chapter 4, is that as legal norms go down the pyramid, and communal and indigenous orderings go up, justice becomes part of everyday transactions and relationships within organizations.

Developing standards from best practice

Quality standards for access to justice policies based on best practice would nurture and take advantage of organizational creativity in developing justice schemes, thus strengthening the upward flow of indigenous institutional orderings that do justice rather than injustice. Accreditation or quality assurance schemes might be introduced, and independent audits imposed as a regulator of the quality of access to justice policies. Each year organizations might be required to publish their access to justice plans including the objectives at which they are aimed, performance indicators, and audit results.[20] One Australian insurance company has voluntarily introduced just such measures to ensure the quality of its consumer justice scheme: following the example of the British Citizens' Charter movement, AAMI has produced a Consumer Charter that sets out exactly what customers can expect of the company in terms of accessibility of claims decision-makers, privacy, how customers' grievances will be handled, and other matters. The company promises to pay a $25 penalty to their customers whenever one of the seventeen guarantees in the charter is not fulfilled. It has hired independent auditors annually to audit its performance in complying with the charter including the consumer complaint scheme and the payout of $25 penalties and publishes the results (AAMI 1997, Smith 1997). The charter was produced in consultation with employees and customers and is updated every year.

External oversight of internal access to justice

A crucial aspect of an effective internal access to justice mechanism will be that the organization provides access to an external mechanism, and ultimately to the law, if claimants do not feel that justice has been done internally. Since internal institutional justice schemes can be criticized for being inherently biased in favour of the powerful organization that operates them, it will be no use introducing internal justice schemes if they are cut off from pyramids of access to justice strategies, which reach up to the apex of formal (external) justice.

In the first instance it might be necessary for institutions to ensure that citizens can go to an independent informal tribunal, ombudsman, or industry complaints scheme. Membership of an association that provides tribunals or an ombudsman may be an access to justice requirement, as membership of the Telecommunications Industry Ombudsman scheme mentioned above is for Australian telecommunications carriers. Ultimately institutional access to justice must be subject to the justice of law. Courts will naturally exercise oversight over

[20] Performance indicators might include things like the results of surveys of complainant satisfaction.

the adequacy of internal justice arrangements if people have sufficient opportunities to go to formal justice when they are not satisfied with private justice. Even Laura Nader (1979: 1020) recognizes that keeping channels of access to formal justice available can make non-judicial internal organizational justice alternatives work better:

> Courts should be available, especially in cases in which the parties have unequal power; parties with relatively equal power are more likely to resolve disputes without the aid of the judiciary. Access to court for parties of unequal power could itself shape opportunities for satisfactory settlement without the exercise of legal authority. Even now, settlements of claims that could have been resolved legally almost universally reflect the level of awards available in small claims court. Expanding judicial relief for minor claims could lead to better nonjudicial solutions.

Even in the fifth wave of justice it remains essential that people can go outside the organization to formal means of justice and it will also become important that internal access to justice policies comply with benchmarks from external law, that they be transparent to the state, the legal profession, and citizens by being subject to public reporting of justice processes and outcomes. In sexual harassment cases, courts are willing to look at internal corporate policies to judge whether they contain adequate processes for identifying and dealing with problems (Conte 1994: 349–51, Ronalds 1991: 144). There is no reason why courts could not show a similar interest in examining access to justice policies more generally. In order to facilitate this, an element of institutional access to justice policies might be that the institution provide finances to assist dissatisfied grievants access legal advice and the court system.[21] However it is important that judicial review of organizational access to justice policies be 'flexible, strategic and contextual' (Black 1996: 51). Rather than forcing rigid and legalistic interpretations of principles of natural justice, proportionality, and illegitimacy on organizations, judges, and lawyers should take a reflexive approach in pointing out where the organization has failed and sending the matter back to the organization to come up internally and democratically with its own way to respect rule of law values and implement a solution (see Black 1996).

In Chapter 4 I outlined the four basic principles that legal justice should enforce in informal and indigenous attempts at justice. First, the

[21] Howells (1994: 65) has made a similar suggestion that credit institutions ought to subsidize their debtors' access to financial counsellors since the credit institutions benefit from their services.

threshold right of someone to be treated as a member of the relevant group to whom justice must be done; secondly, procedural fairness or natural justice in contextually appropriate forms; thirdly, the right of all members of the relevant group to participate in the processes by which the group defines further rights; fourthly, any substantive individual or group rights that have been democratically and deliberatively adopted by the whole society. This approach is consistent with Selznick's (1969) conclusions in his famous study of *Law, Society and Industrial Justice* that wherever there is a 'government', whether it be public or private, wherever authority is exercised, the 'law of governance' should be contextually applied. He concludes from his study of law and justice in industrial organizations that 'the primary source of concepts and doctrines to be used in bringing the rule of law to new settings' is the concept of due process that can be applied as needed (Selznick 1969: 273–4).

In Chapter 4 I also argued that substantive principles of the formal law could be used as a resource to penetrate down the pyramid to improve the justice of more informal justice processes. In the case of organizational access to justice policies this might mean that a doctrine such as conscionability affects internal customer dispute resolution. For example, a non-English-speaking migrant might complain to a bank that they did not understand they were mortgaging their home for the sake of finance for their business until they reneged on the loan and the bank tried to sell the house. During informal dispute resolution, the bank's officers might explain through interpreters that the bank needed security to offer the loan and that offering a mortgage over their house was quite normal for small business people in the migrant's position, and that they thought the complainant had understood this. Due process might be scrupulously followed, the migrant might even agree that the bank was acting reasonably to take the mortgage over the house, and the bank might decide not to disregard the mortgage. But a consumer representative who reviewed the bank's dispute resolution outcomes might suggest that the complainant take the case to court, where the court is likely to decide that the mortgage agreement was unconscionable because of the complainant's language disadvantage and resulting pressure they felt during negotiations. The bank might be required to set the complainant back in the position she would have been, had there never been a loan. The bank's dispute resolution officers might be required to take into account whether the complainant was in a disadvantageous bargaining position in future decision-making, and future standard practice for loans officers might include a check that customers sufficiently understand the deal to which they are agreeing.

Finally, a criticism of internal access to justice schemes (as with informal justice generally) is that they individualize and depoliticize conflict and claims. Edelman et al. (1993: 528) found that internal discrimination complaints schemes for employees were 'primarily geared toward repairing and improving management techniques and relations between employees and their supervisors'. The definition of complaints as individual management problems,

> privatises and depoliticises the public right to equal employment opportunity. Individual complaints are rarely linked to public rights and ideals, and the complaint resolution process does not involve public recognition of those rights or public articulation of a standard to which other employees may appeal. Thus, each employee must renegotiate the meaning of discrimination. Further, IDR [internal dispute resolution] is unlikely to have the general deterrent effect that precedent and publicised lawsuits have on at least some employers. (Edelman et al. 1993: 530)

Chapter 4 argued that informal justice need not privatize disputes unduly if it is placed within a context of concern for and awareness of more structural issues. A quality standard for internal schemes and a responsibility of external overseers might be looking for patterns in complaints, identifying causal structures or practices, and making sure something is done about them (Nader 1979: 1007). In many areas there will be the potential for internal or external groups to take an interest in structural issues surrounding the way justice is meted out. A union, a women's network, an environmental group, telecommunications consumer group, or council for civil liberties may be involved in helping to develop access to justice policies, in overseeing the way they are provided, and advocating that structural issues be dealt with. Effective and just internal access to justice schemes must give such groups a voice.

The interaction of lawyers' justice and indigenous institutional justice

Lawyers' justice is desirable precisely because law and formal legal processes are good at providing an external set of norms against which to judge the way that internal grievance processes protect people's rights. Lawyers might therefore be constructively involved in helping to draw the benefit of law down the pyramid from the apex of formal justice to enhance internal access to justice policies.[22]

In order to preserve the value of informal internal orderings for access to justice, however, we must be careful that penetration does not become domination. Since professionalized justice still has a monopoly of legitimacy, and lawyers have successfully claimed a non-accountable status over large areas of their work, informal justice can easily be captured or co-opted by groups of legal professionals. As Fisse and Braithwaite (1993: 175–6) warn,

> If the law becomes excessively interventionist in proceduralising private justice systems, it creates a hazardous mismatch between the design of private justice and the patterns of particular corporate cultures: it jeopardises that very contextual responsiveness that attracts disputants to informal justice.

If external legal culture will be important in ensuring informal access to justice polices to protect rights, an internally democratic culture and good management practice will be essential to ensure those policies provide accessible, informal processes that have meaning for those they are meant to benefit. Employees, customers, and students need to be involved, as individuals and groups, in making and implementing the policies if they are to find them useful. Just as the involvement of women in developing EEO policies has been demonstrated to be a crucial factor in successfully changing the culture of organizations for affirmative action (V. Braithwaite 1992: 53), so the development of internal justice options must be based on the participation of those they are supposed to benefit.

Contests, privileges and plural professionalisms

As Mnookin and Kornhauser (1979: 986) conclude from their study of lawyers' roles in divorce settlements, the primary function of the legal system ought to be to facilitate private ordering and dispute resolution, not to take it over. Mnookin and Kornhauser (1979: 986) conclude that although 'the participation of lawyers in the divorce process may . . . lead to more disputes and higher costs without improving the fairness of outcomes', lawyers may also facilitate negotiation by minimizing disputes, discovering outcomes preferable to both parties, and increasing

[22] Sigler & Murphy (1988: 93) suggest that corporate lawyers 'form a natural compliance constituency' within companies encouraging them to comply with the letter and spirit of the law.

opportunities for resolution outside of court while ensuring that outcomes reflect legal norms (see also McEwen et al. 1994: 182, 183). In the access to justice policy regime, the goal of lawyers and formal legal processes would be limited to encouraging and supporting informal justice within organizations without allowing legal culture to become impotent. It is better to have robust mutual influence of strong legal culture and strong indigenous ordering in preference to both being weak, or one being so weak as to be neutralized by the other.

If 'law is largely developed, shaped, interpreted and manipulated by that specialised group of experts we know as lawyers' (Shamir 1995: 113–14) the growth of access to justice policies presents the potential for a deregulation of lawyers' work, the opening of a new 'jurisdiction' which invites a re-evaluation of lawyers' relationships with corporate culture and management. The success and quality of institutional access to justice policies will depend to a large extent on the development of non-legal professionalisms, a deeper deregulation of the ability to advise companies and their stakeholders on how to both comply with the law and ensure justice is done in dispute handling.

Both Valerie Braithwaite (1992) and Lauren Edelman et al. (1993: 501) show that the effectiveness of internal procedures for AA and EEO depends on the commitments and role of the professionals responsible for them within the organizations and particularly within management. Valerie Braithwaite's (1992: 94) data showed particularly that the involvement of AA officers in networks of support was an important factor in their effectiveness in changing corporate cultures. Similarly, as occupational health and safety and environmental auditing became professionalized, standards improved because responsible officers developed another source of knowledge and support outside their employer institution. Thus Rees (1988: 228) highlights the importance of a professional safety movement in improving occupational health and safety regulation and compliance within organizations:

> Guided by a distinct body of professional commitments, ideas and aspirations—Safety Management—Safety Department officials converted the workers' compensation system into a safety management tool, not only to highlight job site accident costs, but more importantly, to facilitate consideration of occupational safety as a significant factor of production.

The Regulatory Affairs Professionals Society in the pharmaceutical industry with 4,000 members worldwide and the Society of Consumer Affairs Professionals in Business in the USA, Australia, and a number of other countries are other examples of such organizations. In Europe private sector ombudsmen have met and drawn up their own criteria of the standards which a body must attain before it should be entitled to use the term 'Ombudsman' (Birds 1994: 106, James 1997).[23]

An important question is whether it is possible to replicate with access to justice professionalism what is being accomplished with EEO professionalism—a professionalism where both lawyerly and non-lawyerly voices (such as feminist human resource management voices) are prominent, and contributing to the development of innovative access to justice programmes. This will require the nurture and protection of non-lawyer expertise in preventive, proactive justice procedures. It may require the reform of enduring corporate structures: just as various conventions have grown up to protect the independence of auditors and general counsel, so should the place of 'justice' constituencies within the corporation be protected. The human resources person responsible for internal dispute resolution of employee complaints might be afforded the same status, independence and ability to report directly to the board as the General Counsel. The board audit or compliance committee might have its functions expanded to include access to justice. In some regulatory regimes, companies have been legislatively required to appoint a compliance committee or a senior manager with compliance responsibilities.[24] They could be required to appoint committees or managers with access to justice responsibilities. Non-lawyers within organizations who will be involved in delivering access to justice should also be protected from potential disadvantage because they are not legal professionals (for example through lack of legal professional privilege attaching to communications with them, or through the traditional legal profession's monopoly on 'legal advice'). One option is for the legal profession's monopoly over legal advice and legal professional privilege to be abolished; another is for it to be widened—so that a wider circle of actors can both give legal advice and enjoy privilege in respect of it.

[23] Since this is a purely voluntary association, not all officers called 'ombudsman' actually comply with these standards.

[24] For example the Australian Managed Investments Bill 1997 requires entities that wish to operate a managed investment scheme to have a compliance plan and a compliance committee.

CONCLUSION

This chapter has explored one path to modestly improving citizens' access to justice by simultaneously (1) moving responsibility for creating and financing a large proportion of day-by-day justice options from the state to the organizations in which they occur, and (2) using law to facilitate the doing of justice by non-legal institutional orderings. Requiring private and public organizations above a certain size to develop their own access to justice policies may seem to divert the justice agenda from the crucial and expensive task of improving the court system, legal aid, and the accessibility of lawyers' justice. But while increasing access to law may appear an attractive route to justice, the lesson of Chapter 4 was that it is more effective to improve the integration of legal justice with other forms of justice, so that indigenous orderings become more just.

Edelman et al. (1993: 531) concluded from their study of the implementation of EEO and AA principles within organizations that basic legal norms might infuse and change organizational cultures, but that management practices and indigenous orderings will always affect and change their implementation:

> Even in its peripheral role, *law gradually modifies managerial norms and discourse*; although organisations do not adopt formal legal standards for discerning discrimination, civil rights law has solidified managers' attention to fairness and consistency in organisational governance. But at the same time the infusion of organisation values in internal dispute resolution produces a transformation of civil rights in the workplace. As courts review and (in some cases) legitimate organizational actions and the results of dispute handling, *the symbolic structures that employers create to demonstrate compliance become the vehicles for the infusion of organizational norms and values into law.* Thus, once in the organizational realm, law cannot contain its own appropriation; rather it is shaped and reshaped by management ideology and discourse. (emphasis added)

Where organizational adoption of legal norms is influenced purely by the dominating indigenous orderings of management, justice may not be done. Where legal norms also provide a set of due process and participatory norms which management must meet (see Black 1996, Fisse & Braithwaite 1993: 176, and the discussion above), the conditions are set for creating internal processes which meet the needs of the citizens who have helped to create them. Such mutual interpenetration up and down the pyramid (see Fig. 4.3) helps to create a culture of access to justice in which lawyers, consumer complaints professionals, industrial relations professionals, unions, women's networks, and consumer groups all contribute relevant voices to the way deliberative democracy becomes embedded in our organizations.

9 Lawyers in the Republic of Justice

INTRODUCTION

The main principle for regulatory reform of lawyers that withstands all the normative, phenomenological, and structural challenges of the iterated adjustment employed in the previous chapters is a process of deliberation about how to regulate in which the substantive access to justice concerns of the community are brought to bear on the profession. It is not a model that privileges either the profession or state regulatory institutions. Rather lawyers' regulation would focus on enhancing the culture of legal professionalism in a way that is both subject to and constitutive of deliberative democratic justice. What would the culture of legal professionalism look like in a republic of justice? The first half of this final chapter summarizes the findings of the previous chapters to show how understanding lawyers through the prism of a theory of justice renews the theory of legal professionalism, making it relevant to contemporary democracies. The second half looks through the prism from the other side: it asks what the practical analysis of the world of lawyers and access to justice institutions can contribute to the political theories of deliberative democracy of Habermas (1996) and Pettit (1997). The pragmatist's project of iterated adjustment of the explanatory and the normative requires that the abstract reason of political philosophy be informed by the facts of real-life institutional experience. The detailed study of law and lawyers in this book should challenge political theorists to spend more time considering what law, lawyers, and state legal institutions can*not* do, and more time theorizing beyond them to the practice of justice in many rooms. Just as clients and community are bound to disappointment if they expect lawyers' justice to deliver social justice, so is contemporary normative political theory misguided in its faith in the statist promise of formal law.

LAWYERS THROUGH THE PRISM OF JUSTICE

Legal professional citizenship in the republic of justice

Ordinary citizens turn to law when they fail to solve disputes and problems of violence on their own and they find they have no other resources to bring to bear against domination (as Merry 1990 found). They rely on lawyers being available to help them when they need to use the law (or when the law is used against them) and will complain if they are not served well, if the charges are unaffordable, or if they see lawyers helping other clients achieve unjust goals (see Chapter 2). It is a fundamental contribution to democracy to ensure that regulatory arrangements for lawyers are based upon the insight that lawyers are intermediaries in citizen attempts to use law to ensure that accepted social and political ideals order their lives together. It fits well with traditional functionalist theories which see lawyers as the trustees of the cultural tradition of law, the intermediate mechanism between the organs of the state and individual citizens (Durkheim 1992, Parsons 1954*b*; cf. Brint 1994). But I have also shown that the regulatory practices of legal professional associations and disciplinary authorities have historically tended to disclaim any explicit responsibility for justice. Instead they focused on the high-profile problem of trust account fraud, and on enforcing restrictive advertising and practice rules. They generally ignored the problems of bad service and overcharging that most trouble clients and community. To this extent, the regulatory theory of the legal profession proposed here is also consistent with modern critiques of the profession that see it as engaged in a collective project of market control and status attainment, and individual projects of domination of clients or blind service to the existing social order (Abel 1988*a*, 1989*a*, Larson 1977).

The rhetoric of 'access to justice' is a normative language that can appeal to community, government, and profession alike in the design of regulatory arrangements for lawyers. It provides an ideal of resilient, secure freedom that fits well with political theories that give justice procedures a prominent place in the design of the socio-polity (e.g. Pettit 1993, 1997). It is an ideal of constitutionalism and deliberative democracy in which the procedures that allow citizens to participate in and contest decisions (of public officials and private powers) are what assures freedom and justice.

Access to justice is a fundamental democratic ideal imperfectly put into practice in a world where it has been inadequately buttressed by resilient institutions (see Dunn 1994). Four waves of reform have been employed over the last thirty years to improve on this record: legal aid reform, public interest law, alternative dispute resolution, and competition policy. Chapters 3 and 4 argued that the success of the access to justice movement has been constrained by a dominance of lawyers and legal justice. Improving the culture of justice requires the cumulation of the four waves into a pyramid of justice options. The shadow of the law should cover informal justice so that norms of law ameliorate dominations inherent in indigenous ordering, and informal justice that restores relationships takes precedence in time over litigation. Both legal and informal justice should be set in a context of social and political action by groups who seek to change community attitudes and social/political/legal arrangements in ways that individual citizens cannot do on their own. Chapter 8 suggested how the practical implementation of such a vision of access to justice beyond lawyers might begin in the large institutions where we spend much of our lives. Those institutions could be required to build on the self-regulated justice processes they already operate to develop comprehensive access to justice policies that are permeable to the oversight of law and the just demands of social and political action. Access to justice means creating a workplace culture in which an employee who uses a wheelchair feels able to appeal to shared norms of respect and equality in asking for a toilet with a curtain rather than a door on their floor (Engel & Munger 1996: 22); it means access to a process through which they can pursue their request higher up if it fails in the first instance; and it might mean involvement in a group of disabled workers who proactively advocate and educate for their rights within the company and outside it. It will only rarely mean using court processes to establish rights either individually or as a group, although legal norms might be invoked in advocacy and education and may condition informal relationships.

The access to justice ideal is refreshed when justice in the courtroom gives way to justice in many rooms. Notions of legal professionalism are also revitalized, not by giving lawyers a dominance they do not deserve, but by lending lawyers and what they do the significance of the wider framework of justice and democracy to which they contribute in part. Scholarly theories of the profession have tended to concentrate on the nature of relationships between individual lawyers and clients (Rosenthal 1977, Sarat & Felstiner 1995), the communal socialization of the profession (Dingwall & Fenn 1987, Durkheim 1992, Goode 1957), or the monopolistic strategy of extracting market privileges and social status (Abel 1988*a*, 1989*a*), rather than on the ways lawyers contribute to the constitution of a just community (see Halliday & Karpik 1997: 15). These have been odd priorities for theorizing. In this book I have addressed the 'far more consequential' question of when lawyers will contribute to the constitution of a just socio-polity (see Halliday & Karpik 1997: 60).

A major exception to lack of interest in lawyers' contribution to building the socio-polity is the liberal vision of lawyers as acting autonomously to constitute the separation of powers, to defend the rights of citizens against the power of the state, and to safeguard the rule of law. This conception features prominently in the ideology of many legal professions around the world, as Halliday and Karpik show (1997).[1] On this view lawyers act as leaders of civil society in its efforts to moderate the executive and legislative power of the state. So Tocqueville saw lawyers 'as the most powerful existing security against the excesses of democracy' (1961: 321, 328) because of their 'instinctive love of order and of formalities' (1961: 322, 324) demonstrated in their defence of the rule of law. Halliday and Karpik examine autonomous collective political action by the legal professions (and sometimes the absence of it) in times of political unrest in Germany, France, Britain, and the USA. They show how these political projects have been pursued in addition to market projects (see also Halliday 1987) to form a pillar of modern political liberalism.

It is crucial to have a legal profession which contributes to justice by a self-identity which requires it to advocate for individuals against state power, to defend separations of powers crucial to liberty (including the independence of the judiciary), and to use its expertise to help ensure the state is doing a good and fair job of governing (Halliday 1987, Halliday & Karpik 1997). Yet justice as I have conceived it requires more than that: it also requires a legal profession grounded and oriented by a notion of justice which gives it a role in checking private power, and which gives lawyers' day-to-day work in solving problems and injustices significance in contributing to a just socio-polity. The liberal conception of lawyers' role puts too much emphasis on limiting state power to ground a regulatory theory for the profession which

[1] As Chapter 7 mentioned, Halliday (1987) also develops a political conception of 'civic' legal professionalism which could help the state to govern effectively through the use of its expertise to help define state powers and improve the legal system. Brint (1994) also suggests that the intelligentsia might retain some ideals of traditional 'social trustee' professionalism promoting autonomy and social responsibility which can contribute to the maintenance of liberalism.

could govern lawyers' whole working lives. Indeed, as we have seen, the liberal tradition taken alone can also justify a lawyer in advocacy against the state for wealthy interests who seek to use loopholes and legalism to evade the public-regarding purpose of just laws.

The US republican tradition of the practice of law valorized by Luban (1988) and particularly Gordon (1985, 1988, 1990) gives lawyers a role in moderating not only the influence of the state, but also the power of rapacious private actors. The early American Federalists saw lawyers as particularly suited to being 'impartial arbiters' between private actors as well as checks on the power of the state (Madison et al. 1987: 234–5; see also Gordon 1985). In this vision lawyers are seen as important because they carry the rule of law not only in the ideology and rhetoric they wheel out when they engage in collective political action (as Halliday & Karpik 1997 argue), but also because it is (or ought to be) institutionalized in their day-to-day work practices. Counsel for an insurance company who competently and fairly advises on how to settle motor vehicle or occupational health and safety claims according to law has not only done his or her job, but has contributed to the just functioning of ordinary social relations. He or she has routinely and unspectacularly relieved injustice for a family who must otherwise suffer poverty. But if the lawyer feels that every penny must be saved and every technicality exploited for the benefit of company profits, the socializing and regulatory institutions of the profession have failed to teach him or her what being a lawyer means.

The rhetoric of the Federalist lawyers of the early American republic and their Progressive counterparts of the late nineteenth century described by Gordon and Luban might have been overblown, yet they had a point: lawyers are significant as the cultural bearers of lawyers' justice, the public values inhering in the law that attempt to bind society together justly. Lawyers' work partially constitutes the republic of justice by daily routines which help clients solve everyday problems, challenge private dominations, and stand against state power, as well as in collective political projects which defend the rule of law and make statements about the constitutionality of particular laws and the legality of certain actions. The task of regulatory reform of the profession is to design a regulatory strategy which will ensure that justice is nurtured by a rule of law culture which works itself out in lawyers' daily practices.

Chapters 5 to 7 attempted to develop such a theory. Chapter 5 found that lawyers already hold a specific set of access to justice ideals that citizens might expect them to fulfil to contribute to a wider justice agenda; the advocacy ideal, the social responsibility ideal, the justice ideal, and the ideal of collegiality. The regulatory theory of the legal profession developed in Chapters 6 and 7 gave them a role as citizens within a wider socio-polity alongside government and community groups in deliberating about how they would be regulated. Chapter 6 used theory, empirical evidence, and data from the Australian experience of legal professional reform to show that a deliberative process which keeps open the option of some self-regulation is both possible, and more effective, at achieving long-lasting change than the imposition of competition or accountability reform without listening to the profession. Chapter 7 put these findings into a deliberative model of regulation that takes seriously both the legal profession's citizenship and its domination potential and therefore uses a mix of strategies of self-regulation, communal socialization, competition, state regulation, and community accountability.

The linchpin for ensuring that lawyers contribute to justice is a deliberative process in which the expectations of the community and the knowledge and experience of the legal profession are brought to bear on one another so that a suitable set of regulatory strategies and organizational structures are developed. The 1983 process by which the American Bar Association adopted new *Model Rules of Professional Conduct* is perhaps an example of how not to do this; a mixture of intra-professional politics, deal-making between professional interest groups, and apparently democratic deliberation among lawyers that excluded the public dominated the development of a model set of rules which are gravely criticized but set the agenda for most lawyer regulation in the USA today (Schneyer 1992). A better, yet equally political (and at times equally divisive), example might be the process of reform in the Australian state of New South Wales where the reports of law reform commissions, antitrust enforcers, and community concerns set the agenda, forcing the profession into a process of negotiation with the state resulting in a new regulatory structure (including significant lay involvement and independent oversight of lawyer practices) which is not perfect, but is broadly acceptable to profession, government, and community.

Pyramids of justice

The suggestions for the regulation of the legal profession in Chapters 6 and 7 of this book implement the arguments of Chapters 3 and 4 that long-lasting change and compliance with norms are more likely to occur where dialogic means of social control are used first than when coercive and formalistic ones are applied indiscriminately. Both in the process of reform (a deliberative process) and in its outcome (a regulatory mix in which the profession is brought to account to community and government and where government and community hear what the profession has to say) there is reliance on informal and indigenous orderings in advance of resort to more coercive mechanisms of control.

This theory for regulating the legal profession turns out to be just one pyramid of justice (see Fig. 7.1) for one particular substantive area. Yet the institutions for regulating the legal profession are more than an example of justice in action. The institutions of the legal profession bear a unique relationship to justice in that they can help constitute or help destroy other institutions of access to justice. Fig. 9.1 represents how a pyramid of regulatory strategies for the legal profession contributes to building up more general pyramids of access to justice, at the same time that access to justice pyramids provide the context for deliberating about the regulation of the profession. Indeed the two pyramids pictured in Fig. 9.1 are mirror images of each other (and they could be pictured either way around). Community accountability (at the tip of the pyramid of lawyer regulation) funnels wider access to justice considerations into the profession's own self-regulation and communal practices. Lawyers' justice (at the tip of the access to justice pyramid), which was defined in Chapter 4 as requiring adherence to basic principles of due process, the right to participation in the formulation of further rights, and basic human rights adopted by a whole society, ultimately regulates the indigenous or communal orderings on which most justice (and injustice) depends.

In both cases external norms and communal orderings regulate and balance each other. External norms of access to justice regulate lawyers but are themselves partly constituted by communal orderings in the many 'rooms' in which justice is done in the wider society (Galanter 1981). External norms of formal justice regulate indigenous justice in many rooms, but are constituted by the communal ordering of the legal profession which bears the primary responsibility for carrying the traditions of formal justice. Checking and balancing between profession and community create the channels for justice to flow so that the profession is more likely to contribute adequately to justice, and communal orderings are more likely to become just. It is this funnelling action on which the deliberative processes of regulation of the legal profession described in Chapter 7 rely.

For example, when responsiveness to community concerns began to force national legal professions to admit a small number of women to practise in the 1960s and 1970s, some set up women's legal services, invented new legal categories for the benefit of women (such as sexual harassment; MacKinnon 1979), and used them in their advocacy for women clients. The actions of a small community of feminist lawyers made lawyers' justice more responsive to women's needs. The new legal norms those lawyers created eventually percolated down the pyramid into informal justice processes (such as sexual harassment prevention in human resource management policies within companies and universi-

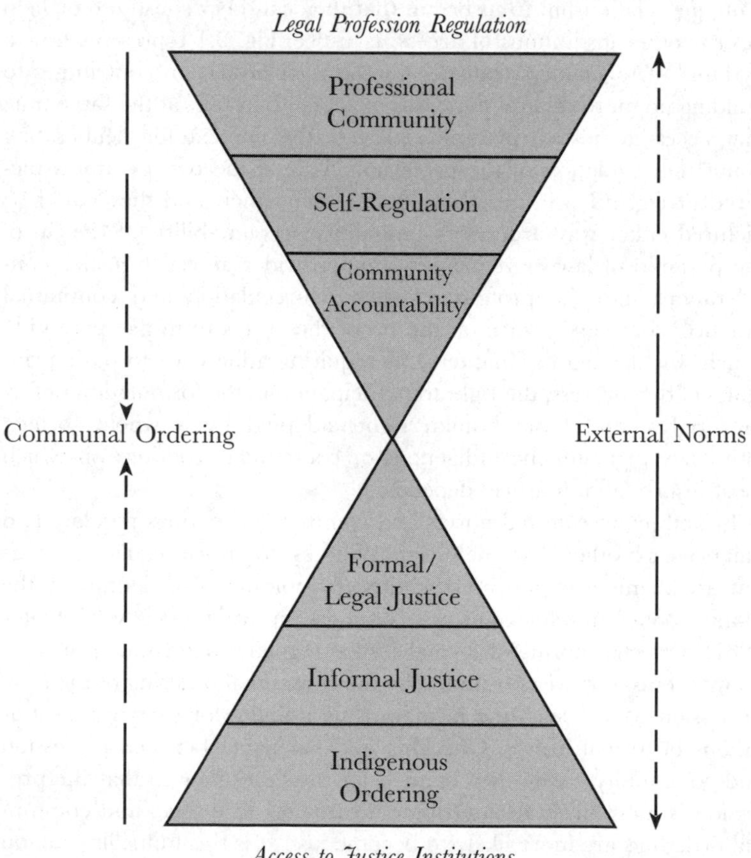

Fig. 9.1 Interplay between access to justice institutions and lawyer regulation

ties) and were also promoted by social movement advocacy in the wider community. Norms of women's equality created by minority feminist lawyers and diffused into the community then looped back up the pyramid into professional practice when law firms themselves became vulnerable to external regulation by the courts and human rights commissions in relation to discrimination and harassment (see Young 1992). Thus changes in law wrought by a small community of feminist lawyers to help their own clients eventually became part of the normative tools with which state and community institutions held the whole legal profession accountable.

This is an ideal model. In most concrete situations either the legal profession will dominate communal orderings and understandings of justice (as some claim is the case in the contemporary USA) or communal orderings will be so strong as to push out the possibilities of legal justice (as regularly occurs in families and workplaces where certain members are discouraged from asserting their legal rights). Deliberative democratic accountability of lawyers is only possible in a republican democracy in which there are many avenues for deliberative justice and in which checks and balances are institutionalized in the design of public and private powers. For example, if the legal profession becomes too arrogant in its service provision and charges, but there is also a strong market, clients will buy services from non-lawyers, forcing lawyers to become more responsive to community concerns in order to compete. Where a workplace or family culture discourages women or workers from asserting their rights, a public sphere in which social movements are encouraged and nurtured might mean that a women's group or industrial advocacy group (which includes lawyers) will take up in legal and political fora the concerns of those who have been silenced in the private sphere of home or work. Journalists will publicize their plight in the media. A state which is willing to step in and hold lawyers accountable to the community when they become too self-interested, or to provide money for individuals or groups to use the courts when they are silenced in their own communities, will counteract the ability of either lawyers or tyrannous majorities to dominate justice.

Halliday and Karpik's (1997) sweeping comparison of the histories of the British, French, German, and US professions shows how hopeless it is to expect lawyers to contribute to the practice of democratic justice if there are no other checks and balances in a democracy. In Britain the modest ability of the profession to act as a restraint on state power is rooted in the long tradition of the bar as an independent institution of civil society with tacit status in a strong but unwritten constitution. In the USA the profession's location between market and state meant that powerful commercial actors who had an interest in a just and independent judicial system underwrote the independence of lawyers from the state early in the century while the strength of the judicial system itself helped the profession to maintain some independence from powerful clients. In France the profession maintained a strong stance against absolutist monarchical power in alliance with the independent parlements, but when the new republican state abolished the parlements, the profession crumbled too. In Germany the profession and the judges only exercised any independence from the civil service from the middle of the seventeenth century. Neither the profession nor the court system was robust enough to withstand the totalitarianism of the Weimar Republic and National Socialist government. Both succumbed together.

CONTRIBUTIONS TO A DELIBERATIVE THEORY OF LAW AND DEMOCRACY

Law and deliberative democracy

The previous section summarized how a deliberative theory of justice can contribute to the understanding of legal professionalism. What can an understanding of law and lawyers contribute to a deliberative theory of justice? Recent political philosophy already takes increasingly seriously the role of law in constituting a just society. As Sunstein (1996: p. ix) writes, 'We are . . . in the midst of a period of enormous enthusiasm for rule-bound justice' particularly in the wake of communism. Indeed much recent theory on deliberative democracy resonates with my analysis of the role of law and regulative institutions in achieving justice (Barber 1984, Dworkin 1986, Habermas 1996, Pettit 1997).

The tradition of freedom under law is an important one in democratic theory. As Barber comments after quoting Rousseau on this topic, 'To obey laws we give to ourselves is in fact a very persuasive definition of democracy' (1994: 264). Chapter 3 has already shown how the republicanism of Pettit construes law as crucial to constituting a society in which freedom is the norm.

> According to the earliest republican doctrine, the laws of a suitable state, in particular the laws of a republic, create the freedom enjoyed by citizens; they do

> not offend against that freedom, even in a measure for which they later compensate . . . As the laws create the authority that rulers enjoy, so the laws create the freedom that citizens share. (Pettit 1997: 35–6)

Yet for republicanism a suitable rule of law is not enough. Law must give support to and be supported by the everyday norms of civil society if it is to make more than a trivial contribution to justice and freedom: 'non-vulnerability can only be guaranteed for each under a law that is internalised by others as a legitimate and welcome form of constraint, not as a forceful imposition that will be systematically resisted and strategically avoided' (Pettit 1997: 252–3). For republicans, the best way for the state to encourage widespread civility, and compliance with the norms enshrined in law, is 'to establish the republican legitimacy of its laws in the public mind, and it can best do this by being an effective, contestatory democracy' (1997: 280).

The process is circular. Law is necessary to advance non-domination, yet it is only effective if it becomes ingrained in the '[just] habits of people's hearts' (Pettit 1997: 241). If the law is to live in everyday interactions and to be supported by cultural norms, it must be contestable and based on the deliberation of the people. Yet law itself is necessary to develop the type of effective, contestatory, or deliberative democracy in which the interests and ideas of the people help formulate the laws. It must ensure that certain public or private powers do not dominate in democratic procedures of deliberation, to provide means by which citizens can contest decisions and actions, and to challenge dominating norms that hold sway in the culture at large.

This circularity or synergy between the law of the state and non-legal norms of decentralized civil society is inescapable for those who seek to understand the role that law can play in building a just society. Krygier (1997) shows how in post-communist societies the success of the rule of law must depend on the extent to which its norms are lived in the culture of a people and in associations of civil society which debate the goodness of the law and ensure that it is kept by government as well as citizens. Tocqueville (1961: 373–8) attributed the vibrancy of democracy in the USA to the fact that even the common people knew the laws and participated in law-making so that legal norms had become a part of their private as well as their public lives: democracy had penetrated into people's 'customs, their opinions, and the forms of social intercourse; it is to be found in all the details of social life equally as in the laws' (Tocqueville 1961: 382). Law and society scholarship, as Chapters 3 and 4 showed, constantly explores the tension between the norms of law and the norms of indigenous ordering and how they either subvert or support one another (e.g. Galanter 1981). Habermas's *Between Facts and Norms* (1996) is likely to become the most influential and detailed normative explication of this synergy between law, deliberation, and institutions of civil society in constituting democracy.

For Habermas, the only norms according to which a socio-polity ought to be organized are those which could be agreed upon in rational discourse (1996: 107). In *Between Facts and Norms* he calls this the 'discourse principle'.[2] However two empirical facts mean that as a matter of practice face-to-face interaction cannot easily be transmitted into deliberation that solves society-wide problems: (1) the problem of oppression and domination which destroys the possibility of free and equal deliberation, and (2) the fact of social complexity which means that we each individually pursue our own 'lifeworlds' in a plurality of social groupings without any overarching worldview (such as religion) to bind us together and allow us to share a common language. 'The limited coordinating power of moral norms in face-to-face interaction cannot be transferred to the integrative functions of large-scale institutions, and this fact presents a limit on the participatory, democratic organization of complex societies' (Bohman 1994: 907). In the terms of Habermas's *Theory of Communicative Action* (1987), the lifeworld (which is made up of everyday culture, civil society, and personality structures) seems to have no effective way of influencing the political and economic systems which govern our lives through power and money.

For Habermas, it is only law that can mediate between these problematic facts and the norms by which we are governed by acting as the 'transmission-belt' between the communicative action of the lifeworld and the administrative power of the political system (Habermas 1996: 448). It is the integrating mechanism[3] that can create and protect the conditions in which deliberation occurs (1) free of domination, and (2) in ways that can have input into the sphere of public decision-making despite social complexity, because it is both coercive and procedural. Only the procedures of law are a sufficient coordinating mechanism to allow everyone to participate in rational debate in a complex society. Only the coercion of law can make this participation possible by ensur-

[2] The discourse principle is in effect a refined application of the idea of the ideal speech situation or communicative action in *The Theory of Communicative Action* (Habermas 1987).

[3] A view akin to that held by Gordon's (1985) Federalist and Progressive lawyers, and also by Parsons (1954*a*, 1954*b*).

ing that citizens have certain fundamental human rights recognized ('private autonomy') as well as the rights that are necessary to allow them to deliberate to make law (to exercise their 'public autonomy') (Habermas 1996: 122–3). Thus as Habermas writes (1996: 8),

> Legal norms of this type make possible highly artificial communities, associations of free and equal legal persons whose integration is based simultaneously on the threat of external sanctions and the supposition of a rationally motivated agreement.

This system of rights must be stable and capable of coercion, and therefore must be promulgated by a constitutional state (Habermas 1996: 133). Yet, with Pettit, Habermas recognizes the problem which lies at the heart of the social science of regulation discussed in Chapter 3: although law is backed by coercion, it cannot achieve even average compliance unless it comes alive in the culture of the people to whom it is addressed (Bohman 1994: 910).[4] For Habermas as for Pettit (1997: 252) this means that the law must be legitimate, it must be capable of meeting the agreement of all citizens in a discursive law-making process that is itself legally constituted.[5] Thus the possibilities of law and deliberation entwine each other in a recursive process wherein deliberation is only possible through the mediation of law, but law itself must be based in deliberation if it is to achieve the goals of making deliberation between free and equal citizens possible:

> The paradoxical achievement of law thus consists in the fact that it reduces the conflict potential of unleashed individual liberties through norms that can coerce only so long as they are recognized as legitimate on the fragile basis of unleashed communicative liberties . . . Social integration thereby takes on a peculiarly reflexive shape: by meeting its need for legitimation with the help of the productive force of communication, law takes advantage of the permanent risk of dissensus to spur on legally institutionalised public discourses. (Habermas 1996: 462)

Like Pettit, then, Habermas's conception of the ideal of human freedom is one of freedom under law. It is an

> idea of autonomy according to which human beings act as free subjects only insofar as they obey just those laws they give themselves in accordance with insights they have acquired intersubjectively. (Habermas 1996: 445–6)

[4] In other words, law must have some support from indigenous orderings or the norms of civil society, if it is to have any effect.

[5] However for Pettit, the notion of deliberation is made more manageable for a large and plural society by saying that decisions and actions need only be contestable, not originally based in deliberation.

One of the practical consequences of this theory for Habermas is that the socio-polity ought to be organized with a centre and periphery of deliberation (a division of labour necessary because of the complexity of society). The centre is the formal decision-making bodies of the constitutional state which ought to be porous to the periphery of the informal public sphere in which the institutions of civil society reign. Discourses developed by institutions of civil society in autonomous public spheres supply legal and administrative discourses with arguments, formulate social needs, and define what issues are relevant at a given moment;

> In the proceduralist paradigm, the public sphere is not conceived simply as the back room of the parliamentary complex, but as the impulse-generating periphery that *surrounds* the political center: in cultivating normative reasons, it affects all parts of the political system without intending to conquer it. Passing through the channels of general elections and various forms of participation, public opinions are converted into a communicative power that authorises the legislature and legitimates regulatory agencies, while a publicly mobilized critique of judicial decisions imposes more-intense justificatory obligations on a judiciary engaged in further developing the law. (Habermas 1996: 442; emphasis in the original)

This need not require all citizens to participate in public deliberation, only a wide enough diversity to ensure that all the rational arguments are considered. Habermas does not theorize how the coercion of law in the service of clients who pay the biggest fees and states whose violence is legitimized can be rendered minimally dominating in practical terms. This is something the model advocated in this book has sought to do with the idea of a pyramid of justice (see Fig. 4.3) in which resort to coercion at the peak of the pyramid is restrained by giving the 'lifeworld' temporal priority in solving injustices.

The limits of law: does anybody listen?

The policy for improving the institutionalization of access to justice developed in Chapter 4 and illustrated in Chapter 5 depended on insights which are also found to a great extent in the democratic theories of Pettit and Habermas. Pyramids of justice strategies that place law in a dynamic mutually supportive relationship with face-to-face social processes and collective social action take account of the facts (1) that law is not effective unless it penetrates into the customs and habits of everyday social intercourse, and is in turn informed and shaped by them, and (2) that law alone can never achieve justice unless collective and widespread social or political action takes place simultaneously. Indeed for these two reasons I have argued that law should be decentred from discussions of the design of institutions for access to justice; and that the regulatory reform of lawyers should be informed by an access to justice discourse wherein lawyers have been removed from the dominant place. Yet both Pettit and Habermas in their different theories of law and democracy concentrate on deliberation in centralist, statist, or legalistic institutions of justice despite their recognition that there must be more to justice than that.

It is standard for political theorists to focus idealistically on law as an output of the central state political system, without a critical focus on law's actual application or effect on the practice of justice in private and everyday contexts (see Campbell 1993). Law and society scholars who document the legal system's domination of the 'lifeworld' and of the economic system, indeed even mainstream lawyers, are wont to see political theory in the ilk of Pettit and Habermas as starry-eyed about the rule of law. As Chapter 4 showed, the design and reform of practical access to justice policies has also tended to fall into the trap of setting too much store on access to central state justice facilitated by lawyers. Failures of institutional design in practice highlight the places where political and social theorists need to focus more thought.

While political theorists concentrate on asking when state-promulgated law is legitimate, socio-legal research is concerned with the real-life question of when it is effective. The issue, as Krygier (1997: 50) says, is whether anyone 'listens' when law is made. Empirical research on regulation shows that while the symbolism and coercion of state law may be important, the way law filters down to everyday life is partial, may cause reactance, and can easily be made a tool of domination. In response to the limitations of state law in achieving justice, I have advocated a principle of parsimony in the use of law (Chapter 3), a theory of the facilitative role of law in nurturing informal and everyday practices that increase access to justice (Chapters 3, 4, and 8), and the need for law to be supplemented by political and social action for doing justice (Chapter 4).

My findings suggest that we should refine the normative theories of both Pettit and Habermas to develop a more realistic conception of a deliberative democracy in which the limits of law and lawyers are recognized so that (1) justice is done in many rooms and through many means, (2) citizens can share in the government of their communities and in the practice of justice by realistic deliberative participation in local and private institutions, not just in public discourses that feed into central law-making processes, and (3) the limiting of private power is as important as the limiting of public power. The following sections consider in turn each of these iterated adjustments to democratic theory.

Justice in many rooms and through many means

Habermas and Pettit see the link between citizen deliberation and law in terms of political and legal action aimed at affecting formal state law-making in the public sphere.[6] So for Habermas, the crucial process is how institutions of civil society funnel interests and arguments into a state centre of formal deliberation:

> Civil society is composed of those more or less spontaneously emergent associations, organisations, and movements that, attuned to how societal problems resonate in the private life spheres, distill and transmit such reactions in amplified form to the public sphere. The core of civil society composes a network of associations that institutionalises problem-solving discourses on questions of general interest inside the framework of organised public spheres. (Habermas 1996: 367)

My vision refines Habermas's theory by seeing citizen deliberation and formal justice as linked through a variety of means of informal justice and social action. The justice of law filters down to everyday social relations through communitarian means of justice like alternative dispute resolution, or through the way people have learnt to solve problems informally among friends, colleagues, and within commercial relationships. The deliberation which informs central state law-making is not always through participation in groups which have political action as their main aim, but by participation in face-to-face deliberations in a workplace or consumer dispute resolution scheme which forms the lower rung of a pyramid of access to justice options which ultimately feeds into court decision-making or centralized policy-making.

I have argued that central state law should not only facilitate deliberation that feeds back into central law-making, but also deliberation and communicative decision-making which feeds primarily into the

[6] Consistent with my argument in the following sections, May 1996: 76–9 also critiques Habermas for ignoring communitarian, participatory democracy in favour of statist representative political institutions in his later writings.

development of norms of justice within private institutions and groups, even within the context of particular relationships (see Waldron 1991). For example, coercive enforcement of state law is largely irrelevant to protecting children from the terrible injustices that can be inflicted by bullies. Yet good schools nurture cultures of deliberation about the regulation of schoolyard violence; and the empirical evidence is that such dialogic regulation can cut bullying by as much as half (Farrington 1993: 419; see also Olweus 1994, Pepler et al. 1993). Face-to-face deliberation in the school is usually more significant in improving the justice quality of everyday transactions than argument in the legislators' chamber. Political philosophers often neglect to theorize the possibility of the development of indigenous 'law' within institutions for their own use, which may never be the topic of discussion in the centre of public and formal deliberation. They lack an emphasis on the significance of justice in many rooms according to (1) norms that are like law but written by non-state institutions, (2) norms that have evolved spontaneously as part of the culture of an organization or community, and (3) totally contextual non-rule-like judgments that are made in relationships, communities, and institutions about the just thing to do.

Consistent with Habermas and Pettit I have argued that interpersonal dispute resolution mechanisms should be linked with central formal justice through recourse to law when informal justice fails. In political theory the emphasis is usually on how linking deliberation in civil society to formal law improves state law. In my model the focus is on how the linkage can make informal justice more effective and more just to obviate the necessity for recourse to state law. Linking formal state justice to informal justice also addresses the criticisms of informal justice made by writers such as Richard Abel (1981*a*, 1982*a*, 1982*b*) and Laura Nader (1979, 1980) that it privatizes disputes and perpetuates domination. Alternative dispute resolution does privatize disputes, yet informal justice can connect private disputes to their public and legal dimensions by ensuring that participants can always walk out and go to court, by involving an advocacy group in their solution, and by ensuring that an external monitor is noting patterns of injustice and bringing them to public attention.

For example in restorative justice conferences, the realities of domination can be confronted by changing conferences from dyadic individualistic encounters into dialogues between communities of care and by connecting private troubles in individual conferences to public issues and patterns of inequality through the involvement of social movement advocacy groups. Thus a youth advocacy service might see a printout of the outcomes of each week's conferences. When it sees that a young first offender who has admitted graffitiing a shop window has agreed to 200 hours' community service, it might contact the offender and advise him to walk away from the agreement to court where a forty-hour requirement is imposed. A youth advocate might observe another conference where a mother complains that the police used excessive force in arresting her son for car theft and complains that they are targeting him. The advocate might be concerned about this and also the fact that no action has been taken against a major car dealing and repairing company who provided the offender with a list of car models it wanted young people to steal (for parts). The conference might decide that the offender should use his 150 hours' community service helping the youth advocacy service prepare a report which criticizes the police for its discriminatory targeting of young people for arrest and exposing the practices of motor vehicle traders in the city supplying desperate young people with lists of cars to be stolen (see Braithwaite & Parker 1999).[7] In a deliberative democracy in which pyramids of access to justice options are generally available (so that individuals can always walk out of informal justice into the courtroom) and are set within a vital social movement politics, public disputes regularly succumb to private reason and private disputes succumb to public reason. The Abel and Nader critiques of informal justice's privatizing tendencies are one-sided, ignoring the great value of facilitating justice in many rooms according to people's justice and evidencing a public-centred myopia that would be rectified in a refined version of deliberative democratic theory.

I have also argued that in most circumstances cultures of injustice are unlikely to be changed unless the symbolic norms of law are supplemented by effective collective action to educate people about injustice and to change habits and attitudes. Citizens are not born democratic; they must be educated for democracy in a way that includes education in respect for just law, resistance to unjust law, and participation in debates about the content of law (see Barber 1994). The native title rally in the park is as important as the High Court decision in accomplishing changed attitudes to justice for indigenous people. Again the

[7] The second example has a basis in fact. In the early 1990s the Motor Vehicle Theft forum in Sydney, New South Wales, found that one factor in an increase in car thefts was white-collar criminals supplying juveniles with lists of parts that had been ordered by customers. The theft rate dropped by a third in two years following the work of the forum (Braithwaite 1993).

political theories of both Habermas and Pettit seem to focus on the way people's involvement in social movement politics allows their concerns to feed into state law-making and administrative decision-making. I have seen social movement politics as significant for its independent potency in educating citizens for justice. With all its symbolism and apparent significance, court-based action, for example, is mostly impotent in achieving social or political change on its own; Martin Luther King in Alabama had more to do with changing public opinion to support school desegregation than the US Supreme Court in *Brown* v. *Board of Education* (Rosenberg 1991). Thus Sunstein can conclude *Legal Reasoning and Political Conflict* (1996) by pointing out that the role of courts in making decisions of justice will always be secondary to more direct methods of citizen involvement:

> We may thus conclude our account of legal reasoning . . . by reflecting on the extraordinary extent to which large-scale social transformations, in America and elsewhere, have had their foundations in popular rather than judicial convictions; and by insisting that in a well-functioning deliberative democracy, the most important social commitments emerge not from courtrooms, but from the reflective judgments of a nation's citizenry. (Sunstein 1996: 195–6)[8]

Law is a deliberative forum with unique qualities that make it of special importance in facilitating other deliberative fora and ensuring their justice. But the real practice of justice occurs, if at all, as a result of the democratic deliberative participation of citizens in the creation and exercise of norms of justice, not as a result of a law being passed. When law embodies norms of justice, it merely symbolizes what has already been deliberated and decided outside the law-makers' chambers. Indeed this is implicit in Habermas (1996: 135; emphasis in original): 'The law receives its full normative sense neither through its legal *form* per se, nor through an a priori moral *content*, but through a *procedure* of lawmaking that begets legitimacy.' What Habermas calls 'a procedure of lawmaking that begets legitimacy' should be broadly construed to mean a culture of justice which permeates everyday life through communitarian dispute resolution and social action, which is (imperfectly) symbolized in the law, and which the law might be able to enforce, in times of last resort.

[8] Here Sunstein makes up for an even more court-oriented republicanism than Pettit's in *Beyond the Rights Revolution* (1990).

Practically feasible deliberative participation

This broad construal of what is meant by the procedures of deliberation that constitute justice in turn renders the ideal of citizens' participation more practical. Rather than idealizing the involvement of every citizen in the public sphere, a broader conception of deliberative democracy puts forward the more realistic goal that most people will participate in decision-making in one or two small local institutions in which they are interested, while some will also participate in the political sphere of law and policy-making.

Within local settings, participation can be more inclusive and more practical by moving beyond the formal, rule-based reasoning of law and the rationality of a political sphere which privileges certain voices and excludes others. Iris Young writes that 'It is no secret that in actual communication situations in our society, poor, or less educated, or non-professionals, or privatised people are often intimidated by the discourse rules of formal organisations, and their speech is often not taken seriously and deemed rational by these organisations' (Young 1993: 127). She argues for an expanded version of deliberation which she calls 'communicative democracy' which would include more than 'the giving and criticising of reasons for proposals' (1993: 128). It would assume 'a starting point of distance and difference' and include all the communicative acts necessary for reaching first understanding of each other and then agreement. It would include everything necessary to explain cultural meanings, ways of life, and points of view to one another 'through whatever modes of expression they judge will be rhetorically effective', through stories, poems, songs, confrontational protests, jokes, and expressions of passion which might otherwise be discounted as irrational. It is in homes, schools, workplaces, and neighbourhoods, local and highly personalized spaces, that such forms of participation are most achievable. A good theory of democracy should encompass 'communicative' participation in many rooms that overcome the difficulties of deliberation in the public sphere of court and legislature.

One problem with Western justice procedures, for example, is that they are based on interrogation; asking questions (usually adversarially) and demanding honest answers. In many of the world's cultures, such as some Australian Aboriginal cultures, it is rude to ask direct questions (Eades 1992, 1995). What one should do is tell a relevant story about oneself that is likely to elicit a desired account of his or her actions from the respondent. It is quite possible to replace formal criminal trials with restorative conferences for Australian Aboriginal offenders within local communities which abandon the usual opening of asking the offender who has admitted guilt to 'tell us in your own words what happened'. Instead, for an assault conference, the facilitator might start by telling a story about how he or she once got into a fight. Recognition of such a radically different and responsively democratized sense of criminal procedure by the formal legal system would create a mechanism for improving the participation of ordinary Aborigines in significant decision-making far more than the limited participation required by voting (even for an Aboriginal government) or other formal means of self-determination. Restorative justice conferences allow involvement from more people than the formal political sphere can sustain and allow an opportunity for radical self-determination by local communities that have been too often dominated by the colonizers' laws in local issues that really count. New Zealand Maori and Canadian First Nations people are already exercising a measure of self-determination through similar initiatives (Consedine 1997, La Prairie 1995).

Where conceptions of deliberative democracy are broadened like this, Young's communicative democracy in many rooms can percolate into public reason through the type of architecture of deliberative democracy shown in the access to justice pyramid of Fig. 9.1. For example, formal recognition of Aboriginal restorative justice conferences might help ameliorate some of the other aspects of the criminal justice system that oppress. Even where a conference has failed and the case ends up in court, official recognition of Aboriginal restorative justice conferences might encourage magistrates to allow examination of witnesses to proceed in a different way, perhaps in narrative form. At present, one reason Australian Aborigines get arrested for minor crimes so regularly is that they refuse to answer questions from the police: the police think they are rude for failing to answer, the Aborigines think the police are rude for their interrogation in the first place. Through their involvement in conferences and court cases, police might learn more appropriate ways of dealing with indigenous people on the street.

Limiting private as well as public power

For both Pettit (1997: 272–3) and Habermas (1996), a just society is first about ensuring that citizens have freedom among themselves and do not dominate one another. For both, the state and public political sphere are necessary only to stabilize and enforce the rights that institutionalize the social ideal of an absence of private domination. Yet, as we have seen, Pettit concentrates on the problem of limiting and moderating public power. Even Habermas, despite his concern with the encroachment of the economic system onto the lifeworld in earlier writings (1987) pays scant attention to controlling private market powers in his theory of law and democracy (1996). For individual citizens, however, the issue of access to justice is more likely to arise in relation to private acts of domination, domination in the family, the workplace, or a consumer transaction. (This is not to deny that access to justice is also of the utmost importance at those times when individuals' freedoms are pitted against the authority of the state, most particularly in criminal prosecutions, and also when taxation, social security, or access to the public political sphere are at issue.) Limiting the private power of large corporations with tens of thousands of employees and the capacity to influence millions of lives ought to be as much the concern of democratic theory as limiting the power of the state.

Like Marxist and feminist critics of traditional political theory who have often pointed out how little it deals with unjust and undemocratic practices in the private spheres of market and family (e.g. Phillips 1991), I have argued that the concept of deliberative democracy ought to be elaborated to encompass the nurture and facilitation of the deliberative practice of justice in all the settings of life, public or private. Chapter 8 set out a practical proposal of what it might mean to take seriously the need to nurture justice and encourage democratic participation across the sites of greatest organizational power in a society. Edelman and various co-authors (Dobbin et al. 1988, Edelman 1990, Edelman et al. 1993) have studied the growth of employee due process rights designed to protect against a wide spectrum of arbitrary management behaviour including indiscriminate firing, failure to promote, safety violations, unequal discipline, sexual harassment, and discriminatory employment opportunity structures in US companies. She argues that the civil rights movement and legal mandates of the 1960s together created a normative environment that put pressure on employers to create formal protections of due process rights. She shows how initially novel models of due process were accepted by some companies as a matter of legitimacy and survival in an environment in which they felt strong public scrutiny and employee expectations of change. Those that were most exposed to public scrutiny and government control changed first. Others followed in an effort to remain 'up to date'. Due process rights that were unheard of for private companies early in the century eventually became institutionalized in the normal bureaucratic structure of the corporation in the role of the personnel department and the professionalism of personnel officers. Now few large companies lack programmes for safeguarding basic rights; they are simply part of the basic operations of a company. Her research gives ground for modest hope that the persuasive and symbolic power of law combined with social action and specific solutions to specific disputes can significantly condition internal corporate management processes and other private cultures so that justice requirements that at first seem imposing and intrusive are eventually accepted as normal (see also Suchman & Edelman 1996). In my vision, the republic of justice is constituted not just by formal legal justice in the public sphere but by deliberative justice (which includes legal institutions) in public and private spheres wherever injustice can be done. All our regulatory design for every private and public institution must be aimed at the development of just deliberative democracy through all the 'capillaries' of life: wherever domination can be exercised so must pyramids of deliberative justice begin.

JUST LAWYERS: A TASK OF INSTITUTIONAL DESIGN

This book embarked upon a task of institutional design, the development of regulatory policies and institutions for the legal profession. For that reason it has intertwined the empirical and the normative—explanatory social science, the theory of deliberative democracy, and policy studies of regulation and access to justice. Like the architectural design of a building which must use principles of aesthetics together with laws of physics and engineering, the design of social institutions must marry normative and empirical considerations (Goodin 1996). A purely empirical consideration of lawyers' regulation, however, could not have grounded a regulatory policy for the profession which envisioned lawyers as much more than technical functionaries. The investigation of lawyers' regulation presented here was informed by a concern with access to justice which was grounded in the data of how people complain about lawyers, how lawyers think about the moral guidance of their professional work, and how lawyering is actually structured. The analysis was enlivened by a republican theory of justice through deliberation and the rule of law. Using this normative basis I have been able to show how lawyers can be of great significance in a democratic socio-polity, and how they might be encouraged to live up to their own and citizens' aspirations of their place in the republic of justice.

While normative visions of justice might enliven research into particular policy areas such as the regulatory reform of lawyers, the translation of normative concerns of political theory into concrete contexts can also show how those theories need to be adjusted; normative theories for sociologically impossible worlds are not very useful. The kind of policy-oriented empirical analysis of lawyers and access to justice attempted here can contribute to a more fine-grained analysis of the role of law in the theory of deliberative democracy, at the same time that democratic theory can be used to throw light on the problem of lawyers' regulation. Ultimately the institutions which are reshaped as a result of such a dialectical process of institutional design can themselves be subject to empirical testing against the ideals they are supposed to achieve.[9]

The regulatory arrangements for the legal profession I have advocated would institutionalize exactly this type of intellectual discourse between theory and policy into a practical discourse between profession, state, and community about how lawyers can continually improve their delivery of access to justice goals. Both the theory of democracy and the practice of access to justice have tended to give law and lawyers too dominating a place in the republic of justice. When the legalism of lawyers' justice is channelled and constrained by the deliberation of citizens, then lawyers can contribute to a community in which the doing of justice is an everyday event, concrete and common, not just the rarefied edicts of legislatures and appellate courts.

[9] For example colleagues in the restorative justice group at the Australian National University have helped implement community justice conferencing in drink driving cases in Canberra and are now testing whether dialogic regulation is more effective than criminal trials in preventing recidivism and securing procedural justice. The data on preventing recidivism and ultimately road deaths are not yet available, but early data on citizens' perceptions that they are treated fairly, with rights respected and some influence over the process, suggest that citizen conferences outperform courts (Barnes 1996).

Appendix: Methodology for Chapter 6 Case Study

SOURCES OF DATA

Forty-one unstructured interviews with lawyers were conducted in the second half of 1994, and two more in 1996. The main aim was to understand how lawyers perceived the reform process by eliciting as many different opinions as possible. Lawyers were interviewed in Sydney, Melbourne, Adelaide, and Canberra, Australian capital cities which have professions of different sizes, structures, and histories. Names were obtained by using an initial two or three well-networked contacts in each place to nominate a range of people with different experiences and different opinions. At the end of each interview, respondents were also asked to nominate potential interviewees with views different from their own. Lawyers with different perspectives were also identified by checking newspaper clippings and professional papers for outspoken participants in public debates.

Of the forty-three interviewees, only nine were women. This reflected the fact that the sampling strategy was biased towards those who were leaders of the private profession or outspoken participants in the debate; women are under-represented in the private profession in Australia, especially its senior echelons (see Thornton 1996). Two of the respondents were full-time bureaucrats working for legal professional associations but many more were at the time or had been office holders of their professional association while maintaining private practice. Six interviewees were officers of relevant independent regulators or government departments. Two were judicial officers and the rest were private practitioners (five of whom were barristers). Two additional lawyers refused an interview due to unavailability, and two more refused for other reasons.

Each interviewee has been allocated a code so that the reader can see how often different interviewees are quoted without risking anonymity. The first letter in the code indicates gender (M or F). The second letter indicates whether the person is a barrister (B), a member of a government department or independent regulatory authority (R), a legal professional association bureaucrat (A), a judicial officer (J), or a solicitor (S). Solicitors are given a third letter to indicate whether they work in a small firm or solo practice (S), a community legal centre (C), government (G), a medium firm (M), or a very large, national firm (L). Each interviewee is also given their own number.

The interview data were supplemented by the collection of newspaper clippings from major Australian papers from December 1993 to October 1996, as well as policy documents and other written material produced by the profession in each state.

SAMPLING: THE DIFFERENCE DISCOVERY METHOD

The data presented in this book are limited in what they can say about the prevalence of different views. The forty-three respondents were not selected randomly nor were they stratified to secure representativeness. Rather the sample was assembled through a theoretically purposive snowballing technique developed for the study, a difference discovery method. While snowballing techniques traditionally follow networks of friendship and sameness (McCall & Simmons 1969: 64–65, Minichiello et al. 1990: 198), the difference discovery method is oriented towards the pursuit of diversity in views and experiences, and was designed to reveal new and unanticipated perspectives (see generally Burgess 1982, Glaser & Strauss 1967: 61, Lofland 1971). The assurance sought was that the full diversity of perspectives in the profession was revealed, that 'saturation' of the categories would be reached (Minichiello et al. 1990: 199). In relation to any topic of public discussion there are likely to be 'a plethora of at best loosely connected and fragmented discourses in which many groups of individuals arrive at partial insights into issues' (Bohman 1994: 918 discussing Habermas 1996). The different discourses that different people articulate will represent a number of different considerations corresponding to their interest positions, values, and types of argument they see as valid. Together these different perspectives represent a pool of reasons that individuals draw on in public deliberation according to their own taste and experience. The sampling method used here was designed to reveal the full potential of reasons relevant to regulatory reform of the legal Australian legal profession by sampling perspectives rather than representatively sampling persons.

Thus initial contacts were asked not to name friends and associates, but to suggest those who were different from them. Respondents were asked to do the same, and the clippings and other policy statements were used to ensure that no obviously different perspectives were missed. As the interviews proceeded, fewer and fewer of the suggestions for new people to interview were of people who had views which had not been aired in earlier interviews. (These suggestions were generally not pursued.) After less than thirty interviews, no significantly different views about the issues were discovered among interviewees, suggesting that the sampling strategy of maximizing difference had succeeded in finding most of the different views that existed in the profession. By the time the sample had reached forty-one it seemed clear that there was no significant way of thinking about the reform debate amongst Australian lawyers which had not been captured, although a further two interviews were conducted in Victoria in 1996 to ensure that the unique characteristics of the Victorian reform process were understood.

These patterns of opinion were independently confirmed by 'data source triangulation' (Denzin 1970: 308) using other research on the legal profession (from Australia and overseas), the published positions of certain lawyers and legal associations, and their commentary reported in newspaper clippings. Some patterns of professional opinion are so robust they are apparent even in a sample of forty-three lawyers, and can be confirmed by the interviewees' own reports of these patterns among their colleagues, combined with credible data (i.e. other research and newspaper clippings) independent of the interviews. Where there are illuminating data in the published literature that complemented or qualified the picture from other countries, they are used. The convergences with the Australian picture were more striking than the divergences from it, and the model developed should apply equally well to other common law countries.

ANALYSIS: THE CONSTANT COMPARATIVE METHOD

The difference discovery method of sampling complemented the constant comparative method of data analysis (Glaser & Strauss 1967). Copious notes were taken during each interview including much verbatim material. They were typed immediately afterwards. It was decided not to tape record the interviews as much of the material under discussion was politically sensitive at the time and lawyers are often over-concerned about the possibility of their confidence being breached. It was hoped that they would be more relaxed and open in their expression of opinion without a tape recorder running. An opening statement that I was interested in hearing their views on the current reform debate was usually sufficient to start a conversation in which most of the topics I hoped to cover were discussed. When conversation faltered, I would ask the interviewee what they thought of another issue in the reform debate or perhaps reported (anonymously) what other lawyers had said and asked for their reaction. In this way we could cover the lawyer's opinion on most of the specific reforms and arguments at issue in the debate that was then running.

Interviews and clippings were then analysed by dividing them into bites each concerned with one topic. These were placed together in categories according to topic, constantly comparing each new piece of information with all the previous bites in a category until nothing new was being discovered. This 'constant comparative method' is the pursuit of difference in data analysis, just as the difference discovery method is the pursuit of difference in sampling.[1] Finally the

[1] It is odd that so much qualitative research applies a difference-enhancing method of analysis on a snowballed sample that is difference-restricting.

relationships between the categories were examined and incorporated into the analysis presented below. Quotations in Chapter 6 are examples from each category.

References

AAMI 1997, *AAMI Customer Charter: First Annual Report 1996–1997*, AAMI, Melbourne. (http://www.aami.com.au/report/report97.htm)

Abbott, A. 1988, *The System of Professions*, University of Chicago Press, Chicago.

Abel, R. 1981*a*, 'Conservative conflict and the reproduction of capitalism: The role of informal justice' 9 *International Journal of the Sociology of Law*, 245–67.

—— 1981*b*, 'Why does the ABA promulgate ethical rules?' 59(4) *Texas Law Review*, 639–88.

—— 1982*a*, 'Introduction' in Abel, R. (ed.) *The Politics of Informal Justice*, i: *The American Experience*, Academic Press, New York, 1–13.

—— 1982*b*, 'The contradictions of informal justice' in Abel, R. (ed.) *The Politics of Informal Justice*, i: *The American Experience*, Academic Press, New York, 267–320.

—— 1985, 'Lawyers and the power to change' 7(1) *Law & Policy*, 5–18.

—— 1988*a*, *The Legal Profession in England and Wales*, Basil Blackwell, Oxford.

—— 1988*b*, 'United States: The contradictions of professionalism' in Abel, R. & Lewis, P. (eds.) *Lawyers in Society: The Common Law World*, University of California Press, Berkeley and Los Angeles, 186–243.

—— 1989*a*, *American Lawyers*, Oxford University Press, New York.

—— 1989*b*, 'Between market and state: The legal profession in turmoil' 52(3) *Modern Law Review*, 285–325.

Abel-Smith, B. & Stevens, R. 1967, *Lawyers and the Courts: A Sociological Study of the English Legal System 1750–1965*, Heinemann, London.

Access to Justice Advisory Committee 1994, *Access to Justice: An Action Plan*, Australian Government Publishing Service, Canberra.

Ackland, R. 1994, 'Power moves to consumer' 4 May *Financial Review*, 39.

ACT Consumer Affairs Bureau 1996, 'New international business charter' June *ACT Alert*, 8.

Affirmative Action Agency 1992, *Quality and Commitment: The Next Steps: The Final Report of the Effectiveness Review of the Affirmative Action (Equal Employment Opportunity for Women) Act 1986*, Australian Government Publishing Service, Canberra.

—— 1998, *Facts and Figures*, Affirmative Action Agency, Sydney.

Akerlof, G. 1970, 'The market for "lemons": Quality uncertainty and the market mechanism' 84 *Quarterly Journal of Economics*, 488–500.

Albon, R. & Lindsay, G. (eds.) 1984, *Occupational Regulation and the Public Interest*, The Centre for Independent Studies, Sydney.

Alexander, R. 1984, 'The history of the law as an independent profession and the present English legal system' in Alexander, R., Brow, P., Cox, A. & MacKay, R. (eds.) *The Lawyer's Professional Independence: Present Threats/Future*

Challenges, Tort and Insurance Practice Section, American Bar Association, Chicago, 1–21.

AMES, J. 1996, 'Anarchy in the U.K.' 31(7) *Australian Lawyer*, 28–9.

ANLEU, S. ROACH 1992, 'The legal profession in the United States and Australia: Deprofessionalization or reorganization?' 19(2) *Work & Occupations*, 184–204.

—— & MACK, K. 1995, 'Balancing principle and pragmatism: Guilty pleas' 4(4) *Journal of Judicial Administration*, 232–9.

ARNOLD, B. & HAGAN, J. 1992, 'Careers of misconduct: The structure of prosecuted professional deviance among lawyers' 57 *American Sociological Review*, 771–80.

—— —— 1994, 'Self-regulatory responses to professional misconduct within the legal profession' 31(2) *Canadian Review of Sociology & Anthropology*, 168–83.

—— & KAY, F. 1995, 'Social capital, violations of trust and the vulnerability of isolates: The social organization of law practice and professional self-regulation' 23 *International Journal of the Sociology of Law*, 321–46.

ARROW, K. 1963, 'Uncertainty and the welfare economics of medical care' 53(3) *American Economic Review*, 941–73.

ARTHURS, H., WEISMAN, R. & ZEMANS, F. 1988, 'Canadian lawyers: A peculiar professionalism' in Abel, R. & Lewis, P. (eds.) *Lawyers in Society: The Common Law World*, University of California Press, Berkeley and Los Angeles, 123–85.

ARTHURS, S. 1970, 'Discipline in the legal profession in Ontario' 7(3) *Osgoode Hall Law Journal*, 235–69.

ASTOR, H. & CHINKIN, C. 1992, *Dispute Resolution in Australia*, Butterworths, Sydney.

ATTORNEY GENERAL'S DEPARTMENT AND DEPARTMENT FOR WOMEN 1996, *Gender Bias and the Law: Women Working in the Legal Profession: Report of the Implementation Committee*, Sydney.

AUERBACH, J. 1983, *Justice without Law?* Oxford University Press, New York.

AYRES, I. & BRAITHWAITE, J. 1992, *Responsive Regulation: Transcending the Deregulation Debate*, Oxford University Press, New York.

BAKER, J. 1996, *Conveyancing Fees in a Competitive Market*, Justice Research Centre, Law Foundation of NSW, Sydney.

BALDWIN, J. & MCCONVILLE, M. 1977, *Negotiated Justice: Pressures to Plead Guilty*, Martin Robertson, London.

BALDWIN, R. 1997, 'Regulation after "command-and-control"' in Hawkins, K. (ed.) *Human Face of Law*, Clarendon Press, Oxford, 65–84.

BARBER, B. 1983, *The Logic and Limits of Trust*, Rutgers University Press, New Brunswick, NJ.

—— 1984, *Strong Democracy: Participatory Politics for a New Age*, University of California Press, Berkeley and Los Angeles.

—— 1994, *An Aristocracy of Everyone: The Politics of Education and the Future of America*, Oxford University Press, New York.

Bardach, E. & Kagan, R. 1982, *Going by the Book: The Problem of Regulatory Unreasonableness*, Temple University Press, Philadelphia.

Barnes, G. 1996, 'An experimental trial of restorative justice and drunk-driving offenders: Preliminary results from Australia' Paper presented to the 1996 Annual Meeting of the American Society of Criminology, Chicago.

Basten J., Graycar, R. & Neal, D. 1985, 'Legal centres in Australia' 7(1) *Law & Policy*, 113–41.

Bayles, M. 1989, *Professional Ethics*, Wadsworth Publishing Coy, Belmont, Calif.

Becker, G. 1975, *Human Capital: A Theoretical and Empirical Analysis with Special Reference to Education*, National Bureau of Economic Research, New York.

Begun, J. 1986, 'Economic and sociological approaches to professionalism' 13(1) *Work & Occupations*, 113–29.

Bell, K. 1985, 'The politics of reforming the legal profession in Australia: A case study' 3 *Law in Context*, 1–44.

Belloni, F. 1996, 'British solicitors and barristers: Change in the legal profession' Paper presented to the Joint Meeting of the Law & Society Association & the Research Committee on the Sociology of Law, University of Strathclyde, Glasgow.

Benson, H. 1979, *The Royal Commission on Legal Services*, vols. i and ii, Her Majesty's Stationery Office, London.

Birds, J. 1994, 'Legal access and private sector ombudsmen' in Shapland, J. & Le Grys, R. (eds.) *The Changing Shape of the Legal Profession*, Institute for the Study of the Legal Profession, Sheffield, 100–7.

Birkinshaw, P. 1994, *Grievances, Remedies and the State*, Sweet & Maxwell, London.

Black, J. 1996, 'Constitutionalising self-regulation' 59 *Modern Law Review* 24–55.

Blankenburg, E. 1994, 'The infrastructure for avoiding civil litigation: Comparing cultures of legal behaviour in the Netherlands and West Germany' 28(4) *Law & Society Review*, 789–808.

Bloch, R. 1992, 'Corporate compliance programs and antitrust enforcement' September *Preventive Law Reporter*, 3–6.

Blumberg, A. 1967, 'The practice of law as confidence game' 1(1) *Law & Society Review*, 15–39.

Boggiano, A., Barrett, M., Weiher, A., McLelland, G. & Lusk, C. 1987, 'Use of the maximal-operant principle to motivate children's intrinsic interest' 53 *Journal of Personality and Social Psychology*, 866–79.

Bohman, J. 1994, 'Complexity, pluralism, and the constitutional state: On Habermas's *Faktizitat und Geltung*' 28(4) *Law & Society Review*, 897–930.

Bottomley, S., Gunningham, N. & Parker, S. 1994, *Law in Context*, Federation Press, Leichardt.

Boucher, D. & Vincent, A. 1993, *A Radical Hegelian: The Political and Social Philosophy of Henry Jones*, University of Wales Press, Cardiff.

BRAITHWAITE, J. 1985, *To Punish or Persuade: Enforcement of Coal Mine Safety*, State University of New York Press, Albany.

—— 1989, *Crime, Shame and Reintegration*, Cambridge University Press, Cambridge.

—— 1991, 'Thinking about the structural context of international dispute resolution' in Bustelo, M. & Alston, P. (eds.) *Whose New World Order: What Role for the United Nations?* Federation Press, Sydney, 58–68.

—— 1993, 'Beyond positivism: Learning from contextual integrated strategies' 30 *Journal of Research in Crime and Delinquency*, 383–99.

—— 1995*a*, 'Inequality and republican criminology' in Hagan, J. & Peterson, R. (eds.) *Crime and Inequality*, Stanford University Press, Stanford, Calif., 277–305.

—— 1995*b*, 'Reintegrative shaming, republicanism, and policy' in Barlow, H. (ed.) *Crime and Public Policy: Putting Theory to Work*, Westview Press, Boulder, Colo., 191–205.

—— 1995*c*, 'Domination, quiescence and crime' Plenary address to the British Criminology Conference, Loughborough.

—— 1997, 'On speaking softly and carrying sticks: Neglected dimensions of a republican separation of powers' 47 *University of Toronto Law Journal*, 305–61.

—— forthcoming, 'The new regulatory state and the coming decline of criminology' *British Journal of Criminology*.

—— & DALY, K. 1994, 'Masculinities, violence and communitarian control' in Newburn, T. & Stanko, E. (eds.) *Just Boys Doing Business? Men, Masculinities and Crime*, Routledge, London, 189–213.

—— & MAKKAI, T. 1991, 'Testing an expected utility model of corporate deterrence' 25 *Law & Society Review*, 7–40.

—— —— 1994, 'Trust and compliance' 4 *Policing & Society*, 1–12.

—— & MUGFORD, S. 1994, 'Conditions of successful reintegration ceremonies' 34 *British Journal of Criminology*, 139–71.

—— & PARKER, C. 1999, 'Restorative justice is republican justice' in Bazemore, G. & Walgrave, L. (eds.) *Restorative Juvenile Justice: Repairing the Harm of Youth Crime*, Criminal Justice Press, Monsey, NY, 103–26.

—— & PETTIT, P. 1990, *Not Just Deserts: A Republican Theory of Criminal Justice*, Oxford University Press, Oxford.

BRAITHWAITE, V. 1992, *First Steps: Business Reactions to Implementing the Affirmative Action Act*, A report to the Affirmative Action Agency, Australian National University, Canberra.

—— 1993, 'The Australian government's affirmative action legislation: Achieving social change through human resource management' 15(4) *Law & Policy*, 327–54.

BRAZIER, M., LOVECY, J., MORAN, M. & POTTON, M. 1993, 'Falling from a tightrope: Doctors and lawyers between the market and the state' 41 *Political Studies*, 197–213.

Brehm, S. & Brehm, J. 1981, *Psychological Reactance: A Theory of Freedom and Control*, Academic Press, New York.

Brint, S. 1994, *In an Age of Experts: The Changing Role of Professionals in Politics and Public Life*, Princeton University Press, Princeton.

Brockman, J. 1996, 'Dismantling or fortifying professional monopolies? On *Regulating Professions and Occupations*' 24 *Manitoba Law Journal*, 301–10.

—— 1997, 'The use of self-regulation to curb discrimination and sexual harassment in the legal profession' 35 *Osgoode Hall Law Journal*, 209–41.

—— & McEwen, C. 1990, 'Self-regulation in the legal profession: Funnel in, funnel out or funnel away?' 5 *Canadian Journal of Law & Society*, 1–46.

Brookman, J. 1997, 'How effectively are the cost disclosure requirements operating?' 35(2) *Law Society Journal*, 73.

Brown, L. 1986, *Lawyering through Life: The Origin of Preventive Law*, Fred B. Rothman & Co, Littleton, Colo.

—— & Kandel, A. 1995 (looseleaf service), *The Legal Audit: Corporate Internal Investigation*, Clark Boardman Callaghan, Deerfield, Ill.

Buchanan, R. 1997, 'Constructing virtual justice in the global arena' 31 *Law & Society Review*, 363–75.

Burchell, G., Gordon, C. & Miller, P. (eds.) 1991, *The Foucault Effect: Studies in Governmentality*, University of Chicago Press, Chicago.

Burgess, R. 1982, 'The unstructured interview as a conversation' in Burgess, R. (ed.) *Field Research: A Sourcebook and Field Manual*, Allen & Unwin, London, 107–10.

Burgmann, V. 1993, *Power and Protest: Movements for Change in Australian Society*, Allen & Unwin, St Leonards.

Burton, C. 1991, *The Promise and the Price: The Struggle for Equal Opportunity in Women's Employment*, Allen & Unwin, Sydney.

Cain, M. 1983, 'The general practice lawyer and the client: Towards a radical conception' in Dingwall, R. & Lewis, P. (eds.) *The Sociology of the Professions*, Macmillan, London, 106–30.

—— 1985, 'Beyond informal justice' 9 *Contemporary Crises*, 335–73.

—— 1994, 'The symbol traders' in Cain, M. & Harrington, C. (eds.) *Lawyers in a Postmodern World: Translation and Transgression*, New York University Press, New York, 15–48.

Callick, R. 1995, 'Legal eagle shows its talons' 13 April *Financial Review*, 19.

Campbell, T. 1988, *Justice*, Macmillan Education, Basingstoke.

—— 1993, 'The contribution of legal studies' in Goodin, R. & Pettit, P. (eds.) *A Companion to Contemporary Political Philosophy*, Basil Blackwell, Oxford, 183–211.

Canadian Bar Association Task Force on Gender Equality in the Legal Profession 1993, *Touchstones for Change: Equality, Diversity and Accountability*, Canadian Bar Association, Ottawa.

Cappelletti, M. (ed.) 1978, *Access to Justice*, i: *A World Survey*, Sijthoff and Noordhoff, Amsterdam.

Cappelletti, M. & Garth, B. 1978, 'Access to justice: The newest wave in the worldwide movement to make rights effective' 27 *Buffalo Law Review*, 181–292.

Carlin, J. 1966, *Lawyers' Ethics: A Survey of the New York City Bar*, Russell Sage Foundation, New York.

—— 1994 (revised edition), *Lawyers on their Own: Solo Practitioners in an Urban Setting*, Austin & Winfield Publishers, San Francisco.

Cascio, J. 1994, 'International environmental management standards: ISO 9000's less tractable siblings' April *ASM Standardization News*, 44–9.

Cass, M. & Sackville, R. 1975, *Legal Needs of the Poor: Commission of Inquiry into Poverty: Law and Poverty Series*, Australian Government Publishing Service, Canberra.

Chayes, A. & Chayes, A. 1985, 'Corporate counsel and the elite law firm' 37 *Stanford Law Review*, 277–304.

Chesterman, J. 1996, *Poverty Law and Social Change: The Story of the Fitzroy Legal Service*, Melbourne University Press, Carlton South.

Christie, N. 1977, 'Conflicts as property' 17(1) *British Journal of Criminology*, 1–15.

Clarkson Committee (Committee of Inquiry into the Future Organisation of the Legal Profession in Western Australia) 1983, *Inquiry into the Future Organisation of the Legal Profession in Western Australia: Report*, Government Printer, Perth.

Clifton-Steele, R. 1994, 'Peak bodies tell the TPC the legal profession is already most competitive' March *Law Society Journal*, 66–7.

Coglianese, C. 1996, 'Litigating within relationships: Disputes and disturbance in the regulatory process' 30 *Law & Society Review*, 735–65.

Colebatch, T. 1995, 'Consumers get say in competition law' 21 January *Age*, 9.

Coleman, J. 1985, *The Criminal Elite: The Sociology of White Collar Crime*, St Martin's Press, New York.

Conroy, P. 1995, 'Wade's law reforms to be reported to UN' 29 March *Age*, 5.

—— & Wilson, D. 1995, 'Lawyer to lobby against reforms' 27 March *Age*, 3.

Consedine, J. 1997, *Restorative Justice: Healing the Effects of Crime*, Ploughshares Publications, Christchurch.

Consumer Action 1995, 'Consumer coalition demands justice system reform' February/March 1995 *Consumer Action: Newsletter of the Australian Federation of Consumer Organisations*, 3.

Conte, A. 1994, *Sexual Harassment in the Workplace: Law and Practice*, vol. i, John Wiley & Sons, New York.

Cooper, J. 1983, *Public Legal Services: A Comparative Study of Policy, Politics and Practice*, Sweet & Maxwell, London.

Cornish, W. & Clark, G de N. 1989, *Law and Society in England 1750–1950*, Sweet & Maxwell, London.

CORONES, S. 1996, 'Solicitors subject to Trade Practices Act' 16(6) *Proctor*, 10–11.

COWNIE, F. 1990, 'The reform of the legal profession or the end of civilization as we know it' in Patfield, F. & White, R. (eds.) *The Changing Law*, Leicester University Press, Leicester, 213–34.

COX, S. 1989, 'Advertising restrictions among professionals: *Bates v State Bar of Arizona*' in Kwoka, J. & White, L. (eds.) *The Antitrust Revolution*, Scott, Foresman & Coy, Glenview, Ill., 134–59.

CRAGG, W. 1992, *The Practice of Punishment: Towards a Theory of Restorative Justice*, Routledge, London.

CRANSTON, R. 1995*a*, '"The rational study of law": Social research and access to justice' in Zuckerman, A. & Cranston, R. (eds.) *Reform of Civil Procedure: Essays on 'Access to Justice'*, Clarendon Press, Oxford, 31–59.

—— 1995*b*, 'Legal ethics and professional responsibility' in Cranston, R. (ed.) *Legal Ethics and Professional Responsibility*, Clarendon Press, Oxford, 1–34.

CRAVEN, G. 1995, *Reforming the Legal Profession: Report of the Attorney-General's Working Party on the Legal Profession*, Department of Justice, Melbourne.

CROFT, C. 1992, 'Reconceptualising American legal professionalism: A proposal for deliberative moral community' 67 *New York University Law Review*, 1256–353.

CURRAN, B. 1985, 'Surveying the legal needs of the public: What the public wants and expects in the lawyer–client relationship' in Gibson, D. & Baldwin, J. (eds.) *Law in a Cynical Society? Opinion and Law in the 1980's*, Carswell Legal Publications, Calgary, 107–19.

CURRAN, C. 1993, 'The American experience with self-regulation in the medical and legal professions' in Faure, M., Finsinger, J., Siegers, J. & Van den Burgh, R. (eds.) *Regulation of Professions: A Law and Economics Approach to the Regulation of Attorneys and Physicians in the US, Belgium, the Netherlands, Germany and the UK*, Maklu, Antwerp, 47–87.

DAL PONT, G. 1996, *Lawyers' Professional Responsibility in Australia and New Zealand*, Law Book Company Information Services, Sydney.

DANIEL, A. 1983, *Power, Privilege and Prestige: Occupations in Australia*, Longman Cheshire, Melbourne.

—— 1998, *Scapegoats for a Profession: Uncovering Procedural Injustice*, Harwood Press, Sydney.

DELANEY, M. & WRIGHT, T. 1997, *Plaintiffs' Satisfaction with Dispute Resolution Processes*, Justice Research Centre, Law Foundation of NSW, Sydney.

DENZIN, N. 1970, *The Research Act in Sociology*, Nelson, London.

DEZALAY, Y. 1993, 'The forum should fit the fuss: The economics and politics of negotiated justice' in Cain, M. & Harrington, C. (eds.) *Lawyers in a Postmodern World: Translation and Transgression*, New York University Press, New York, 155–82.

—— 1996, 'Between the state, law and the market: The social and professional stakes in the construction and definition of a regulatory arena' in McCahery, J., Bratton, W., Picciotto, S. & Scott, C. (eds.) *International Regulatory Competition and Coordination*, Clarendon Press, Oxford, 59–87.

DEZALAY, Y. & GARTH, B. 1996, *Dealing in Virtue: International Commercial Arbitration and the Construction of a Transnational Legal Order*, University of Chicago Press, Chicago.

DIERKES, M. 1985, 'Corporate social reporting and auditing: Theory and practice' in Hopt, K. & Teubner, G. (eds.) *Corporate Governance and Directors' Liabilities: Legal, Economic and Sociological Analyses on Corporate Social Responsibility*, Walter de Gruyter, Berlin, 354–79.

DINGWALL, R. & FENN, P. 1987, '"A respectable profession"? Sociological and economic perspectives on the regulation of professional services' 7 *International Review of Law & Economics*, 51–64.

DINNEN, S. 1996, Challenges of Order in a Weak State–Crime, Violence and Control in Papua New Guinea, Unpublished Ph.D. thesis, Australian National University, Canberra.

DISNEY, J. 1975, 'Appendix: Salaried legal aid lawyers and the courts' in Sackville, R. *Legal Aid in Australia: Commission of Inquiry into Poverty: Law and Poverty Series*, Australian Government Publishing Service, Canberra, 193–201.

——REDMOND, P., BASTEN, J. & ROSS, S. 1986, *Lawyers*, Law Book Company, Sydney.

DIXON, J. & SERRON, C. 1995, 'Stratification in the legal profession: Sex, sector and salary' 29 *Law & Society Review*, 381–412.

DOBBIN, F., EDELMAN, L., MEYER, J., SCOTT, W. R. & SWIDLER, A. 1988, 'The expansion of due process in organizations' in Zucker, L. (ed.) *Institutional Patterns and Organizations: Culture and Environment*, Ballinger Publishing Coy, Cambridge, Mass., 71–98.

DOMBERGER, S. & SHERR, A. 1989, 'The impact of competition on pricing and quality of legal services' 9 *International Review of Law & Economics*, 41–56.

DORSEY, S. 1983, 'Occupational licensing and minorities' 7(2/3) *Law & Human Behaviour*, 171–81.

DOWNES, T., HOPKINS, P. & REES, W. 1981, 'The future of legal services in Britain: A client or lawyer oriented approach?' 1 *Windsor Yearbook of Access to Justice*, 121–62.

DRINKER, H. 1980, *Legal Ethics*, Greenwood Press Publishers, Westport, Conn.

DRYZEK, J. 1990, *Discursive Democracy: Politics, Policy and Political Science*, Cambridge University Press, Cambridge.

DUNN, J. 1994, 'The identity of the bourgeois liberal republic' in Fontana, B. (ed.) *The Invention of the Modern Republic*, Cambridge University Press, Cambridge, 206–25.

DURKHEIM, E. 1992 (new edition), *Professional Ethics and Civic Morals*, Routledge, London.

DWORKIN, R. 1986, *Law's Empire*, Fontana, London.

Eades, D. 1992, *Aboriginal English and the Law: Communicating with Aboriginal English Speaking Clients: A Handbook for Legal Practitioners*, Queensland Law Society, Brisbane.

——(ed.) 1995, *Language in Evidence: Issues Confronting Aboriginal and Multicultural Australia*, University of New South Wales Press, Sydney.

Edelman, L. 1984, 'Institutionalising dispute resolution alternatives' 9 *Justice System Journal*, 134–49.

——1990, 'Legal environments and organisational governance: The expansion of due process in the American workplace' 95 *American Journal of Sociology* 1401–40.

——Erlanger, H. & Lande, J. 1993, 'Internal dispute resolution: The transformation of civil rights in the workplace' 27(3) *Law & Society Review*, 497–534.

Ekland-Olson, S., Lieb, J. & Zurcher, L. 1984, 'The paradoxical impact of criminal sanctions: Some microstructural findings' 18 *Law & Society Review*, 159–78.

Eldred, T. & Schoenherr, T. 1993–4, 'The lawyer's duty of public service: More than charity?' 96(2) *West Virginia Law Review*, 367–403.

Engel, D. & Munger, F. 1996, 'Rights, remembrance, and the reconciliation of difference' 30(1) *Law & Society Review*, 7–53.

Epstein, C. 1993, *Women in Law*, University of Illinois Press, Urbana.

Ericson, R. & Baranek, P. 1982, *The Ordering of Justice: A Study of Accused Persons as Defendants in the Criminal Process*, University of Toronto Press, Toronto.

Erlanger, H., Epp, C., Cahill, M. & Haines, K. 1996, 'Law student idealism and job choice: Some new data on an old question' 30 *Law & Society Review*, 851–64.

Etheridge, C. 1973, 'Lawyers versus indigents: Conflicts of interest in professional–client relations in the legal profession' in Freidson, E. (ed.) *The Professions and their Prospects*, Sage Publications, Beverly Hills, Calif., 245–65.

Evans, A. 1994, 'Holy cow no more!' 19(6) *Alternative Law Journal*, 292.

——1995, '"Acceptable, but not entirely satisfied": Client perceptions of Victorian lawyers' 20(2) *Alternative Law Journal*, 57–62.

Evans, H. 1996, *Lawyers' Liabilities*, Sweet & Maxwell, London.

Evans, R. & Trebilcock, M. 1982, *Lawyers and the Consumer Interest: Regulating the Market for Legal Services*, Butterworths, Toronto.

Eveline, J. 1994, 'Care with compliance: Changing the worlds of men' Paper presented to the Administration, Compliance and Governability Workshop, August 1994, Australian National University, Canberra.

Faine, J. 1993, *Lawyers in the Alice: Aboriginals and Whitefellas' Law*, The Federation Press, Sydney.

Fairlie, D. 1994, 'Commencement of the Reform Act', July *Law Society Journal*, 2.

Falk Moore, S. 1978, *Law as Process: An Anthropological Approach*, Routledge & Kegan Paul, London.

Farmer, J. 1994, 'The application of competition principles to the organisation of the legal profession' 17(1) *University of New South Wales Law Journal*, 285–97.

Farrington, D. 1993, 'Understanding and preventing bullying' in Tonry, M. (ed.) 17 *Crime & Justice: Annual Review of Research*, University of Chicago Press, Chicago, 381–458.

Felstiner, W. 1997, 'Professional inattention: Origins and consequences' in Hawkins, K. (ed.) *The Human Face of Law*, Clarendon Press, Oxford, 121–50.

—— Abel, R. & Sarat, A. 1980–1, 'The emergence and transformation of disputes: Naming, blaming, claiming . . . ' 15 *Law & Society Review*, 631–54.

—— & Sarat, A. 1992, 'Enactments of power: Negotiating reality and responsibility in lawyer–client interactions' 77 *Cornell Law Review*, 1447–98.

Fennell, P. 1982, 'Advertising: Professional ethics and the public interest' in Thomas, P. (ed.) *Law in the Balance: Legal Services in the 1980s*, Martin Robertson, Oxford, 144–60.

Fife-Yeomans, J., Gunn, M. & Staff Reporters 1994, 'TPC report puts lawyers on notice' 8 March *Australian*, 3.

Finkle, P. & Cohen, D. 1993, 'Consumer redress through alternative dispute resolution and small claims court: Theory and practice' 13 *Windsor Yearbook of Access to Justice*, 81–116.

Fischer, K. & Schot, J. (eds.) 1993, *Environmental Strategies for Industry: International Perspectives on Research Needs and Policy Implications*, Island Press, Washington.

Fisse, B. 1989, 'Corporate compliance programmes: The Trade Practices Act and beyond' 17 *Australian Business Law Review*, 356–99.

—— & Braithwaite, J. 1993, *Corporations, Crime and Accountability*, Cambridge University Press, Cambridge.

Fitzgerald, J. 1985, 'Thinking about law and its alternatives: Abel et al and the debate over informal justice' *American Bar Foundation Research Journal*, 637–57.

Fitzpatrick, P. 1984, 'Law and societies' 22(1) *Osgoode Hall Law Journal*, 115–38.

—— 1988, 'The rise and rise of informalism' in Matthews, R. (ed.) *Informal Justice*, Sage Publications, London, 178–98.

—— 1992, *The Mythology of Modern Law*, Routledge, London.

Fleming, D. 1996, 'The social significance of the phenomenon of "legal aid" in the Australian welfare state' Paper presented at the Joint Meeting of the Law & Society Association and the Research Committee on the Sociology of the Law, Glasgow, 10–13 July 1996.

Fogg, R. 1994, *Nursing Home Regulations: Survey, Certification and Enforcement Manual*, Thompson Publishing Group, New York.

Foucault, M. (Gordon, C. ed.) 1980, *Power/Knowledge: Selected Interviews and Other Writings 1972–1977*, Harvester Press, Brighton.

FOWLER, S. 1995, 'A disturbing threat to legal independence' 31 March *Age*, 14.

FREIDSON, E. 1975, *Doctoring Together: A Study of Professional Social Control*, Elsevier, New York.

—— 1983, 'The reorganisation of the professions by regulation' 7(2/3) *Law & Human Behaviour*, 279–90.

—— 1986, *Professional Powers: A Study of the Institutionalization of Formal Knowledge*, University of Chicago Press, Chicago.

—— 1992, 'Professionalism as model and ideology' in Nelson, R., Trubek, D. & Solomon, R. (eds.) *Lawyers' Ideals/Lawyers' Practices: Transformations in the American Legal Profession*, Cornell University Press, Ithaca, NY, 215–29.

FRIEDMAN, M. 1962, 'Chapter IX: Occupational licensure' in *Capitalism and Freedom*, University of Chicago Press, Chicago, 137–60.

GALANTER, M. 1974, 'Why the haves come out ahead: Speculation on the limits of legal change' 9 *Law & Society Review*, 95–160.

—— 1981, 'Justice in many rooms' in Cappelletti, M. (ed.) *Access to Justice and the Welfare State*, Sijthoff, Alphen aan den Rijn, 147–81.

—— 1992, 'Law abounding: Legalisation around the North Atlantic' 55 *Modern Law Review*, 1–24.

—— 1994, 'Predators and parasites: Lawyer-bashing and civil justice' 28(3) *Georgia Law Review*, 633–81.

—— & PALAY, T. 1991, *Tournament of Lawyers: The Transformation of the Big Law Firm*, University of Chicago Press, Chicago.

—— —— 1995*a*, 'Public service implications of evolving law firm size and structure' in Katzmann, R. (ed.) 1995, *The Law Firm and the Public Good*, Brookings Institution, Washington, 19–58.

—— —— 1995*b*, 'Large law firms and professional responsibility' in Cranston, R. (ed.) *Legal Ethics and Professional Responsibility*, Clarendon Press, Oxford, 189–202.

—— & ROGERS, J. 1991, 'A transformation of American business disputing? Some preliminary observations' *Institute for Legal Studies, Working Paper DPRP 10-3*, University of Wisconsin.

GALAWAY, B. & HUDSON, J. 1990, *Criminal Justice, Restitution and Reconciliation*, Criminal Justice Press, Monsey, NY.

GARLING, K. 1983, 'Trust account defalcations: How and why? The system and the motive' in Institute of Criminology, *Crime and the Professions: The Legal Profession*, Proceedings of the Institute of Criminology No. 55, University of Sydney, 11–25.

GARNER, H. 1995, *The First Stone: Some Questions about Sex and Power*, Pan Macmillan, Sydney.

GARTH, B. 1980, *Neighbourhood Law Firms for the Poor: A Comparative Study of Recent Developments in Legal Aid and in the Legal Profession*, Sijthoff & Noordhoff, Alphen aan den Rijn.

Gatfield, G. & Gray, A. 1993, *Women Lawyers in New Zealand: A Survey of the Legal Profession*, 1993 Suffrage Centennial Project, New Zealand.

Geerts, P. 1980, 'The issue of delegalization' in Blankenburg, E. (ed.) *Innovations in the Legal Services*, Oelgeschlager, Gunn & Hain, Cambridge, Mass., 209–30.

Gellhorn, W. 1956, 'Chapter Three: The right to make a living' in *Individual Freedom and Governmental Restraints*, Louisiana State University Press, Baton Rouge, 105–51.

Genn, H. 1987, *Hard Bargaining: Out of Court Settlement in Personal Injury Actions*, Clarendon Press, Oxford.

Germov, J. 1995, 'Equality before the law: The limits of legal aid and the cost of social justice' 30(2) *Australian Journal of Social Issues*, 162–78.

Giffen, P. 1961, 'Social control and professional self-government: A study in the legal profession in Canada' in Clark, S. & Ashley, C. (eds.) *Urbanism and the Changing Canadian Society*, University of Toronto Press, Toronto, 117–34.

Glaser, B. & Strauss, A. 1967, *The Discovery of Grounded Theory: Strategies for Qualitative Research*, Aldine, Chicago.

Glendon, M. 1994, *A Nation under Lawyers: How the Crisis in the Legal Profession is Transforming American Society*, Farrar, Straus & Giroux, New York.

Godfrey, E. (ed.) 1995, *Law without Frontiers: A Comparative Study of the Rules of Professional Ethics Applicable to the Cross-Border Practice of Law*, Kluwer Law International & International Bar Association, London.

Goldberg, S., Green, E. & Sander, F. 1985, *Dispute Resolution*, Little, Brown & Company, Boston.

Goldring, J., Maher, L. & McKeough, J. 1993, *Consumer Protection Law*, Federation Press, Annandale.

Goldsmith, A. 1995, 'Warning: Law school can endanger your health!' 21 *Monash University Law Review*, 272–304.

—— 1996, 'Heroes or technicians? The moral capacities of tomorrow's lawyers', 14 *Journal of Professional Legal Education*, 1–23.

Goode, W. 1957, 'Community within a community: The professions' 22 *American Sociological Review*, 194–200.

Goodin, R. 1996, 'Institutions and their design' in Goodin, R. (ed.) *The Theory of Institutional Design*, Cambridge University Press, Cambridge, 1–53.

Gordon, R. 1984, '"The ideal and the actual in the law": Fantasies and practices of New York city lawyers, 1870–1910' in Gawalt, G. (ed.) *The New High Priests: Lawyers in Post-Civil War America*, Greenwood Press, Westport, Conn., 51–74.

—— 1985, 'Lawyers as the American Aristocracy', Unpublished Holmes Lectures, Harvard Law School.

—— 1988, 'The independence of lawyers' 68 *Boston University Law Review*, 1–83.

—— 1990, 'Corporate law practice as a public calling' 49 *Maryland Law Review*, 255–92.

——& Simon, W. 1992, 'The redemption of professionalism?' in Nelson, R., Trubek, D. & Solomon, R. (eds.) *Lawyers' Ideals/Lawyers' Practices: Transformations in the American Legal Profession*, Cornell University Press, Ithaca, NY, 230–57.

Goriely, T. 1995, 'The government's legal aid reforms' in Zuckerman, A. & Cranston, R. (eds.) *Reform of Civil Procedure: Essays on 'Access to Justice'*, Clarendon Press, Oxford, 347–69.

——& Paterson, A. 1996, 'Introduction: Resourcing civil justice' in Paterson, A. & Goriely, T. (eds.) *A Reader on Resourcing Civil Justice*, Oxford University Press, Oxford, 1–35.

Government of South Australia 1992, *A White Paper: The Legal Profession*, Adelaide.

Grabosky, P. 1990, 'Professional advisers and white collar illegality: Towards explaining and excusing professional failure' 13(1) *University of New South Wales Law Journal*, 73–96.

—— 1995, 'Using non-governmental resources to foster regulatory compliance' 8 *Governance: An International Journal of Policy and Administration*, 527–50.

——& Braithwaite, J. 1986, *Of Manners Gentle: Enforcement Strategies of Australian Business Regulatory Agencies*, Oxford University Press, Melbourne.

Granfield, R. 1992, *Making Elite Lawyers: Visions of Law at Harvard and Beyond*, Routledge, New York.

Gray, R., Owen, D. & Adams, C. 1996, *Accounting and Accountability: Changes and Challenges in Corporate Social and Environmental Reporting*, Prentice Hall, London.

Green, S. 1995 'Minister attacks "cosy' lawyers" 5 April *Age*, 1.

Greenbaum, E. 1996, 'Development of law firm training programs: Coping with a turbulent environment' 3 *International Journal of the Legal Profession*, 315–52.

Greenfield, S. & Osborn, G. 1995, 'Where cultures collide: The characterization of law and lawyers in film' 23 *International Journal of the Sociology of Law*, 107–30.

Gruner, R. 1994, *Corporate Crime and Sentencing*, Michie Company, Charlottesville, Va.

Gunningham, N. 1984, *Safeguarding the Worker: Job Hazards and the Role of Law*, Law Book Company, Sydney.

——& Sinclair, D. 1999, 'Environment management systems, regulation and the pulp and paper industry: ISO 14001 in practice' 16 *Environmental and Planning Law Journal*, 5–24.

Haakonssen, K. 1993, 'Republicanism' in Goodin, R. & Pettit, P. (eds.) *A Companion to Contemporary Philosophy*, Basil Blackwell, Oxford, 568–74.

Habermas, J. (McCarthy, T. trans.) 1987, *The Theory of Communicative Action*, ii: *Lifeworld and System: A Critique of Functionalist Reason*, Polity Press, Cambridge.

——(Rehg, W. trans.) 1996, *Between Facts and Norms: Contributions to a Discourse Theory of Law and Democracy*, MIT Press, Cambridge, Mass.

HAGAN, J. & KAY, F. 1995, *Gender in Practice: A Study of Lawyers' Lives*, Oxford University Press, New York.

HALLIDAY, T. 1987, *Beyond Monopoly: Lawyers, State Crises, and Professional Empowerment*, University of Chicago Press, Chicago.

—— & CARRUTHERS, B. 1996, 'The moral regulation of markets: Professions, privatization and the English Insolvency Act 1986' 21(4) *Accounting, Organizations & Society*, 371–413.

—— & KARPIK, L. 1997, 'Politics matter: A comparative theory of lawyers in the making of political liberalism' in Halliday, T. & Karpik, L. (eds.) *Lawyers and the Rise of Western Political Liberalism*, Clarendon Press, Oxford, 15–64.

HANDLER, J. 1967, *The Lawyer and his Community: The Practicing Bar in a Middle-Sized City*, University of Wisconsin Press, Madison.

—— 1980, 'Social movements and the legal system: A theoretical perspective' in Blankenburg, E. (ed.) *Innovations in the Legal Services: Research on Legal Service Delivery*, i, Oelgeschlager, Gunn & Hain, Cambridge, Mass., 109–29.

HANSEN, O. 1994, *The Solicitors Complaints Bureau: A Consumer View*, National Consumer Council, London.

HARRINGTON, C. & MERRY, S. 1988, 'Ideological production: The making of community mediation' 22(4) *Law & Society Review*, 709–35.

HARRIS, N. 1994, *Solicitors and Client Care: An Aspect of Professional Competence*, National Consumer Council, London.

HARVARD LAW REVIEW 1996, 'Growing the carrot: Encouraging effective corporate compliance' 109 *Harvard Law Review*, 1783–800.

HAUG, M. 1980, 'The sociological approach to self-regulation' in Blair, S. & Rubin, S. (eds.) *Regulating the Professions*, Lexington Books, Lexington, Mass., 61–80.

HAUHART, R. 1989, 'The legal aid sector of the legal services economy' 9(2/3) *International Journal of Sociology & Social Policy*, 51–69.

HAWKINS, K. 1984, *Environment and Enforcement: Regulation and the Social Definition of Pollution*, Clarendon Press, Oxford.

HAYNES, P. 1983, 'Crime and the professions: The legal profession: A comparative view' in Institute of Criminology, *Crime and the Professions: The Legal Profession*, Proceedings of the Institute of Criminology No. 55, University of Sydney, 44–53.

HAZARD, G. & RHODE, D. 1985, *The Legal Profession: Responsibility and Regulation* Foundation Press, Mineola, NY.

HEIMER, C. 1996, 'Explaining variation in the impact of law: Organizations, institutions and professions' 15 *Studies in Law, Politics & Society*, 29–59.

—— 1998, *For the Sake of the Children: Responsibility and Social Control in Neo-natal Intensive Care Units*, University of Chicago Press, Chicago.

HEINZ, J. & LAUMANN, E. 1982, *Chicago Lawyers: The Social Structure of the Bar*, Russell Sage Foundation & American Bar Foundation, New York.

HELD, D. 1995, *Democracy and the Global Order: From the Modern State to Cosmopolitan Governance*, Stanford University Press, Stanford, Calif.

HENRY, S. 1983, *Private Justice: Towards Integrated Theorising in the Sociology of Law*, Routledge & Kegan Paul, London.

HILMER, F., RAYNER, M. & TAPERELL, G. 1993, *National Competition Policy (The Hilmer Report)*, Australian Government Publishing Service, Canberra.

HOFFMAN, A. 1997, *From Heresy to Dogma: An Institutional History of Corporate Environmentalism*, The New Lexington Press, San Francisco.

HOLDSWORTH, W. S. 1937, *A History of English Law*, vol. vi, Methuen & Co., London.

HOOD, C. & SCOTT, C. 1996, 'Bureaucratic regulation and new public management in the United Kingdom: Mirror-image developments?' 23(3) *Journal of Law & Society*, 321–45.

HOPKINS, A. 1978, *Crime, Law and Business: The Sociological Sources of Australian Monopoly Law*, Australian Institute of Criminology, Canberra.

—— 1995, *Making Safety Work*, Allen & Unwin, St Leonards.

HOROWITZ, I. 1980, 'The economic foundations of self-regulation in the professions' in Blair, R. & Rubin, S. (eds.) *Regulating the Professions*, Lexington Books, Lexington, Mass., 3–28.

HOSTICKA, C. 1979, 'We don't care about what happened, we only care about what is going to happen: Lawyer–client negotiations of reality' 26(5) *Social Problems*, 599–610.

HOWELLS, G. 1994, 'Funding money advice services: Ensuring that advisers are not beggars and that creditors cannot be choosers' in Shapland, J. & Le Grys, R. (eds.) *The Changing Shape of the Legal Profession*, Institute for the Study of the Legal Profession, Sheffield, 65–73.

HUGHES, E. 1963, 'Professions' 92 *Daedalus*, 655–68.

HUGHES COMMISSION, 1980, *The Royal Commission on Legal Services in Scotland: Report*, Her Majesty's Stationery Office, Edinburgh.

HUME, D. (Selby-Bigge, L. ed. & Nidditch, P. rev.) 1978, *A Treatise of Human Nature*, Clarendon Press, Oxford.

INNS OF COURT SCHOOL OF LAW 1989, *Professional Conduct and Practical Background: Materials for the Bar Vocational Course*, Blackstone Press, London.

INTERNATIONAL AUDITING PRACTICES COMMITTEE 1995, *The Audit Profession and the Environment*, International Federation of Accountants & the Auditing Standards Board of the Australian Accounting Research Foundation, Caulfield.

JACKSON, J. 1993, 'Public satisfaction with the criminal courts: Lessons for legal professionals' in Shapland, J. & Le Grys, R. (eds.) *The Changing Shape of the Legal Profession*, Institute for the Study of the Legal Profession, Sheffield, 92–9.

JAMES, R. 1997, *Private Ombudsmen and Public Law*, Dartmouth Publishing Company, Aldershot.

—— & SENEVIRATNE, M. 1995, 'The legal services ombudsman: Form versus function?' 58 *Modern Law Review*, 187–207.

JENKINS, J. 1994, 'Practice management: What do we know about how solicitors manage their practices?' 1 *International Journal of the Legal Profession*, 223–36.

JOHNSON, T. 1972, *Professions and Power*, Macmillan, London.

KAFKA, F. (Muir, W. & E. trans.) 1992, 'Before the law' reprinted in Wishingard, J. (ed.) *Legal Fictions: Short Stories about Lawyers and the Law*, Overlook Press, Woodstock, NY, 285–6.

KAGAN, R. & ROSEN, R. 1985, 'On the social significance of large law firm practice' 37 *Stanford Law Review*, 399–457.

—— & SCHOLZ, J. 1984, 'The "criminology of the corporation" and regulatory enforcement strategies' in Hawkins, K. & Thomas, J. (eds.) *Enforcing Regulation*, Kluwer Nijhoff Publishing, Boston, 67–95.

KAKABADSE, M. 1996, 'The general agreement on trade in services: Implications for international trade in legal services' in Tyrrell, A. & Yaqub, Z. (eds.) *The Legal Professions in the New Europe: A Handbook for Practitioners*, Cavendish Publishing, London, 443–50.

KATZMANN, R. (ed.) 1995, *The Law Firm and the Public Good*, Brookings Institution, Washington.

KAVANAUGH, K. 1976, 'Performance evaluation, education, and testing: Alternatives to punishment in professional regulation' 30 *University of Miami Law Review*, 953–83.

KERRUISH, V. 1991, *Jurisprudence as Ideology*, Routledge, London.

KEYS YOUNG, 1995, *Gender Bias and the Law: Women Working in the Legal Profession in NSW: Research on Gender Bias and Women Working in the Legal System*, Department for Women, Sydney.

KIDDER, R. 1976, 'Lawyers for the people: Dilemmas of legal activists', in Gersh, J. & Jacobs, G. (eds.) *Professions for the People: The Politics of Skill*, Schenkman Publishing Coy, New York, 153–74.

KING, M. & ISRAEL, M. 1989, 'The pursuit of excellence, or how solicitors maintain racial inequality' 16 *New Community*, 107–20.

KIRK, H. 1976, *Portrait of a Profession: A History of the Solicitors' Profession 1100 to the Present Day*, Oyez Publishing, London.

KIRK, S. 1994, 'Anger at plans to deregulate professions' 28 February *Sydney Morning Herald*, 6.

KOHN, A. 1993, *Punished by Rewards: The Trouble with Gold Stars, Incentive Plans, A's, Praise and Other Bribes*, Houghton Mifflin Coy, Boston.

KRAAKMAN, R. 1985, 'The economic functions of corporate liability' in Hopt, K. & Teubner, G. (eds.) *Corporate Governance and Directors' Liabilities: Legal, Economic and Sociological Analyses on Corporate Social Responsibility*, Walter de Gruyter, Berlin, 178–207.

KRITZER, H. 1991, 'Abel and the professional project: The institutional analysis of the legal profession' *Law & Social Inquiry*, 529–52.

KRONMAN, A. 1993, *The Lost Lawyer: Failing Ideals of the Legal Profession*, Belknap Press of Harvard University Press, Cambridge, Mass.

KRYGIER, M. 1997, 'Virtuous circles: Antipodean reflections on power, institutions, and civil society' 11 *East European Politics and Societies*, 36–88.

LAFONTAINE, Y. 1985, 'Are lawyers a vivid contradiction?' in Gibson, D. & Baldwin, J. (eds.) *Law in a Cynical Society? Opinion and Law in the 1980's*, Carswell Legal Publications, Calgary, 175–81.

LAGAN, B. 1998, 'Fee estimate rules too difficult, say lawyers' 18 February *Sydney Morning Herald*, 3.

LANDON, D. 1985, 'Clients, colleagues, and community: The shaping of zealous advocacy in country law practice' *American Bar Foundation Research Journal*, 81–111.

LA PRAIRIE, C. 1995, 'Altering course: New directions in criminal justice and corrections: Sentencing circles and family group conferences' *Australian and New Zealand Journal of Criminology*, 78–99.

LARSON, M. 1977, *The Rise of Professionalism*, University of California Press, Berkeley and Los Angeles.

LAW COUNCIL OF AUSTRALIA 1994*a*, *Blueprint for the Structure of the Legal Profession: A National Market for Legal Services*, Canberra.

—— 1994*b*, *Legal Aid Funding in the '90s*, Law Council of Australia, Canberra.

LAW INSTITUTE OF VICTORIA 1994, *Special Report: An Independent Legal Profession: An Integral Part of the Justice System*, Law Institute of Victoria, Melbourne.

LAW REFORM COMMISSION OF VICTORIA 1991, *Access to the Law: Accountability of the Legal Profession*, Law Reform Commission of Victoria, Melbourne.

—— 1992*a*, *Access to the Law: Restrictions on Legal Practice: Report No. 47*, Law Reform Commission of Victoria, Melbourne.

—— 1992*b*, *Competition Law: Report No. 49*, Law Reform Commission of Victoria, Melbourne.

LAWRENCE, E. 1978, 'Lawyers and clients: Some methodological questions' in Tomasic, R. (ed.) *Understanding Lawyers: Perspectives on the Legal Profession in Australia*, Allen & Unwin, Sydney, 305–18.

LEGAL ACCESS MARKETING GROUP 1985, *Legal Access: A Marketing Report and Plan Prepared for the Legal Profession of New South Wales*, Sydney Technical College, Ultimo.

LEGAL AID & FAMILY SERVICES 1994, *Legal Aid in Australia 1992–1993 Statistical Yearbook*, Attorney General's Department, Canberra.

—— 1995, *Legal Aid in Australia 1993–1994 Statistical Yearbook*, Attorney General's Department, Canberra.

LEIBFRIED, S. & RIEGER, E. 1995, 'The welfare state and globalisation: Conflicts over Germany's competitiveness: Exiting from the global economy?' *Occasional Paper*, Center for German and European Studies, University of California at Berkeley.

LELAND, H. 1979, 'Quacks, lemons, and licensing: A theory of minimum quality standards' 87 *Journal of Political Economy*, 1328–46.

LEMPERT, R. & MONSMA, K. 1988, 'Lawyers and informal justice: The case of a public housing eviction board' 51 *Law & Contemporary Problems*, 135–80.

LENTZ, B. & LABAND, D. 1995, *Sex Discrimination in the Legal Profession*, Quorum Books, Westport, Conn.

LERMAN, L. 1994, 'Gross profits? Questions about lawyer billing practices' 22 *Hofstra Law Review*, 645–53.

LEUBSDORF, J. 1982, 'Three models of professional reform' 67 *Cornell Law Review*, 1021–54.

LEVI, M. 1988, *Of Rule and Revenue*, University of California Press, Berkeley and Los Angeles.

LIEBERMAN, J. 1981, *The Litigious Society*, Basic Books, New York.

LIND, E. & TYLER, T. 1988, *The Social Psychology of Procedural Justice*, Plenum Press, New York.

LINOWITZ, S. 1994, *The Betrayed Profession: Lawyering at the End of the Twentieth Century*, Charles Scribner's Sons, New York.

LISTER, R. 1995, 'Dilemmas in engendering citizenship' 24(1) *Economy & Society*, 1–40.

LLOYD, D. 1979, *The Idea of Law*, Penguin Books Ltd., Harmondsworth.

LOCKLEY, A. (ed.) 1993, *The Pursuit of Quality: A Guide for Lawyers*, Tolley Publishing Coy, Surrey.

LOFLAND, J. 1971, *Analysing Social Settings: A Guide to Qualitative Observation and Analysis*, Wadsworth, Belmont, Calif.

LOPEZ, G. 1992, *Rebellious Lawyering: One Chicano's Vision of Progressive Law Practice*, Westview Press, Boulder, Colo.

LOVE, J., STEPHEN, F., GILLANDERS, D. & PATERSON, A. 1992, 'Spatial aspects of deregulation in the market for legal services' 26(2) *Regional Studies*, 137–47.

LOWY, M. 1978, 'A good name is worth more than money: Strategies of court use in urban Ghana' in Nader, L. & Todd, H. (eds.) *The Disputing Process: Law in Ten Societies*, Columbia University Press, New York, 181–208.

LUBAN, D. 1987, 'Law: The decline of the people's lawyer?' in Jennings, B., Levine, C. & Bermel, J. (eds.) *The Public Duties of the Professions: A Hastings Center Report Special Supplement/February 1987*, 11–12.

—— 1988, *Lawyers and Justice: An Ethical Study*, Princeton University Press, Princeton, NJ.

—— 1994, 'Introduction' in Luban, D. (ed.) *The Ethics of Lawyers*, Dartmouth, Aldershot, pp. xi–xxxiv.

LUHMANN, N. 1985, 'The self-reproduction of law and its limits' in Teubner, G. (ed.) *Dilemmas of Law in the Welfare State*, Walter de Gruyter, Berlin, 111–27.

MACAULAY, S. 1963, 'Non-contractual relations in business: A preliminary study' 28 *American Sociological Review*, 55–69.

MCBARNET, D. 1994, 'Legal creativity: Law, capital and legal avoidance' in Cain, M. & Harrington, C. (eds.) *Lawyers in a Postmodern World: Translation and Transgression*, New York University Press, New York, 73–84.

McCall, G. & Simmons, J. 1969, *Issues in Participant Observation: A Text and Reader*, Addison-Wesley, Reading, Mass.

McConville, M. & Mirsky, C. 1995, 'Guilty plea courts: A social disciplinary model of criminal justice' 42(2) *Social Problems*, 216–34.

MacDonald, D. 1994, 'Gross profits: A client's perspective' 22 *Hofstra Law Review*, 655–60.

Macdonald, K. 1995, *The Sociology of the Professions*, Sage Publications, London.

Macdonald, R. 1990, 'Access to justice and law reform' 10 *Windsor Yearbook of Access to Justice*, 287–337.

McEwen, C. 1987, 'Differing visions of alternative dispute resolution and formal law' 12(2) *Justice System Journal*, 247–59.

—— & Maiman, R. 1981, 'Small claims mediation in Maine: An empirical assessment' 33 *Maine Law Review*, 237–68.

—— —— 1984, 'Mediation in small claims court: Achieving compliance through consent' 18 *Law & Society Review*, 11–49.

—— —— 1988, 'Coercion and consent: A tale of two court reforms' 10 *Law & Policy*, 3–24.

—— —— & Mather, L. 1994, 'Lawyers, mediation, and the management of divorce practice' 28(1) *Law & Society Review*, 149–86.

McGuinness, P. 1995, 'Victoria's conservative lawyers crying wolf to reforms' 5 April *Age*, 16.

McKechnie, W. 1914, *Magna Carta: A Commentary on the Great Charter of King John*, Burt Franklin, New York.

Mackie, K. 1989, *Lawyers in Business: And the Law Business*, Macmillan Press, Houndsmills.

MacKinnon, C. 1979, *Sexual Harassment of Working Women: A Case of Sex Discrimination*, Yale University Press, New Haven.

MacMillan, L. 1995, *Client Care: A Report of a Survey on the Client Care Provided by Solicitors in Scotland*, Scottish Consumer Council, Glasgow.

McQueen, R. 1993, 'The Law Institute of Victoria 1885–1930: "A very powerful and far reaching trade union"' *University of Manitoba Canadian Legal History Project Working Paper Series*, University of Manitoba.

Madison, J., Hamilton, A. & Jay, J. (Kramnick, I. ed) 1987, *The Federalist Papers*, Penguin Books, London.

Majone, G. 1994, 'The rise of the regulatory state in Europe' 17 *West European Politics*, 77–101.

—— 1996, *Regulating Europe*, Routledge, London.

Makkai, T. & Braithwaite, J. 1993, 'Praise, pride and corporate compliance' 21 *International Journal of the Sociology of Law*, 73–91.

—— —— 1994*a*, 'Reintegrative shaming and regulatory compliance' 32 *Criminology*, 361–85.

—— —— 1994*b*, 'The dialectics of corporate deterrence' 31 *Journal of Research in Crime & Delinquency*, 347–73.

MALEY, B. 1974, 'Professionalism and professional ethics' in Edgar, D. (ed.) *Social Change in Australia: Readings in Sociology*, Cheshire Publishing, Melbourne, 391–408.

MANIN, B. 1994, 'Checks, balances and boundaries: The separation of powers in the constitutional debate of 1787' in Fontana, B. (ed.) *The Invention of the Modern Republic*, Cambridge University Press, Cambridge, 27–62.

MANN, K. 1985, *Defending White-Collar Crime: A Portrait of Attorneys at Work*, Yale University Press, New Haven.

MANNING, P. 1987, 'Ironics of compliance' in Shearing, C. and Stenning, P. (eds.) *Private Policing*, Sage Publications, Newbury Park, Calif.

MARK, S. 1995, 'Bringing lawyers to the table' in Selby, H. (ed.) *Tomorrow's Law*, Federation Press, Sydney, 235–50.

—— 1996, *The Role of the Legal Services Commissioner*, Office of the Legal Services Commissioner, Sydney.

MARQUESS, J. 1994, 'Legal audits and dishonest legal bills' 22 *Hofstra Law Review*, 637–44.

MARSHALL, T. 1985, *Alternatives to Criminal Courts*, Gower, Aldershot.

—— & MERRY, S. 1990, *Crime and Accountability: Victim/Offender Mediation in Practice*, Her Majesty's Stationery Office, London.

MASON, A. 1993, 'The independence of the bench; the independence of the bar and the bar's role in the judicial system' 10 *Australian Bar Review*, 1–10.

MATHER, L. 1998, 'Theorizing about trial courts: Lawyers, policymaking, and tobacco litigation' 23 *Law & Social Inquiry*, 897–940.

MAY, L. 1996, *The Socially Responsive Self: Social Theory and Professional Ethics*, University of Chicago Press, Chicago.

MEADOWS, H. 1996, 'Attorney defends Bill' 70 *Law Institute Journal*, 10–11.

MEADOWS, R. 1994, 'Comment II' 4 *Journal of Judicial Administration*, 85–93.

MELLINKOFF, D. 1973, *The Conscience of a Lawyer*, West Publishing Coy, St Paul, Minn.

MENTOR, K. 1996, 'Strategic choices in legal services: Funding, case selection, and litigation strategy' Paper presented to the Joint Meeting of the Law & Society Association and the Research Committee on the Sociology of Law, Glasgow.

MERRY, S. E. 1990, *Getting Justice and Getting Even: Legal Consciousness Among Working Class Americans*, University of Chicago Press, Chicago.

—— 1993, 'Sorting out popular justice' in Merry, S. E. & Milner, N. (eds.) *The Possibility of Popular Justice: A Case Study of Community Mediation*, University of Michigan Press, Ann Arbor, 31–66.

—— & MILNER, N. 1993, 'Introduction' in Merry, S. E. & Milner, N. (eds.) *The Possibility of Popular Justice: A Case Study of Community Mediation in the United States*, University of Michigan Press, Ann Arbor, 3–29.

MESSMER, H. & OTTO, H. 1992, 'Restorative justice: Steps on the way toward a good idea' in Messmer, H. & Otto, H. (eds.) *Restorative Justice on Trial*, Kluwer, Dordrecht, 1–12.

Mew, G. 1989, 'Lawyers: The agony and the ecstasy of self-government' 9 *Windsor Yearbook of Access to Justice*, 210–47.

Minichiello, V., Aroni, R., Timewell, E. & Alexander, R. 1990, *In-Depth Interviewing: Researching People*, Longman Cheshire, Melbourne.

Mnookin, R. & Kornhauser, L. 1979, 'Bargaining in the shadow of the law: The case of divorce' 88(5) *Yale Law Journal*, 950–97.

Moore, R. 1985, 'Reflections of Canadians on the law and the legal system: Legal Research Institute survey of respondents in Montreal, Toronto and Winnipeg' in Gibson, D. & Baldwin, J. (eds.) *Law in a Cynical Society? Opinion and Law in the 1980s*, Carswell Legal Publications, Calgary, 41–87.

Moorhead, R. 1998, 'Legal aid in the eye of a storm: Rationing, contracting and a new institutionalism' 25(3) *Journal of Law & Society*, 365–87.

—— Sherr, A. & Paterson, A. 1994, 'Judging on results? Outcome measures: quality, strategy and the search for objectivity' 1 *International Journal of the Legal Profession*, 191–210.

Morgan, T. & Rotunda, R. 1993, *1993 Selected Standards on Professional Responsibility*, Foundation Press, Westbury, NY.

Muris, T. & McChesney, F. 1979, 'Advertising and the price and quality of legal services: The case for legal clinics' *American Bar Foundation Research Journal*, 179–209.

Nader, L. 1979, 'Disputing without the force of law' 88(5) *Yale Law Journal*, 998–1021.

—— (ed.) 1980, *No Access to Law: Alternatives to the American Judicial System*, Academic Press, New York.

Nader, R. & Smith, W. 1996, *No Contest: Corporate Lawyers and the Perversion of Justice in America*, Random House, New York.

Naffine, N. 1990, *Law and the Sexes: Explorations in Feminist Jurisprudence*, Allen & Unwin, Sydney.

—— & Wundersitz, J. 1991, 'Lawyers in the children's court: An Australian perspective' 37(3) *Crime & Delinquency*, 374–92.

National Consumer Council 1995, *Seeking Civil Justice*, National Consumer Council, London.

Nelsen, J. 1996, *Positive Discipline*, Ballantine Books, New York.

Nelson, R. 1988, *Partners with Power: The Social Transformation of the Large Law Firm*, University of California Press, Berkeley and Los Angeles.

—— 1996, 'Uncivil litigation: Problematic behaviour in large law firms' 7(4) *Researching Law*, 1, 7–9.

Newman, R. 1987, 'Laymen as lawyers in the processing of dismissal disputes' 14 *Journal of Law & Society*, 217–28.

New South Wales Law Reform Commission 1980, *The Legal Profession: Background Paper III*, New South Wales Law Reform Commission, Sydney.

New South Wales Law Reform Commission 1982, *First Report on the Legal Profession: General Regulation and Structure: Report 31*, New South Wales Law Reform Commission, Sydney.

—— 1993, *Scrutiny of the Legal Profession: Complaints against Lawyers: Report 70*, New South Wales Law Reform Commission, Sydney.

Norrie, A. 1993, *Crime, Reason and History: A Critical Introduction to Criminal Law*, Weidenfeld & Nicolson, London.

North, R. 1997, 'Encouraging clients to complain' 35(3) *Law Society Journal*, 33.

Nosworthy, E. 1995, 'Ethics and large law firms' in Parker, S. & Sampford, C. (eds.) *Legal Ethics and Legal Practice: Contemporary Issues*, Clarendon Press, Oxford, 57–72.

Office of the Legal Services Commissioner 1997, *Annual Report 1995–96*, Office of the Legal Services Commissioner, Sydney.

Ogus, A. 1994, *Regulation: Legal Form and Economic Theory*, Clarendon Press, Oxford.

Oldfield, A. 1990, *Citizenship and Community: Civic Republicanism and the Modern World*, Routledge, London.

Olweus, D. 1994, 'Annotation: Bullying at school: Basic facts and effects of a school based intervention program' 35 *Journal of Child Psychology & Psychiatry*, 1171–190.

O'Malley, P. 1983, *Law, Capitalism and Democracy*, George Allen & Unwin, Sydney.

Osborne, D. & Gaebler, T. 1992, *Reinventing Government: How the Entrepreneurial Spirit is Transforming the Public Sector*, Addison-Wesley, Reading, Mass.

Page, A. 1987, 'Financial services: The self-regulatory alternative?' in Baldwin, R. & McCrudden, C. (eds.) *Regulation and Public Law*, Weidenfeld & Nicolson, London, 298–322.

Palmer, A. & Sampford, C. 1994, 'Retrospective legislation in Australia: Looking back at the 1980s' 22(2) *Federal Law Review*, 217–77.

Pannick, D. 1992, *Advocates*, Oxford University Press, Oxford.

Parker, C. 1994, 'The logic of professionalism: Stages of domination in legal service delivery to the disadvantaged' 22 *International Journal of the Sociology of Law*, 145–68.

—— 1997*a*, 'Some questions about sex and justice and power: Legal fantasies in *The First Stone*', 22(3) *Alternative Law Journal*, 122–5.

—— 1997*b*, 'Justifying the New South Wales legal profession' 2(2) *Newcastle Law Review*, 1–29.

—— 1999, 'How to win hearts and minds: Corporate compliance policies for sexual harassment' 21 *Law & Policy*, 21–48.

—— & Goldsmith, A. 1998, '"Failed sociologists" in the marketplace: Law schools in Australia' 25 *Journal of Law & Society*, 33–50.

Parker, S. 1996, 'Islands of civic virtue? Lawyers and civil justice reform' Inaugural Professorial Lecture, 5 December 1996, Griffith University.

PARSONS, T. 1954*a*, 'The professions and social structure' in Parsons, T. *Essays in Sociological Theory*, Free Press, Glencoe, Ill., 34–49.

—— 1954*b*, 'A sociologist looks at the legal profession' in Parsons, T. *Essays in Sociological Theory*, Free Press, Glencoe, Ill., 370–85.

PARTINGTON, M. 1991, 'Change or no-change? Reflections on the Courts and Legal Services Act 1990' 54(5) *Modern Law Review*, 702–12.

PATERNOSTER, R., BRAME, R., BACHMAN, R. & SHERMAN, L. 1997, 'Do fair procedures matter? The effect of procedural justice on spouse assault' 31 *Law & Society Review*, 163–204.

—— & SIMPSON, S. 1996, 'Sanction threats and appeals to morality: Testing a rational choice model of corporate crime' 30 *Law & Society Review*, 549–83.

PATERSON, A. 1995, 'Legal ethics: Its nature and place in the curriculum' in Cranston, R. (ed.) *Legal Ethics and Professional Responsibility*, Clarendon Press, Oxford, 175–88.

—— 1996, 'Professionalism and the legal services market' 3 *International Journal of the Legal Profession*, 137–68.

—— FARMER, L., STEPHEN, F. & LOVE, J. 1988, 'Competition and the market for legal services' 15(4) *Journal of Law & Society*, 361–73.

—— & NELKEN, D. 1996, 'The evolution of legal services in Britain: Pragmatic welfarism or demand creation?' in Paterson, A. & Goriely, T. (eds.) *A Reader on Resourcing Civil Justice*, Oxford University Press, Oxford, 201–10.

PAVLICH, G. 1996, 'The power of community mediation: Government and formation of self-identity' 30 *Law & Society Review* 707–33.

PEARSON, J. 1982, 'An evaluation of alternatives to court adjudication' 7 *Justice System Journal*, 420–44.

PENGILLEY, W. 1994, 'Some issues arising from deregulation of legal costs' Paper given at Law Society of New South Wales conference, Australian Lawyers, National Practice and Competition, New South Wales Parliament House, Sydney.

PEPLER, D, CRAIG, W., ZEIGLER, S. & CHURCH, A. 1993, 'A school-based anti-bullying intervention: Preliminary evaluation' in Tattum, D. (ed.) *Understanding and Managing Bullying*, Heinemann, London, 76–91.

PERKIN, H. 1989, *The Rise of Professional Society: England since 1880*, Routledge, London.

PETTIT, P. 1993, 'Liberalism and republicanism' 28 *Australian Journal of Political Science*, 162–89.

—— 1996, 'Freedom as antipower' 106 *Ethics*, 576–604.

—— 1997, *Republicanism: A Theory of Freedom and Government*, Oxford University Press, Oxford.

—— with BRAITHWAITE, J. 1993, 'Not just deserts, even in sentencing' 3(4) *Current Issues in Criminal Justice*, 225–39.

PHELPS, M. 1995, 'Who are these people?' 30(11) *Australian Lawyer*, 3.

PHILLIPS, A. 1991, *Engendering Democracy*, Polity Press, Cambridge.

Pleasence, P., Maclean, S. & Morley, A. 1996, *Profiling Civil Litigation: The Case for Research*, Legal Aid Board Research Unit, London.

Porter, M. 1990, *The Competitive Advantage of Nations*, Macmillan Press, London & Basingstoke.

—— & van der Linde, C. 1995, 'Green and competitive: Ending the stalemate' September–October *Harvard Business Review*, 120–34.

Post, R. 1987, 'On the popular image of the lawyer: Reflections in a dark glass' 75 *California Law Review*, 379–89.

Pound, R. 1953, *The Lawyer from Antiquity to Modern Times*, West Publishing Co, St Paul, Minn.

Powell, M. 1985, 'Developments in the regulation of lawyers: Competing segments and market, client, and government controls' 64(2) *Social Forces*, 281–305.

—— 1986, 'Professional divestiture: The cession of responsibility for lawyer discipline' *American Bar Foundation Research Journal*, 31–54.

—— 1993, 'Professional innovation: Corporate lawyers and private lawmaking' 18 *Law & Social Inquiry*, 423–54.

Power, M. 1997, *The Audit Society: Rituals of Verification*, Oxford University Press, Oxford.

Public Interest Law Clearing House 1996, *Annual Report 1995–1996*, Melbourne.

Pue, W. 1987*a*, 'Rebels at the bar: English barristers and the county courts in the 1850s' 16 *Anglo-American Law Review*, 303–52.

—— 1987*b*, 'Exorcising professional demons: Charles Rann Kennedy and the transition to the modern bar' 5(1) *Law & History Review*, 135–74.

—— 1990*a*, 'Moral panic at the English bar: Paternal vs commercial ideologies of legal practice in the 1860s' 15 *Law & Social Inquiry*, 49–118.

—— 1990*b*, '"Trajectories of professionalism?": Legal professionalism after Abel' 19 *Manitoba Law Journal*, 384–418.

—— 1995, 'In pursuit of better myth: Lawyers' histories and histories of lawyers' 33 *Alberta Law Review*, 730–67.

Pusey, M. 1991, *Economic Rationalism in Canberra: A Nation Building State Changes its Mind*, Cambridge University Press, Cambridge.

Rawls, J. 1972, *A Theory of Justice*, Oxford University Press, Oxford.

Rayner, M. 1995, 'Independent lawyers are a protection for democracy' 3 April *Age*, 14.

Reasons, C., Bray, B. & Chappell, D. 1989, 'Ideology, ethics and the business of law: Varying perceptions of the ethics of the legal profession' 13(2) *Legal Studies Forum*, 171–88.

—— & Chappell, D. 1985, 'Crooked lawyers: Towards a political economy of deviance in the profession' in Fleming, T. (ed.) *The New Criminologies in Canada: State, Crime and Control*, Oxford University Press, Toronto, 206–22.

—— —— 1986, 'Continental capitalism and crooked lawyering' 26 *Crime & Social Justice*, 38–59.

Reed, J. 1972, 'The lawyer–client: A managed relationship?' in Bryant, C. (ed.) *The Social Dimensions of Work*, Prentice Hall, Englewood Cliffs, NJ, 420–34.

Rees, J. 1988, *Reforming the Workplace: A Study of Self-Regulation in Occupational Safety*, University of Pennsylvania Press, Philadelphia.

Regan, F, 1996, 'Criminal legal aid: Does defending liberty undermine citizenship?' in Young, R. & Wall, D. (eds.) *Access to Criminal Justice: Legal Aid, Lawyers and the Defence of Liberty*, Blackstone Press, London, 70–97.

—— & Fleming, D. 1994, 'International perspectives on legal aid' 19(4) *Alternative Law Journal*, 183–5.

Reichstein, K. 1965, 'Ambulance chasing: A case study of deviation and control within the legal profession' 13 *Social Problems*, 3–17.

Rhode, D. 1994, *Professional Responsibility: Ethics by the Pervasive Method*, Little Brown & Company, Boston.

—— 1995, 'Into the valley of ethics: Professional responsibility and educational reform' 58 *Law & Contemporary Problems*, 139–51.

Rickman, N. & Gray, A. 1995, 'The role of legal expenses insurance in securing access to the market for legal services' in Zuckerman, A. & Cranston, R. (eds.) *Reform of Civil Procedure: Essays on 'Access to Justice'*, Clarendon Press, Oxford, 305–25.

Riekert, J. 1990, 'Alternative dispute resolution in Australian commercial disputes: Quo vadis?' 1(1) *Australian Dispute Resolution Journal*, 31–45.

Roberts, S. 1995, 'Litigation and settlement' in Zuckerman, A. & Cranston, R. (eds.) *Reform of Civil Procedure: Essays on 'Access to Justice'*, Clarendon Press, Oxford, 447–57.

Roeber, A. 1981, *Faithful Magistrates and Republican Lawyers: Creators of Virginian Legal Culture, 1680–1810*, University of North Carolina Press, Chapel Hill.

Ronalds, C. 1991, *Affirmative Action and Sex Discrimination: A Handbook on Legal Rights for Women*, Pluto Press, Sydney.

Rose, J. 1983, 'Professional regulation: The current controversy' 7(2/3) *Law & Human Behavior*, 103–16.

Rosen, R. 1989, 'The inside counsel movement, professional judgment and organizational representation' 64 *Indiana Law Journal*, 479–553.

Rosenberg, G. 1991, *The Hollow Hope: Can Courts Bring about Social Change?* The University of Chicago, Chicago.

Rosenthal, D. 1977, *Lawyer and Client: Who's in Charge?* Transaction Books, New Brunswick, NJ.

Ross, S. 1995, *Ethics in Law: Lawyers' Responsibility and Accountability in Australia*, Butterworths, Sydney.

Ross, W. 1996, *The Honest Hour: The Ethics of Time-Based Billing by Attorneys*, Carolina Academic Press, Durham, NC.

Rowley, C. 1992, *The Right to Justice: The Political Economy of Legal Services in the United States*, Edward Elgar, Brookfield.

RUESCHEMEYER, D. 1983, 'Professional autonomy and the social control of expertise' in Dingwall, R. & Lewis, P. (eds.) *The Sociology of the Professions*, Macmillan Press, London, 38–58.

SAINSBURY, R. & GENN, H. 1995, 'Access to justice: Lessons from tribunals' in Zuckerman, A. & Cranston, R. (eds.) *Reform of Civil Procedure: Essays on 'Access to Justice'*, Clarendon Press, Oxford, 413–29.

SALTER, R. & FRIEND, J. 1996, 'One firm's approach to quality' 70(2) *Law Institute Journal*, 36.

SAMPFORD, C. with PARKER, C. 1995, 'Legal regulation, ethical standard setting and institutional design' in Parker, S. & Sampford, C. (eds.) *Legal Ethics and Legal Practice: Contemporary Issues*, Clarendon Press, Oxford, 11–24.

SARAT, A. 1986, 'Access to justice: Citizen participation and the American legal order' in Lipson, L. & Wheeler, S. (eds.) *Law and the Social Sciences*, Russell Sage Foundation, New York, 519–80.

—— & FELSTINER, W. 1995, *Divorce Lawyers and their Clients: Power and Meaning in the Legal Process*, Oxford University Press, New York.

—— & SCHEINGOLD, S. 1998, 'Cause lawyering and the reproduction of professional authority' in Sarat, A. & Scheingold, S. (eds.) *Cause Lawyering: Political Commitments and Professional Responsibility*, Oxford University Press, New York, 3–28.

SCHEFF, T. 1990, *Microsociology: Discourse, Emotion and Social Structure*, University of Chicago Press, Chicago.

SCHEINGOLD, S. 1994, 'The contradictions of radical law practice' in Cain, M. & Harrington, C. (eds.) *Lawyers in a Postmodern World: Translation and Transgression*, New York University Press, New York, 265–85.

SCHNEYER, T. 1992, 'Professionalism as politics: The making of a modern legal ethics code' in Nelson, R., Trubek, D. & Solomon, R. (eds.) *Lawyers' Ideals/Lawyers' Practices: Transformations in the American Legal Profession*, Cornell University Press, Ithaca, NY, 95–143.

SCHROETER, J., SMITH, S. & COX, S. 1987, 'Advertising and competition in routine legal service markets: An empirical investigation' 36 *Journal of Industrial Economics*, 49–60.

SCHULTZ, T. 1961, 'Investment in human capital' 51(1) *American Economic Review*, 1–17.

SCHWARTZ, R. & ORLEANS, S. 1967, 'On legal sanctions' 34 *University of Chicago Law Review*, 274–300.

SCOTT, C. 1995, 'Criminalising the trader to protect the consumer: The fragmentation and consolidation of trading standards regulation' in Loveland, I. (ed.) *Frontiers of Criminality*, Sweet & Maxwell, London, 149–72.

SELF, R. 1985, 'Legal services and the emergence of a service economy: Practical and theoretical considerations' *Issues of Transnational Legal Practice: 1985 Michigan Yearbook of International Legal Studies*, 269–76.

SELINGER, C. 1994, 'Inventing billable hours: Contract v fairness in charging attorney's fees' 22 *Hofstra Law Review*, 671–8.

SELZNICK, P. 1969, *Law, Society and Industrial Justice*, Russell Sage Foundation, New York.

—— 1980, 'Jurisprudence and social policy: Aspirations and perspectives' 68 *California Law Review*, 206–20.

—— 1992, *The Moral Commonwealth*, University of California Press, Berkeley and Los Angeles.

SERON, C. 1992, 'Managing entrepreneurial legal services: The transformation of small-firm practice' in Nelson, R., Trubek, D. & Solomon, R. (eds.) *Lawyers' Ideals/Lawyers' Practices: Transformations in the American Legal Profession*, Cornell University Press, New York, 63–92.

—— 1996, *The Business of Practicing Law: The Work Lives of Solo and Small Firm Attorneys*, Temple University Press, Philadelphia.

SHAFFER, T. & COCHRAN, R. 1994, *Lawyers, Clients and Moral Responsibility*, West Publishing Co., St Paul, Minn.

SHAMIR, R. 1995, *Managing Legal Uncertainty: Elite Lawyers in the New Deal*, Duke University Press, Durham, NC.

SHEIKH, S. 1996, *Corporate Social Responsibilities Law and Practice*, Cavendish Publishing, London.

SHERMAN, L. 1993, 'Defiance, deterrence, and irrelevance: A theory of the criminal sanction' 30(4) *Journal of Research in Crime & Delinquency*, 445–73.

SHERR, A., Moorhead, R. & Paterson, A. 1994, 'Assessing the quality of legal work: Measuring process' 1 *International Journal of the Legal Profession*, 135–58.

SHILS, E. & RHEINSTEIN, M. (eds. & trans.) 1954, *Max Weber on Law in Economy and Society*, Harvard University Press, Cambridge, Mass.

SIGLER, J. & MURPHY, J. 1988, *Interactive Corporate Compliance: An Alternative to Regulatory Compulsion*, Quorum Books, New York.

SILVERSTEIN, D. 1987, 'Managing corporate social responsibility in a changing legal environment' 25 *American Business Law Journal* 524–66.

SIMON, J. 1992, '"The long walk home' to politics" 26 *Law & Society Review*, 923–41.

SIMON, R. 1994, 'Gross profits? An introduction to a program on legal fees' 22 *Hofstra Law Review*, 625–35.

SIMON, W. 1988, 'Ethical discretion in lawyering' 101 *Harvard Law Review*, 1083–145.

SINGER, L. 1994, *Settling Disputes: Conflict Resolution in Business, Families, and the Legal System*, Westview Press, Boulder, Colo.

SKINNER, Q. 1984, 'The idea of negative liberty: Philosophical and historical perspectives' in Rorty, R., Schneewind, J. & Skinner, Q. (eds.) *Philosophy in History: Essays on the Historiography of Philosophy*, Cambridge University Press, Cambridge, 193–221.

SLAYTON, P. & TREBILCOCK, M. (eds.) 1978, *The Professions and Public Policy*, University of Toronto Press, Toronto.

SLOTER, P. & SORENSON, A. 1983, 'Corporate legal ethics: An empirical study: The Model Rules, the Code of Professional Responsibility and counsel's continuing struggle between theory and practice' *Journal of Corporation Law*, 601–711.

SMIGEL, E. 1964, *The Wall Street Lawyer*, Free Press of Glencoe, New York.

SMITH, I., GODDARD, C. & RANDALL, N. 1993, *Health and Safety: The New Legal Framework*, Butterworths, London.

SMITH, R. 1989, 'The green papers and legal services' 52 *Modern Law Review*, 527–39.

—— 1994, 'Last chance saloon' 144 *New Law Journal*, 1741.

—— 1996, 'Introduction' in Smith, R. (ed.) *Achieving Civil Justice: Appropriate Dispute Resolution for the 1990s*, Legal Action Group, London, 1–5.

—— 1997, *Justice: Redressing the Balance*, Legal Action Group, London.

SMITH, S. 1997, 'Customer charters: The next dimension in consumer protection?' 22 *Alternative Law Journal* 138–40.

SPANGLER, E. 1986, *Lawyers for Hire: Salaried Professionals at Work*, Yale University Press, New Haven.

SPEISER, S. 1993, *Lawyers and the American Dream*, Blackstone Press Ltd., London.

STEELE, E. & NIMMER, R. 1976, 'Lawyers, clients, and professional regulation' *American Bar Foundation Research Journal*, 917–1019.

STEELE, J. & BULL, G. 1996, *Fast, Friendly and Expert? Legal Aid Franchising in Agencies without Solicitors*, Policy Studies Institute, London.

STEPHENS, M. 1985, 'Law centres, citizenship and participation' 7(1) *Law & Policy*, 77–95.

STERETT, S. 1990, 'Comparing legal professions' 15 *Law & Social Inquiry*, 363–84.

STOVER, R. 1989, *Making It and Breaking It: The Fate of Public Interest Commitment During Law School*, University of Illinois Press, Urbana.

STRETTON, R. 1994, 'In-house lawyers study how to get top value out of reform' 17 February *Financial Review*, 16.

STRINGHAM, R. 1966, *Magna Carta: Fountainhead of Freedom*, Aqueduct Books, Rochester.

SUCHMAN, M. & EDELMAN, L. 1996, 'Legal rational myths: The new institutionalism and the law and society tradition' 21 *Law & Social Inquiry*, 903–41.

SUDNOW, D. 1965, 'Normal crimes: Sociological features of the penal code in a public defender's office' in Chambliss, W. (ed.) *Crime and the Legal Process*, McGraw-Hill, New York, 237–61.

SUNSTEIN, C. 1988, 'Beyond the republican revival' 97 *Yale Law Journal*, 1539–90.

—— 1990, *After the Rights Revolution: Reconceiving the Regulatory State*, Harvard University Press, Cambridge, Mass.

—— 1993, *Democracy and the Problem of Free Speech*, Free Press, New York.

—— 1996, *Legal Reasoning and Political Conflict*, Oxford University Press, New York.

SUTTON, A. & WILD, R. 1978, 'Corporate crime and social structure' in Wilson, P. & Braithwaite, J. (eds.) *Two Faces of Deviance*, University of Queensland Press, St Lucia, 177–98.

TABAKOFF, N. 1994*a*, 'Lawyers attack plea to cut powers of state societies' 25 May *Financial Review*, 5.

—— 1994*b*, 'Accountants take law into their own firms' 23 September *Financial Review*, 1 and 12.

TARP 1995*a*, *American Express–SOCAP Study of Complaint Handling in Australia: Report One: Consumer Complaint Behaviour in Australia*, Society of Consumer Affairs Professionals in Business Australia, Geelong.

—— 1995*b*, *American Express–SOCAP Study of Complaint Handling in Australia: Report Two: A Profile of Enquiry and Complaint Handling by Australian Business*, Society of Consumer Affairs Professionals in Business Australia, Geelong.

TEUBNER, G. 1987, 'Juridification: Concepts, aspects, limits, solutions' in Teubner, G. (ed.) *Juridification of Social Spheres: A Comparative Analysis of the Areas of Labor, Corporate, Antitrust and Social Welfare Law*, Walter de Gruyter, Berlin, 3–48.

THOMAS, T. 1992, 'Thatcher's will' in Thomas, T. (ed.) *Tomorrow's Lawyers*, Blackwell Publishers, Oxford, 1–12.

THORNTON, M. 1996, *Dissonance and Distrust: Women in the Legal Profession*, Oxford University Press, Melbourne.

TITTLE, C. 1980, *Sanctions and Social Deviance*, Praeger, New York.

TOCQUEVILLE, A. (Reeve, H. trans.) 1961, *Democracy in America*, vol. i, Schocken Books, New York.

TOMASIC, R. 1990, 'Law, legal institutions and commerce: Widening the disciplinary boundaries of access to justice research' 10 *Windsor Yearbook of Access to Justice*, 422–35.

—— & BOTTOMLEY, S. 1993, *Directing the Top 500: Corporate Governance and Accountability in Australian Companies*, Allen & Unwin, Sydney.

TOMSEN, S. 1992, 'Professionalism and state engagement: Lawyers and legal aid policy in Australia in the 1970s and 1980s' 28 *Australian & New Zealand Journal of Sociology*, 307–29.

TRADE PRACTICES COMMISSION 1992, *The Legal Profession, Conveyancing and the Trade Practices Act*, Trade Practices Commission, Canberra.

—— 1993, *Study of the Professions: Legal: Draft Report*, Australian Government Publishing Service, Canberra.

—— 1994, *Study of the Professions: Legal: Final Report*, Trade Practices Commission, Canberra.

—— 1995*a*, *Utility Reform: Corporate Compliance Programs*, Trade Practices Commission, Canberra.

Trade Practices Commission 1995*b*, *Utility Reform: Information Disclosure and Redress Mechanisms*, Trade Practices Commission, Canberra.

Travers, M. 1994, 'Measurement and reality: Quality assurance and the work of a firm of criminal defence lawyers in Northern England' 1 *International Journal of the Legal Profession*, 173–89.

Trebilcock, M. & Reiter, B. 1982, 'Licensure in law' in Evans, R. & Trebilcock, M. (eds.) *Lawyers and the Consumer Interest: Regulating the Market for Legal Services*, Butterworths, Toronto, 65–103.

—— Tuohy, C. & Wolfson, A. 1979, *Professional Regulation*, Professional Organisations Committee, Ontario.

Trubek, D. 1990, 'Critical moments in access to justice theory: The quest for the empowered self' in Hutchinson, A. C. (ed.) *Access to Civil Justice*, Carswell, Toronto, 107–28.

—— & Trubek, L. 1981, 'Civic justice through civil justice: A new approach to public interest advocacy in the United States' in Cappelletti, M. (ed.) *Access to Justice and the Welfare State*, Sijthoff, Alphen aan den Rijn, 119–44.

Tuohy, C. 1976, 'Private government, property, and professionalism' 9(4) *Canadian Journal of Political Science*, 668–81.

Turow, S. 1977, *One L*, Penguin Books, New York.

Tyler, T. 1998, 'Trust and democratic governance' in Braithwaite, V. & Levi, M. (eds.) *Trust and Governance*, Russell Sage, New York, 269–94.

—— & Dawes, R. 1993, 'Fairness in groups: Comparing the self-interest and social identity perspectives' in Mellers, B. & Baron, J. (eds.) *Psychological Perspectives on Justice: Theory and Applications*, Cambridge University Press, Cambridge, 87–108.

Van Ness, D. 1986, *Crime and its Victims*, Intervarsity Press, Downers Grove, Ill.

Vaughan, D. 1992, 'Theory elaboration: The heuristics of case analysis' in Ragin, C. & Becker, H. (eds.) *What is a Case? Exploring the Foundations of Social Inquiry*, Cambridge University Press, Cambridge, 173–202.

—— 1996, *The Challenger Launch Decision: Risky Technology, Culture and Deviance at NASA*, University of Chicago Press, Chicago.

Vidmar, N. 1984, 'The small claims court: A reconceptualisation of disputes and an empirical investigation' 18 *Law & Society Review*, 515–50.

Wade, J. 1994, *Discussion Paper: Reforming the Legal Profession: An Agenda for Change*, Attorney General's Department, Melbourne.

Waldron, J. 1991, 'When justice replaces affection: The need for rights' in *Liberal Rights: Collected Papers 1981–1991*, Cambridge University Press, Cambridge, 370–91.

Webb, J. 1998, 'Ethics for lawyers or ethics for citizens? New directions for legal education' 25 *Journal of Law & Society*, 134–50.

Weinstein, H. 1993, 'Attorney liability in the savings and loan crisis' *University of Illinois Law Review*, 53–65.

Weisbrot, D. 1990, *Australian Lawyers*, Longman Cheshire, Melbourne.

——1993, 'Competition, cooperation and legal change' 4 *Legal Education Review*, 1–27.

Wilkins, D. 1992, 'Who should regulate lawyers?' 105(4) *Harvard Law Review*, 799–887.

——1993, 'Making context count: Regulating lawyers after Kaye, Scholer' 66 *Southern California Law Review*, 1145–220.

Will, K. 1996, 'Formal quality systems: An introduction' 70(2) *Law Institute Journal*, 31–3.

Wilson, D. 1995, 'Lawyers face new watchdog' 8 January *Sunday Herald Sun*, 4.

Wilton, H. 1983, 'The incidence of crime in the legal profession: A pattern of criminality or bumbling inefficiency' in Institute of Criminology, *Crime and the Professions: The Legal Profession*, Proceedings of the Institute of Criminology No. 55, University of Sydney, 29–36.

Wissler, R. 1995, 'Mediation and adjudication in the small claims court: The effects of process and case characteristics' 29 *Law & Society Review*, 323–58.

Wolfram, C. 1978, 'Barriers to effective public participation in the regulation of the legal profession' 62 *Minnesota Law Review*, 619–47.

Wollstonecraft, M. (Tomaselli, S. ed.) 1995, *A Vindication of the Rights of Men and a Vindication of the Rights of Woman*, Cambridge University Press, Cambridge.

Woods, J. 1993, 'Lawyers defend the system' 14 October *Courier Mail*, 22.

Woolf, Lord, 1995, *Access to Justice: Interim Report to the Lord Chancellor on the Civil Justice System in England and Wales*, Lord Chancellor's Department, London.

Yale, J. 1982, 'Public attitudes towards lawyers: An information perspective' in Evans, R. & Trebilcock, M. (eds.) *Lawyers and the Consumer Interest: Regulating the Market for Legal Services*, Butterworths, Toronto, 33–63.

Young, I. 1990, *Justice and the Politics of Difference*, Princeton University Press, Princeton, NJ.

——1993, 'Justice and communicative democracy' in Gottlieb, R. (ed.) *Radical Philosophy: Tradition, Counter-Tradition, Politics*, Temple University Press, Philadelphia, 123–43.

Young, M. 1992, 'Affirmative action in the legal profession' 66 *Law Institute Journal*, 1094–6.

Young, R. & Wall, D. 1996, *Access to Criminal Justice: Legal Aid, Lawyers and the Defence of Liberty*, Blackstone Press, London.

Zander, M. 1968, 'Restrictions on lawyers working for the poor' in Zander, M. *Lawyers and the Public Interest*, Wiedenfield & Nicholson, London, 234–51.

Zemans, F. 1982, 'The non-lawyer as a means of providing legal services' in Evans, R. & Trebilcock, M. (eds.) *Lawyers and the Consumer Interest: Regulating the Market for Legal Services*, Butterworths, Toronto, 263–302.

Zuckerman, A. & Cranston, R. (eds.) 1995, *Reform of Civil Procedure: Essays on 'Access to Justice'*, Clarendon Press, Oxford.

Index